Lecture Notes in Computer Scien

Commenced Publication in 1973
Founding and Former Series Editors:
Gerhard Goos, Juris Hartmanis, and Jan van Leeuwen

T0237838

Zhigeng Pan   Adrian David Cheok
Wolfgang Müller   Maiga Chang (Eds.)

Transactions on Edutainment III

Springer

Editors-in-Chief

Zhigeng Pan
Zhejiang University
State Key Lab of CAD&CG
Hangzhou, 310027, China,
E-mail: zhigengpan@gmail.com

Adrian David Cheok
Mixed Reality Lab
National University of Singapore
Singapore
E-mail: adriancheok@mixedrealitylab.org

Wolfgang Müller
University of Education
Media Education and Visualization Group
Leibnizstr. 3, 88250 Weingarten, Germany
E-mail: mueller@md-phw.de

Guest Editor

Maiga Chang
Athabasca University
School of Computing and Information Systems
CIS, 1 University Drive, T9S 3A3, Canada
E-mail: maigac@athabascau.ca

CR Subject Classification (1998): K.3.1-2, I.2.1, H.5, H.3, I.3

ISSN   0302-9743 (Lecture Notes in Computer Science)
ISSN   1867-7207 (Transactions on Edutainment)

ISBN   978-3-642-11244-7 Springer Berlin Heidelberg New York

springer.com

Typesetting: Camera-ready by author, data conversion by Scientific Publishing Services, Chennai, India
Printed on acid-free paper   SPIN: 12824861   06/3180   5 4 3 2 1 0

Preface

With great pleasure we would like to present the third volume of the journal *Transactions on Edutainment*. This journal, part of the Springer series *Lecture Notes in Computer Science*, is devoted to research and development in the field of edutainment. Edutainment, also known as educational entertainment or entertainment-education, denotes all forms of entertainment designed to educate as well as to provide fun. This approach is motivated by the growing demands on individuals for life-long learning and the need to integrate effective learning opportunities throughout life. As such, edutainment has attracted increasing interest in the last few years.

The first 12 articles of this issue represent a selection of outstanding contributions from *Edutainment 2009*, the 4th International Conference on E-Learning and Games held in Canada, in August 2009. The main purpose of the Edutainment conferences is the discussion, presentation, and information exchange of scientific and technological developments in the new community. These 12 papers cover mainly the topic of using games to stimulate learners' learning motivation, i.e., learning by playing, including: "Engaging Kids with the Concept of Sustainability Using a Commercial Videogame— A Case Study," "Doing It Right: Combining Edutainment Format Development and Research," "Edutainment Robotics as Learning Tool," "SoundTag: RFID-Based Wearable Computer Play Tool for Children," "Do Improve Typing Skill but No Significant Difference Between Drill-Based and Game-Based Typing Software," "Widget-Based Simulator for Testing Smart Space," "Entertaining Education – Using Games-Based and Service-Oriented Learning to Improve STEM Education," "Learning English Through Serious Games – Reflections on Teacher and Learner Performance," "Motivational Factors in Educational MMORPGs: Some Implications for Education," "A Distributed Multi-agent Architecture in Simulation-Based Medical Training," "Designing a Trading Card Game as Educational Reward System to Improve Students' Learning Motivations," and "Sketch Learning Environment with Diagnosis and Drawing Guidance from Rough Form to Detail Contour."

The following ten papers are regular papers. In "Application of Visualization in Virtual Endoscopy System," Yanjun et al. developed an efficient algorithm to solve path planning based on distance transform. In "Design and Implementation of Virtual Museum Based on Web3D," Zhang and Yang explain how to develop a Web3D-based virtual museum. In "Large Area Interactive Browsing for High-Resolution Digitized Dunhuang Murals," Yuan et al. use a Gaussian pyramid structure on Dunhuang Mural arts and allowed visitors to interact with the system by gestures. In "Research of Autonomous Active Control for Virtual Human Based on Emotion-Driven Model," Wang et al. create an emotion-driven virtual human on the smartphone. In "An XML-Based Interface Customization Model in Digital Museum," Wang et al. propose an XML-based Web interface customization model which can be used to construct a digital museum. In "Animation as an Aid for Higher Education Computing Teaching," Taylor and Pountney examine the potential use of animation for supporting teaching courses in UK higher education. In "Bringing Integrated Multimedia Content into

Virtual Reality Environments," Sampaio and Rodríguez Peralta propose a solution for the integrated presentation of different kinds of media objects inside virtual environments based on the Graphical Engine OGRE. In "Virtual Reality House for Rehabilitation of Aphasic Clients," Horváth et al. develop an innovative virtual reality house therapy, Virtual ELA®-House, for patients with language and speech disorders and cognitive neuropsychological disorders, e.g., aphasia, apraxia of speech, and neglect. In "Investigating the Effects of Educational Game with Wii Remote on Outcomes of Learning," Ho et al. develop a health education-based game with the Nintendo Wii remote. In "Using Computer Games for Youth Development," Yun et al. describe how to use games to assist students learning declarative knowledge, developing intellectual skills and psychomotor skill, and forming attitude structure.

The papers in this issue present a large number of application examples of edutainment, which gives more evidence of the great potential and high impact of edutainment approaches. We would like to express our thanks to all those people who contributed to this issue. They are authors of all papers, the reviewers of the regular papers, and the IPC of Edutainment 2009 for recommending high-quality to this new journal. Special thanks go to Yi Li, Ruwei Yun and Qiaoyun Chen from the journal's Editorial Office in Nanjing Normal University: they put in a lot of effort in contacting authors, managing the reviewing process, checking the format of all papers, and collecting all the material.

October 2009   Maiga Chang
                                                         Adrian David Cheok
                                                               Zhigeng Pan
                                                         Abdennour El Rhalibi

LNCS Transactions on Edutainment

This journal subline aims to provide a highly visible dissemination channel for remarkable work that in one way or another addresses research and development on issues related to this field. It targets to serve as a forum for stimulating and disseminating innovative research ideas, theories, emerging technologies, empirical investigations, state-of-the-art methods, and tools in all the different genres of Edutainment, such as game-based learning and serious games, interactive storytelling, virtual learning environments, VR-based education, and related fields. It will cover aspects of educational and game theories, human–computer interaction, computer graphics, artificial intelligence, and systems design.

Abdennour El Rhalibi	JMU, UK
Daniel Thalmann	EPFL, Switzerland
Kok-Wai Wong	Murdoch University, Australia
Gangshan Wu	Nanjing University, China
Xiaopeng Zhang	IA-CAS, China
Stefan Goebel	ZGDV, Germany
Michitaka Hirose	University of Tokyo, Japan
Hyun Seung Yang	KAIST, Korea

Editorial Assistants

Ru-wei Yun	Nanjing Normal University, China
Qiao- yun Chen	Nanjing Normal University, China

Editorial Office

Address: Ninghai Road 122, Edu-Game Research Center,
        School of Education Science, Nanjing Normal University,
        Nanjing, 210097, China
E-mail: edutainment@njnu.edu.cn;   njnu.edutainment@gmail.com
Tel/Fax: 86-25-83598921

Table of Contents

Regular Papers

Engaging Kids with the Concept of Sustainability Using a Commercial Video Game – A Case Study

Panagiotis Tragazikis[1] and Michael Meimaris[2]

[1] Msc in Models of Educational Planning and Development, Department of Sciences of Pre-school Education & Educational Design, University of Aegean, Metsovou 26. 17563, Athens, Greece
ptragaz@sch.gr
[2] Professor, Director of the New Technologies Laboratory in Communication, Education and the Mass Media, Faculty of Communication and Media Studies, University of Athens

Abstract. This paper focuses on the use of a commercial game, [COTS (Commercial off-the-shelf games for learning)], as a main motivating and educational tool, to make kids of 11 years old aware of the relationship, between every day actions and activities with emissions. It also intends to prove that, with the use of the game, a satisfactory level of modified behaviour towards the concept of sustainability is achieved by changing attitudes and taking actions. Furthermore, it intends to introduce a method, which is related to the efficient implementation of COTS, in primary school, educational projects.

Keywords: COTS (Commercial off-the-shelf games for learning), DGBL (Digital Games Based Learning), Sustainability (Education for Sustainable Development).

1 Introduction

The Game Based Learning has been researched for over 20 years, but its positive implementation in the classroom seems to be rather slow. The incorporation of the games in the curriculum seems to meet with difficulties even if the games are designed for educational purposes. Furthermore, the barriers are increased when you have to plan an activity based on commercial games.

The fact is generally expected because teachers are trained in methods that do not include games in the curriculum. However, we have an increasing number of teachers, who are willing to incorporate videogame activities into subjects of the curriculum. Consequently, the necessity arises to have as many examples of incorporating games in the curriculum, as possible. Furthermore, a variation in applications within school environment is also a necessity. Apart from what we have pointed out above, the efficiency of videogames in a variety of applications is well presented in academic field and considered to enhance learning (Prensky 2001, Gee 2003, De Freitas 2006, and M. & P. Pivec 2008). The question emerging is why COTS should be incorporated in

Z. Pan et al. (Eds.): Transactions on Edutainment III, LNCS 5940, pp. 1–12, 2009.
© Springer-Verlag Berlin Heidelberg 2009

the school curriculum? The idea of choosing commercial game in an educational project is supported on a variety of cases in bibliography. We have a number of cases in primary school. We have some cases focusing on open curriculum activities but no case related to environmental activities and especially the concept of sustainability.

Furthermore, the commercial games incorporate the most up-to-date technical possibilities and the intellectual reserve of a huge group of people, with differences in culture, attitudes, generally their life philosophy. They evaluate the social aspect of the users, because they have to be popular with a very competitive environment. In other words, a commercial videogame reflects social needs and is here to fulfil those needs. Pupils have been familiarised ever since they were born with the videogames and as they grow up they spend more time with the games. The time spend on the games is part of informal knowledge and the abilities are obtained. This part of learning is generally unexploited in school. Furthermore games are a part of the daily life of the young; they look like a world which is in parallel development with the adult world. In the world of games, the young tried to explain and understand adults' world (Turkle, 1984). Additionally, according to Prensky, games serve various types of knowledge and efficiently offer the possibility of modifying in the personal needs of knowledge of the users.Finally the immersion, was a key point to the final target of the activity we introduced, to change attitudes and incorporate the suitable behaviour. We interpret immersion as mind and body role adaptation which leads in our case to understand the relations between every day actions, which occurred unconsciously, with emissions and a sustainable future.

2   Place a Game in an Educational Project

There is a variety of factors which is related to the implementation of a videogame in the school environment. Even more, choosing a commercial game could be a hard procedure to use for a specific educational target. In our opinion, you have to evaluate a considerable number of factors, like fun, game play, interface (optical effects and sound perception), the existence of tutorial, the existence of sandbox (mode that you can play the game without any consequence), the immersion, the expected regression, circle of learning, feedback and control, narration, rules (should be clear) and goals (should be clear and set in an achievable way), challenge and mystery (Garris et al. 2002) , fantasy and curiosity (Malone, 1981). Generally, we need a good balance of all of them.

Furthermore, pupils- players have special needs and abilities. So the age, the sex, the experience, the type of the games played the motivation of the chosen game, the personal preferences and the possible opinion about the chosen game could increase or deteriorate the efficiency of an educational game activity. Generally, with an adaptation of the interactions, as had been described by many scholars (Prensky 2001, Gee 2003, Malone 1980, Garris, 2002 Csikszentmihalyi 1975, Papert, 1997) between the player and the game we introduce the following type of interrelations and feedback (Figure 1).

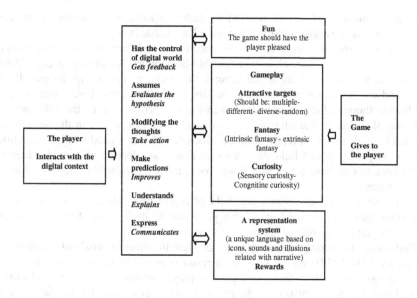

Fig. 1. The duality between a game and a player

3 COTS and Sustainability

The education for sustainability has the human being as a starting point, as biological, intellectual and behavioural, social and finally symbolic unit. The fact is related to systemic education (De Rosnay 1975, 1983), which he also suggests as teaching methods, the self education and the simulation using computers. On the other hand Environmental education has the natural environment and biodiversity as a starting point. (UNESCO- UNEP, 1976). The necessity of social and economic environmental modification has also appeared in order to protect the natural Environment (Agenda 21, 1992).In order to achieve this target the access to education must be improved and educational process must be orientated to Sustainability (Mckeown, Hopkins, 2003).

Furthermore, according to (Sauvé 1999) the education for sustainability is repre-sented as three interactive spheres, the one within the other. On the core is the identity or personal sphere, the next is the others and the interactions which each personality has with others or social groups and the third sphere is the biophysical environment as it is transformed and modified by the actions that took place within the spheres personal and social relations. We also add in the part of social relations, the economy as a main decision starting in contemporary communities. So the fact is that if we need to protect the environment to keep our future sustainable, it is necessary to focus on human beings and create a kind of environmental morality, which act and influence the inner worlds of each of us. In educational terms, the pupils should become capable through their personal investigations and reflections, of evolving the suitable compre-hension of reality which should become perceptible depending on individual and so-cial characteristics related to the way of life, the personal and social frame for action, types and situations of action, restrictions and prospects, as an interactive process (Kyburz-Graber & Hogger modification from Rauch 2002).

This is the point that motivates us to search the implementation of a commercial game in a lesson plan and achieve sustainable behaviours. According to Gee, (2004) we know a few things about social groups, the social practices and the established forms and the norms thought as social buildings. That is to say these processes convert human thought. Gee gives social dimension of learning derived from the fact that each one of us has a characteristic core of identity (his main role in the society, the one that he feels that it represents him e.g. doctor) which is related to all the identities that are adopted in social field. In this social field, the adoption of new identities replaces previous ones faster or at a lower pace, as any personality adapts in various social groups.

That's where precisely comes our field of report that concerns the children that play video games as a social team with particular identities, but also identities that they adopt playing the role of heroes in each video game.

That resembles from pedagogical point of view the zone of proximal development (Vygotsky 1934/1978) and the way that a result is revealed, focusing on the activity theory (Engestrom 1987, 1993). In a game a player adopts three different identities, the real one, the representation of the real one on the avatar and finally the avatar itself on the digital environment. When each of these identities is adopted, a variety of other identities will appear (Garris et al. 2002) who depend on the context where the action takes place.

Moreover, games include representations of the real world and involve the player's fantasy. Fantasies facilitate focalization of attention and the self-absorption that occurs when users become immersed in game activity (Driskell & Dwyer, 1984). Furthermore, according to (Malone & Lepper 1987) fantasies can offer analogies or metaphors for real-world processes that allow the user to experience phenomena from varied perspectives. In brief, it suggests that material may be learned more readily when presented in an imagined context that is of interest than when presented in a generic or decontextualized form. By evaluating the above facts, we consider gaming an important motivating tool to manipulate concepts that could be difficult to be understood by the kids and especially to increase environmental concern of them. The perception we have about the way that games can interact with the environment end the concepts related to them is represented in figure 2.

Finally having a commercial game in educational use, as has been analyzed above, encloses more aspects of the complicate environment which our main purpose in our case is to deal with, understand, modify our behaviours and take the proper actions.

Fig. 2. The Game Interface

4 The Game

The game we used was "THE SIMS" (Fig 3). It is considered a game of simulation, or a metaphor (De Freitas 2006) or a God game (Prensky 2001). Basically, it is a simulation of people, in which the players manage, as small gods, families and neighbourhoods that they have created by themselves (Frasca, 2001, Kline, 2003, Nutt & Railton, 2003). The action took place in an advanced and three-dimensional graphic environment. The game invites their players to be involved in a model of a neighbourhood in the suburbs of the city, (American suburb is related to what American dream calls for) and they manage a model of daily life by creating their own avatars.

As Jenkins (2001) mentioned, the players examine their own lives, simplifying complicated real world in a microcosm. That is to say the game constitutes model at a significance of real life and does not have an end.

Will Wright the creator of the game reports in an interview: "If you're building a solution, how large that solution space is gives the player a much stronger feeling of empathy. If they know that what they've done is unique to them, they tend to care for it a lot more. I think that's the direction I tend to come from". (Interview, Celine Pearce, 2001).

5 The Lesson Plan

5.1 Targets and Establishment

The scheduled activity is based on project method. Titled: "Carbon dioxide- global warming- personal responsibility".

Main objective: The pupils should realize that the model of life that we adopt has strong relation with the emissions of carbon dioxide, Global Warming and it is related to the consumption of energy.

Additional objectives: Create a simple model of life and manage it, realize that their behavior within the management of avatars life must be cooperative, dealing between digital and non digital environments, realize the energy model of growth and its relation with their life model and finally modify behaviors.

We used synthetic work and mixed activities. This choice is incorporated in the activity in order to achieve as many internal references as possible, in any type of educational procedure that the pupils have been faced with before. We are looking for the experiences of children; moreover we focus on various ways of approaching the training process. Furthermore it facilitated work with teams because the digital environment is designed for one player. We first introduced the activity to four 11 year old children of a public school with whom we worked together, allocating time proportional with the one that we intended to allocate in the classes we had chosen to work with. We also made the modifications that were issued by the test. Basically, we intend to take advantage of the immersion (as it described above) in order to achieve the goals we had set.In order to ensure that the pupils were willing to take part in the project with the terms we needed, we visited the two classes and we had a discussion related with their videogame activities and experiences. Additionally, we informed them that in case they agree to take part in the project they will play, considerably less time than they spent in their home videogame activities. The general impression derived from the discussion was extremely positive and together we decided on the dates of our future meetings with both classes.

5.2 Tools

We used four copies of the game Sims 2 (brought by the pupils) and a version for pc which was used for game demonstration. Four TV-screens and four PS2 game consoles. We also used an   Excel sheet, which was structured by the teacher and counts emissions and cost. Informative software related to energy. A translation in Greek of the words which appeared in the game arranged in alphabetical order and in groups related to the buttons of the menu and finally six activity papers.

5.3 Class Management

Each class was organized in four teams (4-5 students per team, figure 3). In each team we took care to have somebody who had played the game. We didn't intend to give a special role to the experts but simply we considered that if somebody exists, who has this game experience, it would be helpful especially in cases where the teacher wouldn't offer any help. The fact during the activity became effective enough. This game engine was preferred for the following reasons:

a. To avoid problems of compatibility related to the equipment of school computer laboratory. b. We wanted to give to the project an orientation as an easy action so we planned a limited amount of changes in the classroom. c. Familiarization with the game engines as part of their leisure time activities. d. The opinion that a quicker circle of learning would be achieved.

The teacher was designed to give instructions and navigate the teams and no other intervention occurred while the game was being played.

Fig. 3. Class management

6 Parts of the Activity

We use one full day of the school program to do the activity and the pupils have their regular brakes.

(1) *Familiarization activity*. The pupils play the game for one educational hour managing the control for five minutes time (one minute real time is one hour

game time) and then passed to the next member of the team. In this part of the activity, they also have the sheet with the word index.

(2)   *Assignment responsibilities.* Each team define certain roles for each member (manager, secretary, player, and translator). Everyone has the role for five minutes time and then adopts the role of the person seated next to him.

(3)   (3) *Starting play the game.* The game starts from the beginning. Teams take the first activity paper   where they have to add details of the personality that they have created. The purpose of the paper is to realise that each personality is related to particular needs. Then, they take the second activity paper where they have to fill the activities that have been done by the avatar and their duration according to the time the game indicates. Simultaneously, they take the activity paper number 3 where they have to fill the need that is in the lower level at the same time that actions filled in the activity paper number two took place. There is also another paper where each member of the team any time can fill thoughts and feelings. Teams can pause any time they want the game especially when they didn't have the time to fill the activity papers. This section of the activity lasts one hour.

(4)   *Evaluating activity papers.* The game stops, teams evaluate the activity papers. We have a discussion managed by the teacher and each team chooses three or four actions and the related need that was in the lower point. They connect actions and needs. Then we connect the needs and the actions with energy consumption. Each action is related to energy consumption. The next step is to group the actions in bigger categories related with energy consumption. To do this they take the next activity paper. This part also lasts one hour.

(5)   *Create a concept map with* the topic energy. They do this firstly within the teams and then on the blackboard as a whole class activity. The teacher gives additional information using a laptop and a projector. Then each team uses the computer Excel calculator that calculates the consumption of energy by performing group of actions through avatar, the emissions for each action and the total emissions from all the actions. It also gives the total cost of energy consumption. Teams also fill another activity paper where each product they have bought is analyzed approximately in its components and using the Excel calculator they add the energy consumption, so it's possible to count the things they have bought totally. This fact feeds a part of the discussion about the necessity of the things we buy. Every team has its own energy calculator and then they save the results. We also need one hour for this part.

(6)   *At the game again, final activity.* In the final part the teams were asked to create the same avatar (they had the data from the activity papers) and try according to the action described in the activity paper, to do the same actions in the same playing time, but keep in mind to save energy. The way the new view of the game works, (target modification) is described in the following example: In the first place, they listened to the music without turning the units off. So in the part the calculations they count a continuously playing machine related to the time they have played the game. Now they have to take care of it. Furthermore, teams competed not for the total reduction of emissions as weight but as percentage in their initial game activity. This had been decided because at the same time some teams had done much more actions than others. It's like a new game using the

SIMS. The reward estimated more to the effort and less to numbers. In this part as meta-cognition activity, it is proposed to create guidelines for modified actions to save energy. This part lasts for the two hours of the school program.

7 The Research

7.1 The Method

The case study method was chosen because it is suitable for social and educational research. Furthermore it takes place in real context, it can be managed either qualitative or quantitative data in any proportion, gives the possibility of generalizations, it permits the participation of the researcher, it can rely on previous development or it can use multiple data recourses. To increase the validity of the findings, we also used two types of focus groups, one with pupils with minor experience in videogames and one with high experience in videogames. We also used two types of questionnaires. A semi-structured questionnaire was given at the end of the activity and a Likert type questionnaire to research the attitudes, was given three months after the activity at the beginning of the new school year. In the meantime, 10 days after the activity we have done the focus groups. The quantitative data was analysed using SPSS for Windows ver.14.0.1. The first part of the analysis was descriptive statistics (Mean, Median, Standard Deviation, Standard Error, and Variance). The second part was Factor analysis to reveal relevant groups of questions and reliability analysis of basic groups of questions with A Cronbach related with the Likert type questionnaire. We also have a field observation form and the observations were combined with the activity paper where the pupils filled their comments while the activity was in progress.

7.2 The Questions

Can pupils understand environmental topics like emissions and energy consumption using a commercial videogame adopted in a scheduled activity? Can pupils realize the relation of emissions, energy consumption with the life model they adopt and modify their behaviour?

Moreover there was a general question, how a commercial game can be highly motivating to deal with difficult concepts like sustainability, and could be an efficient tool which improves the participation of the pupils in educational activities and, knowledge acquisition. How did motivation work? Which were the dimensions covered?

7.3 The Sample

The sample was to classes of pupils of 11 years old, having kids mainly from middle class families. Among the kids were some with high relation with games and some with small relation with them. We have mentioned above the way that we choose the focus groups. The members had been chosen in our first contact when we discussed games generally. We chose this age because we think that it is the starting point for those who play games often, to obtain attitudes and preferences related to videogames.

8 Research Conclusions

8.1 Conclusions Related to the Game

The majority of pupils enjoyed the game even if; we didn't use the game in full operational performances. The "experts" tried to play in fields where they were related with their particular individual interests, they "abused" time and they didn't offer the help expected. Of course we had decided not to give any special assignment to them. We had assumed that they will undertake initiatives. The fact happened but occurred in the following way: they achieved the objectives quickly and afterwards played the game following game targets. Furthermore in teams with them, in the available time, more action and development occurred.

The avatar creation seemed to be a very interesting part but it also created a type of conflict between boys and girls within the groups. Girls wanted a female avatar and boys a male one, but finally, operationally, groups worked efficiently.

The less experienced players enjoyed the game most. The control of the avatar was more pleasant for experienced players. Among the less experienced we had some cases that disliked it and the reason was that they didn't like it to happen to them.

There was a general need for more action and distress. Pupils gave us proposals about games characteristics. Mostly they related them with the previous game experiences. The final issue dominates a perception that would be very motivating and enjoyable to play a game but this game should have the possibility of the adaptation of immersive environment in different time zones e.g. now, life in 100 years from now, or life in 100 years before or play the same game in Paris or in Paris of 18th century.

The project also reveals that one pupil with "dyslexia" put himself apart from the activity. The same happened with a girl who had never played such games. This indicates that in complex projects like the one introduced, deepest and specified modifications for pupils with particularities are required.

8.2 Conclusions Related to the Lesson Plan

Most pupils found the activity pleasant and interesting. There was a small number who indicated negative preferences but not in the full scale of the activity. The opportunity for collaboration and the knowledge that they acquired were considered the most important elements of the activity. The modifications in the classroom, the rules of the game and the relation with new cognitive fields were in smaller scales their next choices. Most of pupils had clarified the objective of activity, four of them focused only on the game. They considered the game as the only important thing of the activity. The pupils had perceived the relation that exists between the satisfaction of every day needs and the consumption of energy.

The error functioned in certain cases pressingly, but despite any existing difficulties the pupils proceeded to correcting themselves. In any case this process presents low degree of cross-correlation with the error and its confrontation in the usual everyday school activity. The error appeared in two aspects: error related with game action and error related with the activity. The error within the game increased the tension to deal experimentally with the errors. That means that finally the pupils managed their mistakes efficiently, without the usual stress appeared in everyday class activities. Despite the fact that there was the will to have a more adventurous game, the activity was satisfactory related with fantasy, challenge and curiosity. Even more the errors and misconceptions of pupils functioned in an efficient way as it was initially scheduled.

The responsibilities (roles within the team) undertaken by the members of the teams indicated a diffusion of preferences. So while it was expected to have the role of the player as the most preferable the fact didn't occur. Moreover differentiations appeared between two sexes, where boys' roles shared between manager and player while girls' roles shared between secretary and player.

Nevertheless existing disagreements and conflicts between the members of certain teams finally functioned positively towards the objectives that were scheduled.

8.3 Conclusions Related to Attitudes

One week after the activity the majority of pupils adopted the expected attitude and even more they were willing to undertake action related to what they had done during playing the game. For example they took care of lights and electric appliances on stand by, and a small change in their attitude toward the waste. We realised a slightly bigger influence on girls and on those who aren't so experienced with games. Pupils perceived in their majority the relation between consuming action and the emissions of coal dioxide. Moreover, they perceived some of the results of emissions and modified the relative attitudes.

We realise after four months that they have adopted the desirable attitude and the willing behaviour related with what they should do with simple habits of daily life, but there is also one important percentage that tries to spread this knowledge. They consider the activity particularly important for the familiarization with coal dioxide as it is the physics and the relative topic that has been taught for a certain period of the school year. They also consider that each one of us is related to the global warming as result of the emissions. Finally, they perceived the relation of energy consumption and saving money and they modified the relative attitude.

Summarising we think, that approaching sustainability concept using a commercial game, evaluating the limitations and the difficulties in generalizing the conclusions of this case study, could be a powerful tool to investigate the human behaviour, modify and finally change it. Furthermore we think that our lesson plan also introduces a method for the implementation of COTS in traditional school environments. Generally we are looking forward to immersive environments that can support actions towards sustainability.

References

1. Ager, R.: Information and Communications Technology in Primary Schools: Children or Computers in Control. David Fulton Publishers, London (1998)
2. Aldrich, C.: Learning by doing. Pfeiffer, San Francisco (2005)
3. Begoña, G.: The impact of digital games in education by First Monday 8(7) (2003), http://firstmonday.org/issues/issue8_7/gros/index.html
4. Becta: Computer Games in Education project. Report (2002), http://partners.org.uk/index.php?section=rh&rid=13595

5. Chumpley, J., Griffiths, M.: Affect and the Computer Game Player: The Effect of Gender, Personality, and Game Reinforcement Structure on Affective Responses to Computer Game play. CyberPsychology and Behavior 9(3), 308–316 (2006)
6. Csikszentmihalyi, M.: Beyond boredom and anxiety: The experience of play in work and games, San Francisco (1975)
7. De Freitas, S.: Learning in Immersive worlds. A review of game-based learning Prepared for the JISC e-Learning Programme (2006), http://www.jisc.ac.uk/media/documents/programmes/elearninginnovation/gamingreport_v3.pdf
8. De Freitas, S.: Building bridges between computer modelling and simulation and games and virtual worlds communities. In: vizNET Workshop. University of Central England, Birmingham (2007)
9. De Rosney, J.: Le macroscope: vers une vision globale. In: Seuil (ed.), Paris (1975)
10. Dainter, J.: A Collaborative Educational Computer Game That Enhances Learning for Key Stage 1 Citizenship Skills, BSc Computing and Management (2005/2006)
11. Engestrom, Y.: Activity Theory and Individual and Social Transformation. In: Engeström, R.M.a.R.P. (ed.) Perspectives on Activity Theory, pp. 19–38. Cambridge University Press, Cambridge (1999)
12. Egeneldt-Nielsen, S.: Beyond Edutainment: Exploring the educational potential of Computer games. Doctoral Thesis, IT-University of Copenhagen, Denmark (2005), http://www.itu.dk/people/sen/egenfeldt.pdf
13. Gee, J.P.: What videogames have to teach us about learning and literacy? Palgrave Macmillan, London (2003)
14. Garris, R., Ahlers, R., Driskell, J.: Games, motivation and learning: a research and practice model. Simulation and Gaming 33, 441–467 (2002)
15. Jenkins, H.: From Barbie to Mortal Combat: Further Reflections, presented at Playing By The Rules: The Cultural Policy Challenges of Video Games, U. Chicago (2001), http://web.mit.edu/cms/People/henry3/publications.html
16. Lepper, M.R., Malone, T.W.: Intrinsic motivation and instructional effectiveness in computer-based education. In: Snow, R.E., Farr, M.C. (eds.) Aptitude, learning, and instruction: III: Cognitive and affective process analyses, pp. 255–286. Erlbaum, Hillsdale (1987)
17. Lo, J., et al.: Developing a Digital Game-Based Situated Learning System for Ocean Ecology. In: Pan, Z., Cheok, D.A.D., Müller, W., El Rhalibi, A. (eds.) Transactions on Edutainment I. LNCS, vol. 5080, pp. 51–61. Springer, Heidelberg (2008)
18. Malone, T.W.: What Makes Games Fun to Learn? heuristics for designing instructional computer games (1990), http://www.educ.msu.edu/DWongLibrary/CEP991/Malone-FunLearning.pdf
19. Malone, T.W.: Heuristics for Designing Enjoyable User Interfaces: Lessons from Computer Games (1982), http://portal.acm.org/citation.cfm?id=801756
20. Mitchell, A., Savill-Smith, C.: The use of computer and video games for learning A review of the literature (2004), http://www.lsda.org.uk/files/PDF/1529.pdf
21. Pivec, M., Pivec, P.: Games in schools, final literature review (2008), http://games.eun.org
22. Mckeown, R., Hopkins, C.: EE/ESD: defusing the worry, Environmental Education Research 9(1) (2003)
23. Papert, S.: Mindstorms: children, computers, and powerful ideas. Basic Books, New York (1980)
24. Prensky, M.: Digital game-based learning. McGraw-Hill, New York (2001)

25. Ricardo, R., Nussbaumb, M., Cumsillea, P., Marianovb, V., Correaa, M., Floresa, P., et al.: Beyond Nintendo: design and assessment of educational video games for first and second grade students. Computers & Education 40, 71–94 (2003)
26. Rauch, F.: Environmental education research 8 (2002)
27. Squire, K.: Replaying history: Learning world history through playing Civilization III, Doctoral Thesis, University of Indiana, USA (2005),
    http://website.education.wisc.edu/kdsquire/
    REPLAYINGHISTORY.doc
28. Sisler, V., Brom, C.: Designing an Educational Game: Case Study of "EUROPE 2045". In: Pan, Z., Cheok, D.A.D., Müller, W., El Rhalibi, A. (eds.) Transactions on Edutainment I. LNCS, vol. 5080, pp. 1–16. Springer, Heidelberg (2008)
29. Squire, K.: From content to context: digital games as designed experiences, Educational Researcher (2006)
30. Sauvé, L.: Environmental education between Modernity and Post modernity. Canadian Journal of Environmental Education 4 (1999)

Doing It Right: Combining Edutainment Format Development and Research

Simon Staffans[1], Annika Wiklund-Engblom[1], Marc Hassenzahl[1,2], and Susanne Sperring[1]

[1] MediaCity, Åbo Akademi University, Box 311, 65101 Vaasa, Finland
[2] Folkwang University, Campus Universitat Duisburg-Essen, Universitatstrasse 12, 45141 Essen, Germany
{Simon.Staffans,Annika.Wiklund-Engblom,Susanne.Sperring}@abo.fi,
Marc.Hassenzahl@folkwang-hochshule.de

Abstract. This paper is an effort to describe the synergy achieved by combining research and cross media edutainment format development. At MediaCity we a) develop formats and b) market them. But to be able to make an efficient development of them we also need to c) research into them, from a user's point of view. A presentation is given to the development process of "The Space Trainees": what is it? How has it been developed? What does it look like at this phase of development? How have we involved testing and research? What kind of methods for combining development and research do we see as the best ones? What results so far and what kind of an impact have they had on the developmental work?

Keywords: Edutainment, language learning games, cross media format development, user experience research.

1 Introduction

This paper is a description of the cross media edutainment format "The Space Trainees" and how we involve research as a tool for assisting the design process. This is the first and foremost aim of the research attempts, in which targets are both usability of the format and user experience of children tested during their interaction with "The Space Trainees" at several stages of the format development. Another aim of involving research is to gain more understanding of the edutainment value this cross media format delivers; i.e. both the value of entertainment and learning. The third aim is to fine-tune research instruments to better target children's user experience, with regard to their attitudes, emotions, actions, and reactions. These three goals of the research investigations are of course interconnected on many levels. In this paper, we will especially elaborate on the synergy effect achieved from combining cross media content development and research at MediaCity.

MediaCity is an independent unit at Åbo Akademi University. We are positioned with one foot in the academic field and the other in the business world. Our work spans media production, media innovations and cross media format development,

Z. Pan et al. (Eds.): Transactions on Edutainment III, LNCS 5940, pp. 13–24, 2009.
© Springer-Verlag Berlin Heidelberg 2009

commercial testing of media solutions, and media research. The cross media format development unit, iDC, within MediaCity has existed since 2005. The aim of the unit is to develop cross media and interactive formats, many in the edutainment genre, for various platforms and for various target groups, and to market these formats on the international media market. The aim is also to co-operate with researchers at MediaCity's audience research unit, iDTV Lab, and thus, obtain valuable information about the formats' usability and user experience during the development process. This co-operation will at the same time provide data to analyse further into edutainment regarding more academically defined issues. It is a win-win situation paired with one further overlaying goal as well; to develop and validate methods to efficiently test different formats, concepts and ideas in the field of interactivity and cross media, during different phases of development.

In the area of media research, the iDTV Lab within MediaCity, is striving towards becoming a leader in the field of user experience (UX) research, especially that which concerns end-users' media experiences and human-media interaction, but also user experience related to technology, human-computer interaction, products, and services. Our research is pragmatic in the sense that we work with companies developing media solutions and test these hands on. This pragmatic perspective influences the methods we apply for answering specific questions in the field of product development. Our main goal is to guide this product development so that the end-product answers to the needs and demands of targeted users. We strive towards outlining guidelines for best practices by looking at both usability issues and user experience, as we see these aspects as two sides of the same coin; ease of use, and fun of use.

2   Current Status of the Project

The project "The Space Trainees" originated in 2005, when the development team at MediaCity decided to explore the possibilities of developing an educational format for interactive television. Finland is amongst the countries to have embraced the DVB-supported MHP (Multimedia Home Platform) solution as the tool for interactivity via set-top-box.

The aim of the project was, from the outset, to create and develop a format that would combine an educational value with an entertaining form. The subject decided on was language learning. This decision was partly based on a survey conducted by the European Commission in 2001 which showed that 93% of all parents within the EU saw learning another European language as an important thing for their children[1], partly on the experience of the development team with regards to the possibilities of interactive television.

The project developed quite rapidly during the first few months, with several ideas created, developed and either encompassed as a part of the project or discarded for different reasons. Several key points were agreed upon; that a strong drama setting was needed, to combine the edutainment, the interactivity and the television show into one logical entity; that this drama would be set in space, to give as much freedom as possible to the developers; that MHP-based set-top-box interactivity was not necessarily the

---

[1] http://ec.europa.eu/public_opinion/archives/ebs/ebs_147_summ_en.pdf

best way forward for the project and that a cross media approach to the project would enable the production of better content, as well as a more logical approach to the inter-activity within the format.

"The Space Trainees" today is a cross media format encompassing television and Internet, with the cross media aspect and solutions integrated in a logical way, striving to make it a natural step for users and viewers to switch between the different media.

The drama setting, mentioned above, is set in space. A gigantic space ship, the Babel, is orbiting Earth, filled with databases of all Earths languages. Now, a virus has breached the databases and is destroying all the languages. The students (Space Trainees) at the International Space Academy are given the task of rescuing the languages. They will travel to Babel, to rescue as much of their languages as possible, by playing an array of language games. The best team gets to go on to the next mission, and is handsomely rewarded.

The viewers at home can sign up at the virtual Space Academy on the Internet, to become Space Trainees themselves, train the same games, practice their language skills, interact with fellow Trainees and, at the end of each semester, take part in tests, where the best Trainees have the chance to go on a real mission; i.e. take part in a television show in the next series.

The games the teams play on the television show, while the teams navigate the labyrinths of the space ship Babel trying to rescue the language(s), are coded in Flash. This means that the same games, looking much the same, are implemented on the web portal, the Space Academy on the Internet. The major difference is that the games on the television show are developed to activate the teams and their members physically, while the games on the Internet are more sedentary.

2.1 Unique Aspects of "The Space Trainees"

Edutainment is the genre created when mixing education and entertainment. There are many examples of edutainment throughout media history, some better and some worse. Learning through edutainment has been a topic of controversy, with critics pointing out that edutainment promises a fun learning environment, and learning does not have to be fun all the time [1]. Supporters or more neutral commentators have pointed out that games, digital learning and edutainment can be valuable as learning and training methods if used and applied correctly [e.g., 2; 3]. Children of today, as researchers have pointed out, are on a different level than the teachers teaching them, or even their own parents. Marc Prensky coined the term "digital natives" to describe these children, growing up in a digital environment, in stark contrast to earlier genera-tions which he called "digital immigrants" [4]. By offering learning through different media in a setting based on a strong drama, not unlike many computer and online games of today, we are aiming at motivating the children to engage themselves to a higher degree. Studies have indicated that subtle educational game design connecting learning elements to gameplay, story and simulation, has a positive effect on the play-ers' engagement and motivation [5], which is one of the aims of this project.

"The Space Trainees" has also been developed, from the start, with a multiple lan-guage aspect in mind. The children, "The Space Trainees" on the television show can try to rescue their own language, training their native language. They can try to rescue a foreign language, training that. Or there could be two teams of Trainees from different countries and different languages, trying to rescue a third language. In this last setting we approach the "real world" take on languages, where often two people from different languages must try to understand each other in a third, more or less common language. Furthermore, "The Space Trainees" offers teachers the possibility to register as a professional user on the web portal. The teacher can put together a sequence of games and edit the content to fit the current curriculum and invite his/her students to play.

2.2 Interactive Elements of "The Space Trainees"

As mentioned above, the teams on the television show play games to try to rescue as much of their languages as possible. The objectives of the games are to (a) train team members in a language, either by making them combine or construct words, letters and sentences, or by finding missing words and parts of sentences in different settings, but also to (b) activate team members physically, to heighten the suspense and the action of the television show. At the same time (c) the same games are used as Flash games on the web portal.

All in all over fifteen different games have been developed to date. One of the games is called the Lyrics Game. In the databases onboard Babel all songs ever recorded are stored. A virus has entered the database system, and is now destroying lyrics of songs. The task is to find missing words of the songs.

On the television show, as can be seen in image one below, the playing field is separated onto several different large screens. The team (consisting of three children) has to move around, communicate and collaborate in order to find the correct answers. The image is a so called heat map taken from one user experience test described later in this paper. The coloured dots visualize the fixations of the user. The red areas indicate most fixations, while the yellow areas indicate fewer fixations. The least viewed areas are shown as green, while the black areas did not attract any fixations.

Fig. 1. Screen shot of the TV-show during the Lyrics Game visualising eye-movements of a viewer

On the web portal, the same game is concentrated to one screen, enabling it to be played by one user. This can be seen in image two below. Other than that, the game is similar as the one on the television show.

Fig. 2. Screen shot of the Lyrics Game featured in the web portal

This game works well as an edutainment game, as it focuses on popular music and lyrics, which themselves have an entertainment value. From an educational perspective the game encourages users to find correct words in sentences, sometimes drawing on memory, but more often drawing on rhyming words, logical sentences etc.

2.3 Final Version of the Format as of April 2009

The format "The Space Trainees" is currently, as of mid-April 2009, in production for the Finnish Broadcasting Company. Together with the production company and the director of the show, the drama setting has been re-developed to better conform to the production schedule and the look and feel of the show. The setting is still space, but a space where space tourism is the newest thing. What every child wants to be, is a captain on one of the luxury Star Cruisers that transport people far and wide throughout the galaxies.

Now, one of the cruisers is in need of new captains, since the old ones are getting, well, old. A competition is staged, between the best Space Trainees at the Space Academy, to find the best of the best.

The teams – with three children in each team – face the challenges any space captain faces. Some challenges are physical, pitting the teams head-to-head against each other, while most are about helping the crew on the cruiser with their problems. For instance, all the electronic postcards have been mixed up. The pictures are correct, but what should the sentences look like? The challenges are many, all leading into language games.

The show will be broadcast from September onwards, with the web portal opening in late August.

3 Research

Research in the area of interaction between end-users and technology has so far been to a large extent focused on the usability of the technological product per se. Usability is most often defined as the efficiency, effectiveness, and satisfaction of a product [6]. Put simple, usability concerns the "ease of use" of a product. Hence, the emphasis is placed on the physical product and whether it works or not [7]. Research into user experience (UX) is looking beyond this technical aspect into human emotions and needs and how these are affected by and related to the use of a product. In contrast to usability testing, which measures "ease of use" of a product, UX measures "joy of use". Joy is a key-factor for success for almost any media solution today. Not to say that usability is not important. However, it is merely not enough. Media users of the 21st century are critical in their judgment of systems and services they choose to use. They take functionality for granted, but also entertainment; if something does not entertain them, they simply go somewhere else [8]. This fact is obvious to designers. Therefore, continuous feedback about users' experiences from using a system is essential during the development process of it. When it comes to edutainment format development, the aim is always two sided: it has to be both entertaining and educational at the same time. This makes the design process even more dependent on expertise from various fields of knowledge, but also the end-users' actual learning experiences as well as enjoyment.

The Space Trainees has been developed utilizing the principles of bridged cross media, i.e. the development of a storyline that continues in a logical way from one media – the television show – to another- the web portal – and back again. The development work has throughout the process of the project been aimed at producing a viable commercial cross media edutainment format for production and international marketing. The research involved in the development work is conducted in convergence with the design phases, and hence, the aims are always pragmatic. One crucial factor has been the correct timing of the tests, so that they are implemented at the right time in the development process and give the best possible impact.

3.1 Research Questions

This paper describes a developmental project, which involves an extensive design process. During this process there are many factors of interest regarding both usability and user experience of the system being created. The usability concerns whether the games function on a practical level, and whether the aims of the games are achieved; in this case both learning and entertainment. The targeted UX involves the users' satisfaction during interaction, as well as their perceived pleasure, which also includes both learning and entertainment. Questions that we are looking into are: what is fun about watching the game show on TV? What is fun about playing the games on the computer? What factors contributed to users' negative experiences? Do users feel that this is a good way to learn? Why? How? How does the collaborative dimension of the games contribute to their experience of learning and entertainment?

3.2 Research Layout

At MediaCity and iDC, "The Space Trainees" is a collaborative creative developmental project. The research involved is conducted in convergence with the design phases, and hence, the aims are always pragmatic. Different variables are of interest at different phases of development. In the following, we will describe how research has been and continues to be involved in the development process.

Right now we are at the point when the language learning games have been developed and tested in order to meet standards of achieving both learning and entertainment. The finalized games will be tested for user experience issues on the targeted population on both forms of delivery: the TV show and the web portal. The final cross media product is released in the fall of 2009, when the TV-show will be aired by YLE FST5. The final product will be subjected to extensive research targeting its value for learning and entertainment. The aim of this research is to build know-how for the cross media design team for future edutainment projects, but also to investigate further into the educational perspective on combining learning and play.

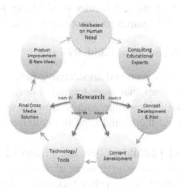

Fig. 3. Illustration of research as an integrated part of the design phases of cross media content development

3.3 Study I: Concept Development and Pilot (2005-06)

Within the scope of "The Space Trainees", we quite rapidly encountered the problem of validating the pedagogical value of the television show and the interactive and cross media applications. Did the viewers learn something at all? To address this issue, we have actively involved professors and researchers of pedagogy and didactics at Åbo Akademi University, who have been evaluating the game concepts and suggesting improvements throughout the development process of the project.

The task of combining games, a television show, real-time interactive services and educational content was a daunting one. As the format began to find its' first form and the games begun to be developed and programmed, testing became inevitable. A short version of the show was shot as a pilot in 2005, with the aim of editing a pilot of the television show, adding Beta-versions of the MHP-interactive games to the concept, and testing it on an audience of children from the targeted age-group.

In 2006 an extensive user experience and usability study was done on a demo of "The Space Trainees". The demo was, as stated above, an edited version of the pilot shot earlier, with interactive MHP-games added. The games that were included were relatively easy and simple games, as more complex games could not be included due to the severe technological limitations that the MHP-technology entailed.

The participants included 12 children between 10 and 13 years; 6 boys and 6 girls. The research design involved three groups of children: one group (N=4) played the interactive games through a MHP-set top box after receiving instructions, the other group (N=4) played the interactive games without any prior instructions, and the third group (N=4) watched the game show without the possibility of being interactive. The third group was furthermore divided into two children who watched the show to-gether, and two children who watched the show individually.

The end result was that – due to a wish to engage all viewers and guide them to in-teractivity through a compelling story, as well as due to the severe limitations the set-top-box-interactivity brought – the project in the end was discontinued as a concept for interactive television, and instead was redeveloped as a cross media concept, in-volving television and web solutions. Should the project have continued as a concept for interactive television, then the test results would have given much needed guid-ance for redeveloping the MHP-games in a more accessible direction [see also 9].

3.4 Study II: Content Development (2008-09)

This phase of the development involved an intensive period of design, testing, redes-ign, and testing. The main issues that were looked at during the testing of paper ver-sions of the games were the logic of the games: how they worked, how the children understood them and enjoyed them; and how the collaboration between participants functioned.

The participants included 12 children between 11 and 12 years; 5 boys and 7 girls. The participants played the games in groups of three. Three to four games were played per day. All the games were video recorded. After each game, the teams switched. Each group of children were interviewed after every game. A separate room was used for these group interviews. After all the games were played, the children filled in the positive-negative part of the self-assessment manikin (SAM) [10]. They also filled in a short version of the positive and negative affect schedule (PANAS) [11] containing five positive and five negative adjectives. We wanted to know if the PANAS questionnaire was suitable for this age-group. Therefore, a semi-structured instant recall (SIR) interview was conducted with each of the children separately, in which the PANAS was used as a recall instrument for the interviewee, in order to discuss their affective experiences triggered by playing the games.

From the development team's point of view there were a number of issues addressed through the tests with the children. Firstly the different language games were tested, 14 games all in all, both with regards to the game logic and game play; i.e., how well did the children understand the games and how to play them, as well as with regards to the content of the games. Some of the games had content based on the current curriculum, with words and phrases they had encountered at school. Other games featured content developed based on the games themselves: which kind of content would suit a certain game the best? There were quite a lot of tweaking of the games going on during and after testing, and a number of general principles regarding all games and certain games in particular were documented. These centred around the difficulty level of the games, the interaction between different parts of the games and so on.

Secondly, the development team wanted to look at the entertainment value of the game play with regards to the future television show. All games tests were therefore documented on video, for the team to better be able to evaluate the games and the settings afterwards. The set in itself was designed without building anything new, instead using regular furniture to symbolize the different parts of the game that should be available when making the TV program itself. The movement of the children, their communication (or lack thereof) and the strategies they came up with spontaneously all gave food for thought and led to changes being made in the concept.

Thirdly, we were curious to hear what the children thought of the overall concept and the different games. The concept and most of the games received resounding approval, although many creative suggestions for improvements were also included.

The observations and interviews further provided needed information for re-developing parts of the show in an even better direction (unpublished results). Analyses for answering academically posed research questions are being done on both quantitative and qualitative data collected in study II.

3.5 Study III: Technology Development (2009)

At the time of writing, the Flash games still need to be tested regarding usability for both the TV-version and web-version. The programming of the Flash-games will be ready by the end of March 2009. Research targets will be the overall appeal, ease of use and learning value, as well as viewers' capability of understanding the games as part of the TV-show. We would ideally be able to use the tests results to bring the games from a Beta stadium to the finished product, which can be integrated both as a part of the television show and of the web portal.

Both the TV-show and the web portal "The Space Academy" will be released in September 2009. This means that further testing will be needed. The research targets are once again many. Firstly, we need to understand if the cross media solution functions as intended. Is the Call to Action in the television series compelling enough and is the content attractive enough to pull the viewers to the web portal? Secondly, when on the portal, we need to test all parts of the portal – the registration, the communication, the touch and feel of the portal, the games, their game-ability and their pedagogical value, to mention a few.

When "The Space Trainees" cross media solution is finalized, it will be researched regarding several perspectives. Variables will be manipulated in order to see how the experience of learning and entertainment changes depending on where the user takes part (context), whether the user is a passive viewer or an active participator (format delivery), and with whom the user is playing (social interaction). Background variables that will be regarded are: age, gender, personality, prior knowledge, expectations, prior gaming experience, and prior TV experience. Table 1 presents a preliminary research design for investigating the learning and entertainment value of the final version of "The Space Trainees".

Table 1. Variables covered in the research design of investigations of "The Space Trainees" project

Input	Action (Controlled Variables)				Output (UX)
Age	Research design:				Entertainment
Gender		School	Home	Lab	Learning
Personality	TV				
Prior	Format				
Knowledge	Web				
Expectations	Format				
Prior Gaming	TV +				
Experience	Web				
Prior TV					
Experience					

3.6 Research Instruments

At MediaCity we have developed a standardized procedure for investigating both usability and user experience, with a wide battery of research instruments that cover attitudes, affect/emotions, psychophysiological reactions, and users' actions/ behaviour.
iDTV Lab, is equipped with the latest gear for testing usability and user experience of
both individual users and large audiences. Figure two illustrates the research targets and
data collection techniques in relation to levels of data, which are applied for investigating usability and user experience of media solutions. Instant recall and triangulation of
data is one of our methods for validating findings from a wide selection of objective and
subjective measurements. Furthermore, earlier studies conducted at iDTV Lab have
confirmed that a combination of methods guarantees a broad and deep understanding of
how humans interact with and experience media interactions [e.g., 12].

In our research design the standardized research instruments (questionnaires, psychophysiological and behavioural recordings) are complemented by other methods
that target more in-depth qualities of users' subjective experiences. For this purpose
we use semi-structured instant recall (SIR) interviews, in which each participant is
subjected to instant recall stimulated by their own replies regarding their self-ratings
of product attributions, affective experience, needs fulfilment, and mental effort, but
also their bodily reactions and behavioural actions. The research tools we have developed for this purpose help us to build bridges between subjective and objective data,
as well as between summative and formative data as shown in figure two. Thus, the
three arrows in the figure point to the targets of SIR interviews: questionnaire items
(self-ratings), psychophysiological measuring (reactions), and behavioural observations (actions).

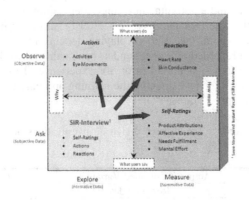

Fig. 4. Targeted aspects of user experience lined up according to type of data generated

"The Space Trainees" show is targeting the age group of 8-12 year olds. This demands research instruments adapted to this specific age group. For this purpose we
are testing age-adapted versions of the standardized methods for measuring user experience, for instance: the 10 item short version of PANAS in combination with
SAM, behavioural recordings, group interviews and individual SIR interviews.

4 Conclusions Regarding the Synergy of Research and Format Development

During the format development phases of "The Space Trainees" (language learning cross media solution) research into both usability issues and user experience has supported the development work. The first study gave indications that the interactivity was well received by viewers and users. The overall concept also received support. Interactivity via set-top-box, however, brought some negative issues that contributed to the switch to cross media solutions instead. Study two on the further developed versions of the concept, involving the content development phase, gave much needed information on the set instructions, the games themselves and the collaboration between the children on the television show, and contributed to changes made during the later development phases.

When developing edutainment and especially in a cross media setting, such as the one developed in the case of the project "The Space Trainees", there are many variables to take into consideration. There is the pedagogical and didactic value of the content; will the participants, the viewers and the active participators learn something? There is of course the entertaining part of the project; will the content be exciting, attractive, or engaging enough to capture the imagination of the target group? And, last but not least, the cross media aspect; will the story carry over to another media flawlessly and logically, and will it be enticing enough to pull the viewers and the users along?

One of the most important things when testing, especially while testing at an early stage when the design alternatives are almost endless, is to know what you want to test and what you need to ask. With a thoroughly developed testing system the design related questions and tests can be narrowed down and pinpointed to a suitable degree, so that the adequate information can be obtained. The information gathered during these standardized tests is of high value to the development process, as costly mistakes can be avoided and the most likely routes to success highlighted. Standardized methods that are flexible enough to fit the chosen target group and context are a corner stone in these test situations.

The results of the studies conducted so far in this development project suggest that while the web portal is designed to be the major form for interaction, viewers also play along in their own minds while just watching the show, thereby taking part and training languages themselves. This type of research has been significant to the development process of the cross media format. It has been a corner stone for assuring the edutainment value.

References

1. Okan, Z.: Edutainment Is learning at risk? British Journal of Educational Technology 34(3), 255–264 (2003)
2. Hogle, J.G.: Considering Games as Cognitive Tools: In Search of Effective "Edutainment", University of Georgia, Department of Instructional Technology (1996)
3. Becker, K.: Digital game-based learning once removed: Teaching teachers. British Journal of Educational Technology 38(3), 478–488 (2007)

4. Prensky, M.: Digital Natives, digital immigrants (2001), http://www.marcprensky.com/writing/Prensky%20-%20Digital%20Natives,%20Digital%20Immigrants%20-%20Part1.pdf (Retrieved August 13, 2008)
5. Wechselberger, U.: Teaching Me Softly: Experiences and Reflections on Informal Educational Game Design. In: Pan, Z., Cheok, D.A.D., Müller, W., El Rhalibi, A. (eds.) Transactions on Edutainment I. LNCS, vol. 5080, pp. 90–104. Springer, Heidelberg (2008)
6. Bevan, N.: UX, usability and ISO standards. In: Proceedings of CHI 2008, Florence, Italy (2008)
7. Hassenzahl, M.: User Experience (UX): Towards an experiential perspective on product quality. Keynote. In: IHM 2008: Proceedings of the 20th French-speaking conference on Human-computer interaction (Conférence Francophone sur l'Interaction Homme-Machine) (2008) (in press)
8. Graffman, K.: Unga och medier: en etnografisk studie. Symposium presentation, November 19, Åbo Akademi University, Vaasa, Finland (2008)
9. Staffans, S.: Developing cross media and interactivity for edutainment purposes. Conclusions drawn from the development work on the project The Space Trainees. In: Proceedings of the DREAM Conference, Odense (September 2008)
10. Lang, P.J.: Behavioral treatment and bio-behavioral assessment: Computer applications. In: Sidowski, J.B., Johnson, H., Williams, T.A. (eds.) Technology in Mental Health Care Delivery Systems, pp. 119–137. Ablex, Norwood (1980)
11. Watson, D., Clark, L.A.: The PANAS-X: Manual for the Positive and Negative Affect Schedule – Expanded Form. The University of Iowa (1994)
12. Sperring, S., Strandvall, T.: Viewers' Experiences of a TV Quiz Show with integrated interactivity. International Journal of Human-Computer Interaction 24(2), 174–196 (2008)

Edutainment Robotics as Learning Tool

Eleonora Bilotta, Lorella Gabriele, Rocco Servidio, and Assunta Tavernise

Department of Linguistics, University of Calabria, via P. Bucci, Cube 17/B,
87036 Arcavacata di Rende, Cosenza, Italy
{bilotta,lgabriele,servidio,tavernise}@unical.it

Abstract. Many constructivist technologies allow students to improve problem-solving strategies and learning in educational settings, encouraging teamwork and creativeness. Hence, in didactic contexts, the building, design and programming of Lego® MindStorms™ robots entertain students, stimulating technological and social factors. In this paper, we investigated the knowledge acquisition of a Lego Robotics system in University students, who had to create a robot able to take part in a race and avoid an obstacle placed in an arena. The learners' documentation of each phase of the task (reports, schemes, photos and videos) was analyzed as cognitive fingerprints of subjects' mental activities.

Keywords: Learning and Instruction; Lego; Edutainment Robotics; Cognitive strategies; Constructivism.

1 Introduction

Over recent decades, a number of robot construction kits for edutainment applications have been designed to improve and increase interaction between users and robotics artifacts [1], [2], [3], [4]. As Lund and Pagliarini assert, [5] some robots have a static morphology (e.g. Furby), while others have one which is variable (e.g. Lego® Mind-Storms™, FischerTechnic robot). The robots with a variable morphology, give the user the opportunity to build, plan and program different kinds of robotics artifacts. This latter Edutainment Robotic kit has been built in accordance with learning principles derived from Piaget and Vygotskij's theories [6], [7], [8] of cognitive development, as revised by Papert [9], which portray learning as the acquisition or 'construction' of knowledge through observation of the effects of one's actions on the world [10]. The constructivist approach promotes a kind of learning in which the educator does not transfer information, but is rather a facilitator of learning, leading the working group, and so the learner enhances his/her knowledge through the manipulation and construction of physical objects.

With regard to specific artefacts, numerous researchers endorse Robotics as an educational tool [11], [12], [13], [14], [15], [16], [17], with a quantity of literature devoted solely to using the Lego MindStorms kit [18, 19, 20, 21], at levels ranging from primary school to University [22], [23], [24], [25], [26], [27], [28]. There are reports of improved performance in Mathematics, Physics, and Engineering courses resulting from educational Robotics projects [29], [30], although most of the evidence is based on the reports of teachers achieving positive outcomes through individual initiatives [31].

Z. Pan et al. (Eds.): Transactions on Edutainment III, LNCS 5940, pp. 25–35, 2009.
© Springer-Verlag Berlin Heidelberg 2009

Moreover, Johnson [32] argues that Robotics offers special educational leverage, because it is multi-disciplinary field involving a synthesis of many technical topics, including Mathematics and Physics, Design and Innovation, Electronics, Computer Science and Programming, and Psychology. Research results suggest that the pedagogical value of robots lies in making them work, through using or extending knowledge to identify problems, and argues that robots are a particularly motivating technology because they are concrete, complex, and relate to deep human needs.

In effect, by constructing physical agents together with the code to control them, students have a unique opportunity to tackle many central issues directly, including the interaction between hardware and software, space complexity in terms of the memory limitations of the robot's controller, and time complexity in terms of the speed of the robot's action decisions. Furthermore, the robot theme provides a strong incentive to learning because students desire to see the success of their invention [12]. Moreover, many researchers underline the positive results in the rehabilitation of autism and cognitive deficits using interactive robots [33], [34].

Another application for Edutainment Robotics is represented by RoboCup [35]. The World-Wide RobCup Championship is a large international competition that aims at involving all sorts of research in Robotics and Artificial Intelligence. It has been developed with the initial idea that the stimulus of competition encourages the integration of different technologies which, once optimized for the engaging and pleasant game of football, may be transferred to significant, practical problems for industry. The RoboCup Championship involves participants in the challenges of competition, as well as in the development of educational skills [36], [37]. Finally, it can be stated that robots are a particularly motivating technology and that the use of Robotics tools in teaching contexts offers the opportunity to build a bridge between entertainment and education [38].

In this paper, we present the results of an empirical research project with university students the purpose of which was to investigate cognitive strategies using the Lego MindStorms robotics kit.

The paper is organized as follows. In section two, we present a description of the research objective. In section three, we describe the subjects. The robot laboratory organization is described in section four. In section five, we describe the materials used. Section six focuses on methods of results analysis. Finally, in sections seven and eight we present analysis of the results and some conclusions.

2   Objectives

Our research aimed at investigating the learning process by using Edutainment Robotics. In particular, we analyzed the cognitive abilities of the University students involved in the Lego robot construction, related to:

- Planning strategies – students are expected to use the Constructopedia (a guide with different examples of robot Lego projects) to plan their robots, by modifying little functional parts of their artefacts. For example, students could use little wheels if large wheels prevented good performance.
- Programming strategies – students should learn to define and manage robot behavior in relation to the final task.

- Students' use of different strategies to complete the task and how these strategies influence the results.

3 Subjects

Twenty-eight students, aged from 19 to 21 and enrolled in an 11-week Robotics laboratory program at the University of Calabria, were divided into 6 groups. From an individual interview, we found that none of the subjects were familiar with the concepts of Educational Robotics or the Lego MindStorms kit.

All of the students were enrolled to the first year of the Humanities degree course and attended the Cognitive Psychology course. The aim of the course was to present an overview of Cognitive Psychology, its findings, theories and approaches. The course was divided into two sections. The first introduced central cognitive processes such as perception, memory, learning, language, reasoning and problem solving. The second focused on Artificial Intelligence and explained the reproduction of human behaviour in artificial agents such as Robotics artefacts.

4 Robotics Laboratory Organization and Assignment

The Robotics laboratory program comprised 22 hours of activities, two hours a week for 11 weeks: preliminary lessons covered elementary concepts of Robotics, the Lego MindStorms kit, the visual programming environment and the Robotics Invention System (RIS). During the laboratory activities, each group had to design, build, program and test the performance of its own robot. The final task was to realize a robot able to cross an arena in order to take part in a race.

The groups had to describe and report on the robot planning, the resolution of the problems encountered in the construction of the robots, the programming methodologies, the number of tests and the dividing up of work within the group. In particular, they had to document each phase of the work through reports, schemes, photos and videos.

At the end of the laboratory activities, a race divided into two rounds took place. Each robot had two minutes to complete its performance in each round.

5 Materials

The MindStorms kit (Fig. 1) includes over 700 traditional Lego pieces, the RCX (Robotics Command System), infrared transmitter, light and touch sensors, motors, gears, and a visual detailed building guide or Constructopedia™. The building guide provides students with direction in their building of working robots, as well as inspiration for more complex robotic inventions models.

The core of the Robotics Invention System is the RCX "brick", a microcomputer that can be programmed using a Personal Computer. The RCX receives input from the environment through sensors, it processes data, and then it transfers the output to the motors. Each user may program the robot, using a specific programming language and a personal computer. The next step is to download the program into the RCX memory using an infrared transmitter or Transceiver. Finally, the robot agent can move in an autonomous way in the environment.

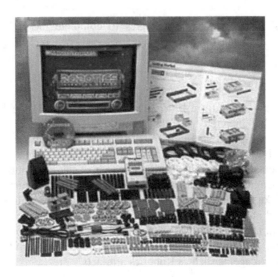

Fig. 1. Lego MindStorms Robotics Invention Systems

6 Method of Results Analysis

We analyzed the reports that students made during their laboratory activities in order to detect the task organization, related to cognitive strategies in problem solving, applying the followings evaluation criteria:

- Work distribution in each group.
- Groups' description of working modalities for task resolution (programming and planning strategies).
- Correctness of programming strategies, related to the results of the robot race.
- The number of programming tests completed before the robot was able to cross the arena.

In particular, the programming analysis methodology pointed out the conceptual aspects of programming, investigating program adjustment in relation to the final task and the cognitive strategies used.

7 Analysis of the Results

From the analysis of the reports, we found that the groups utilized three different typologies of work subdivision:

- The first typology was adopted by three groups. Each member adopted a role in the building work (for example, one person read instructions, another person chose the appropriate piece and others assembled the chosen pieces). All the members programmed the robot.

- The second typology was adopted by two groups. Members did not adopt a fixed rule in building and programming the robot (for example, the same person chose the appropriate piece and assembled it together with the other pieces).
- The third typology was adopted by only one group. Each member adopted a role in building and programming the robot and a leader supervised the work.

Regarding the programming and planning modalities, each group carried out tests to modify the behavior of the robot.

The first group carried out six programming tests (Fig. 2), the second five, while, the third and the fourth carried out four, and the fifth five. The sixth group carried out ten.

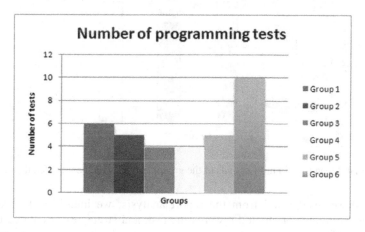

Fig. 2. Number of programming tests carried out before completion of the task

Each group programmed the robot's behaviour correctly. The robots of the first and fourth group obtained a good time in the first round of the race but exceeded the maximum time in the second one (Fig. 3).

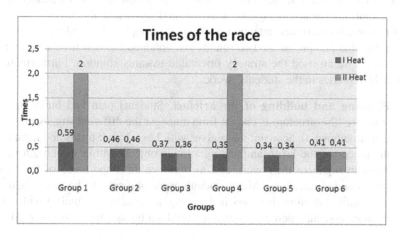

Fig. 3. Times obtained by each group's robot in the two stages of the race

The robots of the first and fourth groups did not complete the race because they exceeded the maximum time in the second stage. Taking into account time achieved for each robot during the rounds, we calculated the mean time, expressed in milliseconds, which ranged from 0,33 to 0,46 (Fig. 4).

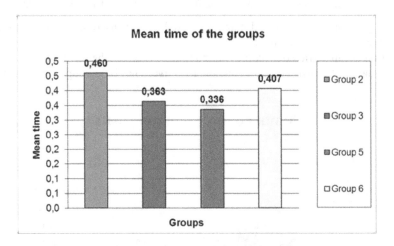

Fig. 4. Mean time in milliseconds of the groups' robots which completed the race

From these results and from the report analysis, we identified two kinds of strategies: strategies orientated towards the task and strategies orientated towards the solution [39].

The groups, which used a strategy orientated towards the task did not test their robot's behaviour many times and focused their attention on comprehension of the task (group 3 and group 4). In fact, in this kind of strategy subjects are skilled at understanding implicit rules quickly, hypothesizing about the trials [40]. In the strategy orientated towards solution, subjects do not analyze the problem but immediately test the possible solution. Groups using this kind of strategy tested the robot's behaviour many times and focused their attention on the goal (groups 1, 2, 5 and 6).

The robot that completed the two rounds and obtained the best time was the robot from group 5 which used the strategy orientated towards solution. Furthermore, we detected three phases in the students' work:

1. **Planning and building of the artefact**. Students plan and build the robot structure (the structure is chosen from amongst the different suggestions in the Constructopedia), acquaint themselves with Lego MindStorms and learn to use the pieces of the kit. Manipulating various objects within the kit allows students to organize their work and to discover the importance of the various pieces and connections. Many students were observed to be using their own personalised design; they enriched an original structure or built it with simply its more essential elements so that it would not be weighed down (Fig. 5).

Fig. 5. An example of a robot built by a group of students

2. **Behavioural programming**. Students learned a programming language that allowed them to control the artificial agent's behavior (Fig. 6). The Figure 6 show the program realized by students to control robot behavior. In this program students use two touch sensors to control the robot movement within the arena during the competition. This program is very simple but it is functional to achieving the final objective.

Programming was divided into two sections (basic programming and sensor programming); the key concepts of this phase included: performance in sequence following the instructions, logical order of the commands, and use of conditional expressions, loop and debugging.

Fig. 6. An example of a program prepared by a group of students

3. **Check**. Students checked the results of their work, in particular the physical structure and the algorithm that controlled the robot's behavior. They also decided on modifications to improve the time taken to cover the path in the arena (Fig. 7).

Fig. 7. The competition arena with Lego MindStorms robot

The best times in the final race were obtained by groups three and five, which had adopted the second typology of work subdivision (without fixed roles, collaborating for every task). These groups carried out a small number of tests in building and programming the robot, paying close attention to task comprehension in a problem-orientated strategy.

8 Conclusions

In this work we focus on the cognitive strategies adopted by University students attending a Robotics laboratory program, working in an Edutainment setting with the Lego MindStorms kit. We analyzed the students' reports on the teamwork during laboratory activities, and we gathered information on the subjects' working modalities during the activities of building and programming basic robots. First of all, we detected three different typologies of work subdivision: each member adopted a role in the building work and all programmed the robot; members did not adopt a fixed rule in building and programming the robot; each member adopted a role in building and programming the robot and a leader supervised the work. We then found that the use of robots stimulated students to explore their own knowledge in a critical way and to share it within the group, and that the activity of realizing an artefact took place through precise phases. These phases were:

1) Planning and building of the artefact, related to problem identification and objective definition, collection and production of ideas, problem conceptualization. During the building and manipulation phases, a fundamental role was played by the perceptive and behavioral functions and by the affordance that the elements of the kit suggested to the subjects. As they progressed with the work, students advanced in the learning process and became able to explore, arrange and recombine, in different ways, the material structures and the creative ideas in order to realize the final artefact.

2) Behavioral programming, in which students detected problems, hypothesized and applied solution strategies. In this way, they were able to enrich their work through new details, looking at different thinking modalities; in particular, in planning strategies students divided the problem into many parts and elaborated each part from the particular to arrive at a general solution. This phase was strictly related to the check phase.

3) Check, in which subjects evaluated the realization of the artefact and decided on the need to go back to the building phase, to the programming phase, to both, or rather to search for new ideas.

Thanks to the results of this analysis we can affirm that the Robotics laboratory stimulated students with regard to problem finding (the subject identifies and formulates the initial idea or the problem to solve), problem solving (the subject elaborates and explores some possible solutions in order to reach the objective) and checking procedures (the subject evaluates the artefact's properties from functional, planning and behavioral points of view). The repetition of each of these phases allowed the subjects to modify and improve the structure and this reflected their mental model of the artefact in relation to the assignment.

We underline that the students followed the basic Constructopedia, instructions and prototype figures for the building of the robot, but the final look of each artefact differed because of their using creativity. Moreover, each group programmed the robot's behavior correctly.

In conclusion, Edutainment Robotics stimulates students to change their artefacts, to modify them for their specific needs and to choose the best strategy to accomplish their tasks. In this view, the use of robotics artefacts in didactic contexts stimulates students to analyze processes and information selection, to observe and to experiment the consequences of their behavior. In this way, students get used to problem solving, are encouraged to work collaboratively and co-operatively and to improve their listening to others. In general, this construction of knowledge and the reflection on the process is essential for the retention and application of learning in every field.

Edutainment Robotics creates a cognitive bridge between educational aims and concrete experience, encouraging in the students, at different levels, the acquisition of new skills in an engaging setting.

References

1. Eguchi, A., Reyes, J.: Engage and Motivate Non-Computer Science Major Undergraduates Using Educational Robotics. In: McFerrin, K., et al. (eds.) Proceedings of Society for Information Technology and Teacher Education International Conference, pp. 2572–2576. AACE, Chesapeake (2008)

2. Miglino, O., Lund, H.H., Cardaci, M.: Robotics as an educational tool. J. of I. Lea. Rese. 10(1), 25–48 (1999)
3. Sklar, E., Parsons, S., Azhar, M.Q., Andrewlevich, V.: Educational Robotics in Brooklyn (short version). In: Proceedings of the AAAI 2006 Mobile Robot Workshop (2006)
4. Balogh, R.: Basic Activities with the Boe-Bot Mobile Robot, In: Proceedings of conference DidInfo 2008, FPV UMB, Banská Bystrica, Slovakia (2008)
5. Lund, H.H., Pagliarini, L.: Edutainment Robotics: Applying Modern AI Techniques. In: Proceedings of International Conference on Autonomous Minirobots for Research and Edutainment, AMIRE 2001 (2001)
6. Piaget, J., Inhelder, B.: La psychologie de L'enfant, P.U.F., Paris (1966)
7. Piaget, J.: L'epistemologia genetica, Roma-Bari, Laterza (1971)
8. Vygotskij, L.S.: Storia dello sviluppo delle funzioni psichiche superiori e altri scritti, Giunti, Firenze (1974)
9. Papert, S.: Constructionism: A New Opportunity for Elementary Science Education. MIT: Media Laboratory-Epistemology and learning group, Cambridge (1986)
10. Papert, S., Harel, I.: Constructionism. Ablex Publishing, Norwood (1991)
11. Denis, B., Hubert, S.: Collaborative learning in an educational robotics environment. C. in Hum Beha 17, 465–480 (2001a)
12. Kumar, D., Meedan, L.: A robot laboratory for teaching artificial intelligence. In: Daniel, J. (ed.) Proceedings of the ACM SIGCSE symposium, pp. 341–344. ACM Press, New York (1998)
13. Nostrand, B.: Autonomous robotics projects for learning software engineering. In: Proceedings of IEEE (2000)
14. Weinberg, J.B., Engel, G.L., Gu, K., Karacal, C.S., Smith, S.R., White, W.W., Yu, X.W.: A multidisciplinary model for using robotics in engineering education. In: Proceedings of the 2001 ASEE AnnualConference and Exposition (2001)
15. Martin, F.: Circuits to control: learning engineering by designing Lego robots, PhD. thesis. MIT Press, Boston (1994)
16. Bertacchini, P.A., Bilotta, E., Gabriele, L., Pantano, P., Servidio, R.: Investigating cognitive processes in robotic programmers developed by children in educational context. In: Roccetti, M., Syed, M.R. (eds.) Proceedings of international conference on simulation and multimedia in engineering education/Western multiconference on computer simulation (ICSEE/WMC 2003), SCS, Orlando, pp. 111–116 (2003)
17. Bertacchini, P.A., Bilotta, E., Gabriele, L., Servidio, R., Tavernise, A.: Investigating Learning Processes Through Educational Robotics. In: Proceedings of II ASLA, Australian online conference, 8-26 Maggio (2006a)
18. Klassner, F., Anderson, S.: Lego MindStorms: Not just for K-12 anymore. IEEE Robotics and Automation Magazine (2003)
19. Bertacchini, P.A., Bilotta, E., Gabriele, L., Pantano, P., Servidio, R.: Apprendere con le mani. Strategie cognitive per la realizzazione di ambienti di apprendimento-insegnamento con i nuovi strumenti tecnologici. Franco Angeli, Milano (2006b)
20. Marcinkiewicz, M., Kunin, M., Parsons, S., Sklar, E., Raphan, T.: Towards a methodology for stabilizing the gaze of a quadrupedal robot. In: Lakemeyer, G., Sklar, E., Sorrenti, D.G., Takahashi, T. (eds.) RoboCup 2006: Robot Soccer World Cup X. LNCS (LNAI), vol. 4434, pp. 540–547. Springer, Heidelberg (2007)
21. Goldman, R., Azhar, M.Q., Sklar, E.: From roboLab to aibo: A behavior-based interface for educational robotics. In: Lakemeyer, G., Sklar, E., Sorrenti, D.G., Takahashi, T. (eds.) RoboCup 2006: Robot Soccer World Cup X. LNCS (LNAI), vol. 4434, pp. 122–133. Springer, Heidelberg (2007)

22. Ma, Y., Williams, D., Lai, G., Prejean, L., Ford, M.: Integrating storytelling into robotics challenges that teach mathematics. Paper presented at the Society for Information Technology and Teacher Education International Conference (2008)
23. Moundridou, M., Kalinoglou, A.: Using LEGO Mindstorms as an Instructional Aid in Technical and Vocational Secondary Education: Experiences from an Empirical Case Study. In: Dillenbourg, P., Specht, M. (eds.) EC-TEL 2008. LNCS, vol. 5192, pp. 312–321. Springer, Heidelberg (2008)
24. Petrovic, P., Balogh, R.: Educational Robotics Initiatives in Slovakia, Teaching with Robotics, SIMPAR (2008)
25. Petre, M., Price, B.: Using robotics to motivate 'back door' learning. E. and Inf. Tech. 9(2), 147–158 (2004)
26. Arcella, A., Bertacchini, P.A., Bilotta, E., Gabriele, L.: Progettare il comportamento di un robot: un esperimento didattico. In: Bertacchini, P.A., Bilotta, E., Nolfi, S., Pantano, P. (eds.) Proceedings of the first Italian workshop of artificial life, Arcavacata di Rende, Cosenza, Italy (2003)
27. Gabriele, L., Arcella, A., Servidio, R., Bertacchini, P.A.: Investigare strategie di problem solving attraverso la robotica: un'esperienza con studenti universitari. In: Baldassarre, G., Marocco, D., Mirolli, M. (eds.) 2nd Workshop Italiano di Vita Artificiale, Istituto di Scienze e Tecnologie della Cognizione, CNR, Roma, Marzo 2-5 (2005a)
28. Gabriele, L., Servidio, R., Tavernise, A.: Acquisire concetti complessi attraverso l'uso di strumenti: un'indagine empirica. In: Atti del Congresso Nazionale della Sezione di Psicologia Sperimentale dell'AIP - Associazione Italiana di Psicologia, Cagliari, settembre 18-20 (2005b)
29. Bers, M.U., Portsmore, M.: Teaching Partnerships: Early Childhood and Engineering Students Teaching Math and Science Through Robotics. J. of S. Edu. and Tech. 14(1), 59–73 (2005)
30. Nagchaudhuri, A., Singh, G., Kaur, M., George, S.: Lego robotics products boost student creativity in pre-college programs at UMES. In: Budny, D., Bjedov, G. (eds.) 32nd ASEE/IEEE frontiers in education conference, pp. S4D-1–S4D-6. IEEE, Piscataway (2002)
31. Yoon, S., Pedretti, E., Pedretti, L., Hewitt, J., Perris, K., Oostveen, R.: Exploring the Use of Cases and Case Methods. J. of S. Tea Educ. 17(1), 15–35 (2006)
32. Johnson, J.: Children, robotics, and education. In: 7th International Symposium on Artificial Life and Robotics (AROB-7), pp. 491–496 (2002)
33. Cardaci, M., Caci, B., D'Amico, A.: La robotica nella riabilitazione di soggetti autistici e con deficit cognitivi, Tecnologie digitali e l'Intelligenza Artificiale al servizio dei disabili, C.I.T.C, Università di Palermo (2004)
34. D'Ambrosio, M., Mirabile, C., Miglino, O.: Uno studio pilota sull'impiego di giocattoli robotici nella riabilitazione cognitiva. In: Bertacchini, P. A., Bilotta, E., Nolfi, S., Pantano, P. (eds.) In: Proceedings of the first Italian workshop of artificial life, Arcavacata di Rende, Cosenza, Italy (2003)
35. Sklar, E., Eguchi, A.: Examining Team Robotics through RoboCup Junior. In: Annual conference of Japan Society for Educational Technology, Nagaoka, Japan (November 2002)
36. Sklar, E., Eguchi, A.: Learning while Teaching Robotics. In: AAAI Spring Symposium 2004 on Accessible Hands-on Artificial Intelligence and Robotics Education (2004)
37. Baltes, J., Sklar, E., Anderson, J.: Teaching with RoboCup. In: AAAI Spring Symposium 2004 on Accessible Hands-on Artificial Intelligence and Robotics Education (2004)
38. Miglino, O., Lund, H.H., Cardaci, M.: Robotics as an educational tool. J. of I. Lea. Rese. 10(1), 25–48 (1999)
39. Lawson, B.R.: How designers think. Architectural Press, Oxford (1997)
40. Arielli, E.: Pensiero e progettazione. La psicologia cognitiva applicata al design e all'architettura, Bruno Mondadori Editore, Milano (2003)

SoundTag:
RFID Based Wearable Computer Play Tool for Children

Ryoko Ueoka[1], Hiroki Kobayashi[2], and Michitaka Hirose[2]

[1] Research Center for Advanced Science and Technology, the University of Tokyo,
4-11-16 Komaba Meguro-Ku Tokyo, Japan
[2] Cyber Interface Laboratory, the University of Tokyo, 7-3-1 Hongo Bunkyo-Ku Tokyo, Japan
{yogurt,hill_koba,hirose}@cyber.t.u-tokyo.ac.jp

Abstract. Outdoor play is an important activity in young children's lives which should be encouraged. Cultural and social demographic data inform of decreasing numbers of children and shortage of playgrounds around urban areas. Technological advancements such as television and computer games have influenced children's recreational activities so that they prefer to play indoors rather than outdoors. In order to motivate children to play outside we propose technologically supported play tool titled 'SoundTag'. This is a Radio Frequency Identification (RFID) based wearable system that uses sound interaction. We deployed two types of SoundTag system. The first one is the interactive wearable system with sound feedback. And the second one is interactive sound feedback with sound recording system. In this paper, we detail the concept of the system and related design theory. A pilot experiment with the first SoundTag system is reported where we observed the system in use. And followed by the observation of the experiment, the second SoundTag system is deployed and the preliminary experiment is reported.

Keywords: Wearable computer, children's interactive play, RFID.

1 Introduction

Societal demographics inform that the number of children is decreasing. Also there is a shortage of playgrounds around urban areas. These are factors that tend to influence the time children spend outdoors playing with friends. This tendency is not exclusive to Japan but also common in urban area in developed countries.[1][2] The decrease of outside playing time is unfortunate for children since outdoor activities contribute to children's well-being and development in ways that are not addressed by academic learning. Although there are many social reasons having decreased outside playing time, technological advancement such as television or computer games are considered to be one of the factors. However the authors suggest that the technological advancement is not the reason to cause this tendency. For example, as Bekkerm et al. stated, Wii game controllers and eye-toy camera's are examples of input game devices that require physical activity.[3] The trend of current computer games induces players doing physical activities indoors. In this study, we take the advantage of technological advancement into positive effect to motivate children playing outdoors. We propose

Z. Pan et al. (Eds.): Transactions on Edutainment III, LNCS 5940, pp. 36–47, 2009.

SoundTag, which is a wearable computer prototype system to motivate them to play outside. It employs RFID tag and reader into wears to realize interactive play with sound feedback.

In this paper, we present the SoundTag concept, design theory and two types of wearable system and experiments. The first SoundTag system was applied to a play scenario, which is an enhanced version of a 'tag' game. We performed a pilot experiment partnered with children (from 5 years old to 10 years old) to observe how SoundTag affected playfulness. Playfulness is discussed from the observation of children while playing it and the comments from their parents after the experiment. Followed by the observations of the first experiment, the second version of the SoundTag system is deployed and is applied to the outdoor sound collection game.

2 Related Research

In this section, related work that deals with technically enhanced educational and playing applications for children is introduced. The authors have previously conducted experiments adapting playful factors into the development of wearable or portable computer systems. This was an outdoor exhibition prototype which included outdoor experiments for studying the use of an exhibition system in public outdoor space. [4][5] In this exhibition experiment, we focused on making educational and playful content for children with a location-based system using Global Positioning System(GPS) equipment. Ubiquitous gaming contents were developed for the location-based exhibition system using a portable stone-looking computer. [6]

Related research has been reported from NESTA Futurelab in the U.K. under the 'Savannah' program.[7] This PDA-based role-playing game is played outside where each player has a role as a wild animal to learn about survival in the jungle.

'Periscope' was a related computer-based educational tool that supported a computer enhanced field trip for children. [8] This tool enhanced a conventional field trip by the networked device being utilized to allow children to access information to learn more about the life cycle of wood. The interactive and tangible device was designed for 10- to 12-year-old children. In this work, RFID tags were effectively used for tagging the wildlife in the wood.

BibPhone was a hyper book system for children that was based upon RFID and Bluetooth. [9] This was an interactive audio recording and playing back system connected to a physical book. The system enabled annotations of books in order for the child to get an overview of the content and also to establish linkages to other books with similar contents.

Huang et al. described an interactive learning-guide and advisor system designed with RFID tags and PDA to assist museum visitors so as to improve their understanding of the museum exhibition. [10] The system guided the visitor through the art works while giving recommendations according to their preferences. This system was used not only for children but for all museum visitors.

The purposes of the related bodies of research described above are mainly for learning. The users interactively learn with or through the targeted objects by receiving additional digital information according to a location tag such as RFID.

By using a RFID system for enhancing physical play, Burleson, Jensen and Raaschou introduced 'Sprock-it', which was a hand-sized robotic character that encourages full-body interaction. [11] The main purpose of this work was to create an experience to promote social interactions through play. The purpose of this research is similar to SoundTag but the system is not a wearable device.

There are not many computer-embedded "wears" especially targeting children, which especially aims at inducing physical activity. As for RFID installed wearable computer for younger children's play platform, Tagaboo was proposed by Konkel et al. [12] The system has not yet been tested with children, therefore the effect of the wearable computing system is still an open question. Another recent system has been developed by Bekkerm and Eggen. [3] The aim with this system is to stimulate children to practice sport-related skills by embedded sensor and actuator technology. The prototypes are based on game design, persuasive technology and sport motivation theories. One of the design sketches called "Virtual Basketball" is a glove type interface, which provides feedback through LEDs according to a user's locomotion. Similar to Tagaboo[12], this work is not tested by children, so the effectiveness of the system is not yet certain.

Although there are few precedents for adapting wearable computer into children's play tools, Fails et al. suggests that embedded technologies in the physical world can positively affect children's learning. [13] According to the research by Fails et al. the embedded technology in a physical environment has advantages compared to a desktop virtual environment. This gave us confidence that wearable computer applications would be effective for use in children's play tools as the wearable computer correlates to the physical world. This helps to draw and keep children's attention to outdoor activity.

3 SoundTag Concept and System

In order to encourage physical activity, it is important to offer enjoyable play tools so as to motivate and engage children's interest. Based on this, we have developed SoundTag, a wearable sound feedback system based upon RFID tag and reader. The system is for children who are not yet capable of exercising highly sports or athletic games but capable of playing with friends for the purpose of improving athletic activity and develop the base of intellect. So the main target users of the system are preschool-age children. The constant physical activity in early childhood is estimated to be effective for growing both mental and physical strength. [2][14] Also Baumgarten stated play helps young children learn about their social world, begin to develop friendships and relationships, learn social rules, and grow creativity. [15] Therefore play is very important for preschool children both from the perspective of improving athletic ability and psycho-social characteristics.

While children play outside, visual perception system is highly dominant. Thus it is not effective to add visual information. Besides visual display system tends to be a large system when it is operated outdoors because display brightness level has to be kept high enough against the sun. It is highly probable for children being unaware of visual feedback while running outdoors. Thus we selected audio perception for interactive feedback system. In Hartley et al. [16], it is stated that basic audio perception and sound localization skills are developed as early as the sensory-motor stages of development. (birth to age two) So sound feedback is reliable for additional information even for pre-school children.

We define the SoundTag technical requirements as follows;

1. SoundTag is a wearable system designed for pre-school-age children to carry while playing outside.
2. SoundTag is a wearable system which is durable against children's active movement.
3. SoundTag is a wearable system which is capable of putting a unique ID on different parts of touching area so as to set the sound mark or scores on each part.
4. SoundTag is a wearable system which is capable of recording players' touching log or scores.
5. SoundTag is a wearable system which has an interface that is easily noticeable for children where to touch.

In order to satisfy those requirements, we employ Hitachi Mu chip RFID[17] and a small size reader for realizing wireless communication with unique ID settings and a board CPU for the control system. Fig.1 illustrates the conceptual sketch of Sound-Tag. Although SoundTag has a lot of potential to create various physical games, we adopt the rule of a conventional "tag" play to SoundTag as a first game scenario. The brief rule of the game is as follows; first, children split up into two parts, those who chase the runners and those who run from chasers. The chasers wear the system, which has a RFID antenna and controller system and the runners wear RFID tags, each of them has unique ID. When chaser touches one of the tags of the runners, sound feedback associated with each ID is played from the worn speakers. The touching log is recorded in the chaser's controller system.

Fig. 1. SoundTag Concept Sketch

4 Design Theory

4.1 Experiment with Wearable System Design

Two types of experiments were performed to test technical requirements of the Sound-Tag system. 1) To examine the percentage of the recognition rate of RFID tag for a given time; 1,2 and 3 Hz. This condition simulates momentary touch of a RFID tag when playing SoundTag. 2) To examine the percentage of the recognition rate of RFID tag when attached on the body since it is possible for tags to be affected by electrolyte in the human body. Tags were attached to bottled electrolyzed water and we examined the difference of the recognition rate under various conditions, i.e. directly attaching a tag on the bottle, attaching one/two/three-millimeter thick felt in between. (see Table 1) By attaching a more than 2mm thick insulator between the tag and the electrolyzed water, the recognition rate of the tag maintained almost the same as the standard environmental condition. (condition 1) Figure 2 shows the recognition rate of each condition listed in Table 1. Based on the result of the experiment, we decided to separate a RFID tag from the body with at least 2mm thickness.

Table 1. Five experimental conditions

case 1	RFID tag
case 2	electrolyzed water + RFID tag
case 3	electrolyzed water + 1mm felt + RFID tag
case 4	electrolyzed water + 2mm felt + RFID tag
case 5	electrolyzed water + 3mm felt + RFID tag

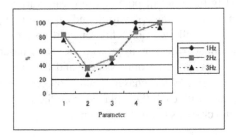

Fig. 2. Recognition rate of each condition

4.2 System Outline and Design

The system outline of SoundTag is shown in Fig.3. The system is constructed of two parts, chaser and runner. The outfit of a wearable computer for a chaser is shown in Fig.4. The antenna of the RFID reader is employed in the glove and two speakers are stitched in the upper side of both chests. A rechargeable 5.0 V battery pack is put in the left side pocket. The control system (board CPU,SD card, audio amplifier and RFID reader controller) are employed in the back of the wear. The total weight of the wear is about 120 g.

As for a runner, a mu chip tag is stitched in the instrumental shaped tag which is made by wool felt of 2mm thickness. Velcro tape is stitched on the back of the instrumental tag for easy attach and detach from the wear of a runner.

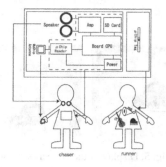

Fig. 3. SoundTag system outline

Fig. 4. SoundTag prototype (chaser(left), runner(right))

5 Pilot Study

5.1 Rules of the Game

In the pilot experiment, we conducted the instrumental sound collection game using SoundTag. The four participants were split up into two groups; two chasers and two runners who had the instrumental tags attached to their bodies. When the runner touches one of the tags, the sound is played appropriate to the shape of the tag. For example, when a runner touches a xylophone tag, the melody of xylophone is played. There were six varieties of tags (piano, xylophone, drum, trumpet, contrabass, cymbal) and each runner wore three kinds of the different tags. The touching logs were recorded in SD card memory. When the children changed the roles, from being a runner to becoming a chaser and the other way around, the location of tags were changed. This showed to be effective in that it kept up the children's interest in playing the game.

After finishing the game, the children were gathered in a room where they performed a common concert using the instruments that they had collected during the outdoor play. The intention with arranging this concert was to provide the children with a sense of achievement, not just showing the scores they had collected but also the common achievement. Fig. 5 shows the concert application.

The number of stars depicts the collected numbers of the instrument (in this case piano) during the outdoor play

All the items collected by one player harmonize a melody in the concert session.

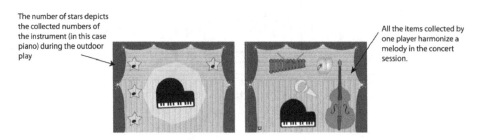

Fig. 5. Display of the concert session

5.2 SoundTag Evaluation

The purpose of the evaluation was to investigate how SoundTag could foster playfulness among children. The subjects in the study were five preschool children (2 boys and 3 girls), two elementary school children (1 boy and 1 girl). The experiment took place in a public park and community center. One set of the game lasted about 30 minutes (two 5-minute 'chase and run' game and 20-minutes concert). In total, 5 sets of the game were performed.

6 Results

High physical activity was observed among all of the participating children whilst they were playing the tag game, no matter if they were a chaser or a runner. The result indicated that SoundTag motivated the children to collect music tags by chasing each other and running to keep away from the chaser. However, it was not solely the chasing and running that motivated the children to keep up their interest in the game, The feature of collecting musical tags seemed to be the primary activity for the children. In traditional tag play, if for example a chaser runs slowly and cannot keep up with the runners and thereby not touch them so as to change roles, he or she sooner or later lose the interest as he or she has to play the same role over and over again. In the SoundTag tag game, on the other hand, the switching of roles was not that important in order to keep up the interest and motivation. The collecting of the different sound tags was an important factor to motivate the children to go on playing the game. These results are preliminary and further user studies are needed so as to be able to be more detailed about the features of the tool and the specific motivation factors. Fig. 6 shows children playing SoundTag game.

Another interesting finding from the video observation was that the subjects played the game collaboratively; they naturally developed team play. A common strategy among the 'chasers' was to be able to touch as many tags as possible. Similarly, the common strategy among the 'runners' was not to be touched by the chasers. Fig. 7 shows the example of this. Two chasers effectively used a slide to tag a runner.

The children created their own rules whilst playing SoundTag game, which was to shout 'touch' when they touched one of the tags.

During the concert session, all children reported the number of instruments they remembered touching and wanted to compare this with the result that the computer showed.

The parent of one of the girls who participated in the game said that she had previously been reluctant to participate in a computer supported reading experiment, but she vigorously participated in this experiment as it was promoting outdoor play. Furthermore one reason to why all the children seemed to enjoy running was that nowadays there are not so many open in the urban areas and this has forced the children to play indoors. Another parent commented that parents in general want to use play tools when playing with their children, especially those tools which motivate physical activity such as SoundTag. The parent furthermore emphasized the problem that nowadays there is too little space available to play outdoor games so a tool which induces playfulness even though the space is small would be helpful to keep up the children's interest in playing outside.

Fig. 6. Children playing with SoundTag

Fig. 7. Example of Team Play

7 Modified SoundTag

The first experiment showed positive effect to support children playing outdoors. However, the system only offers prerecorded sound feedback when touching the designated RFID tag. Recent development of the prototype, the second version of SoundTag enables recording audio when touching the RFID tag. This function enables children collect their favorite sound outdoors, which may offer enhanced creativity possibilities for the children.

The modified SoundTag system added recording function using an amplifier embedded 16.0 x 3.76 x 1.45(mm) mono-microphone. Also an embedded Linux computer with an audio board is used for RFID reader and audio manipulation. [18] The system outline is shown in Fig.8. When a wearer touches a RFID tag inserted card in Fig.9, the system goes to a recording mode. Then the wearer is able to record sound for 30 second with a microphone sewn around the cuff of right sleeve. The tag ID and collected sound are linked digitally so that when the wearer touches the card which has already recorded, the recorded sound is played.

A preliminary test was conducted at Ueno Zoological Gardens, oldest zoo in Japan. [19] Five elementary school children attended the experiment. All children wore SoundTag jacket and hold twelve 5.5(width) x 8.6cm(height) -size cards and a pen. Experimenter raised a topic what sound to collect. The topic was to collect the sound which was different from or similar to those you could listen to the southern island in Japan. By setting the topic, children consciously listen to the local sound which may find varieties of sound in the environment and may enhance creativities. When collected sound, the wearer scribbled down any comments by words and drawings on the back of the card. Fig. 10 shows children wearing SoundTag at the Ueno zoo. While

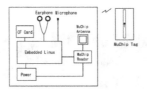

Fig. 8. Modified SoundTag System Outline

Fig. 9. RFID Inserted Card Front and Back with Children's Comments

Fig. 10. Children Wearing Modified SoundTag

conducting the experiment, some of the wearable system became unstable. There were only 15 sounds collected by the five wearers. Therefore the result didn't prove the effectiveness of the system offering enhanced creativity. However the observations of this test showed the positive reaction from children about the interface of recording function as well as RFID inserted card. For recording function, they raise their right hand while recording. This action was very unique and it paid their attention. Also, hands-free recording function was positively accepted for practical reason. And as for RFID inserted card, writing down their comments on the card by hand writing was received positive comment from children. They liked the idea that digitally recorded sound was linked to manually written card.

8 Conclusion and Future Research

In this paper, we propose SoundTag, RFID electronic tags based interactive wearable system using sound feedback in order to motivate children to play outside. We propose the design theory of the SoundTag system and have performed a basic experiment to evaluate the attributes when RFID is worn on the human body. We found that in order to prevent noise from electrolyzed water generated from human body in order to play the game properly, at least 2mm thickness is necessary to separate the body from RFID tag. Taking this result into consideration, we employed SoundTag system into a wearable computer for children and performed a pilot experiment. We have received positive feedback from children enjoying SoundTag game. Talking about the concert session, they seem to enjoy the difference of melody depending on the number of collected items and varieties of them. In this pilot study, we separate physical game and concert session, but we should merge them together for direct interaction system so that children enjoy direct composing while they play. This is one of the future works. Also during the concert session, we perceived that children compared the memorized number of collected items and the computer generated numbers, which supports the idea that they can remember their own performance. We should discuss children's memory schema with professionals and revise it for improving educational effect. We recently modified SoundTag system by adding the recording function. This makes it possible to create children's favorite sound feedback and this may assist developing creativity for children. We need further experiments to find out the relations with wearable interface and enhancing creativity.

In conclusion, SoundTag may enhance playfulness for children to play outside as well as supports to improve physical activity for them by keeping their concentration with computer assisted interface.

Acknowledgement. We appreciate the help of Ms. Tomomi Sato who arranged the pilot experiment as well as yui,shin,yuttan,kou,mocchi,hina,rei who fully enjoyed the play. We also would like to appreciate all the members of Sound Explorer Club in Keio Gijuku Yochisha Primary School for collaborative work for the second SoundTag experiment.

Modified SoundTag system and its experiment were funded by Nissan Science Foundation.

References

1. Study of Future Early Childhood Education Based on the Tendency of Recent Environmental Change. Central Education Council Report (2005) (in Japanese)
2. Amy, K.S.: Children are born to be outside and wild- not stuck inside and mild. EarlychildhoodNEWS (2007),
   http://www.earlychildhoodnews.com/earlychildhood/
   article_view.aspx?ArticleId=49
3. Tilde, B.M., Berry, E.H.: Designing for Children's Physical Play. In: CHI 2008 extended abstracts on Human factors in computing systems, pp. 2871–2876. ACM, New York (2008)
4. Ryoko, U., Michitaka, H., Kengo, K., Michie, S., Kenji, K., Tomohiro, K., Kenichiro, H.: Wearable Computer Application for Open Air Exhibition in EXPO 2005. In: Proceedings of the Second IEEE Pacific-Rim Conference on Multimedia, Beijing, October 2001, pp. 8–15. IEEE Press, New York (2001)
5. Atsushi, H., Ryoko, U., Koichi, H., Hirose, M., Sone, M., Kawamura, T.: Development and Demonstration of Wearable computer based Interactive Nomadic Gallery. In: Proceedings of the Sixth IEEE International Symposium of Wearable Computer, pp. 129–130. IEEE Press, New York (2002)
6. Atsushi, H., Jun, Y., Yuichi, N., Teiichi, N., Koichi, H., Hideaki, K., Michitaka, H.: A Real World Role-Playing Game as an Application of the Guide System in a Museum. In: Procceedings of the Fourteenth International Conference on Artificial Reality and Telexistence, pp. 29–34 (2004)
7. Facer, K., Joiner, R., Stanton, D., Reid, J., Hull, R., Kirk, D.: avannah: mobile gaming and learning? Journal of Computer Assisted Learning 20, 399–409 (2004)
8. Danielle, W., Eric, H., Yvonne, R., Cliff, R.: The Periscope: supporting a computer enhanced field trip for children. In: Personal and ubiquitous computing, July 2003, vol. 7(3), pp. 227–233. Springer, London (2003)
9. Andreas, L.-O., Jesper, N.: BibPhone-Adding Sound to the Children's Library. In: Proceedings of the Sixth international conference on Interaction design and children, Aalborg, June 2007, pp. 145–148. ACM, New York (2007)
10. Huang, Y.-P., Chuang, W.-P., Chang, Y.-T., Frode, S.E.: Enhanced Interactivity in Learning-Guide Systems with RFID. In: RFID Eurasia 2007 First Annual Conference, Istanbul, September 2007, pp. 1–6. IEEE Press, New York (2007)
11. Winslow, B., Camilla, J.N., Trine, R., Stefan, F.: Sprock-it: A physically Interactive Play System. In: Proceedings of the Sixth international conference on Interaction design and children, pp. 125–128. ACM, New York (2007)
12. Mirlam, K., Brygg, L.V.U., Catherine, H.: Tagaboo: a collaborative children's game based upon wearable RFID technology. Personal and Ubiquitous Computing 8(5), 382–384 (2004)
13. Jerry, F.A., Allison, D., Mona, G.L., Gene, C., Sante, S., Wayne, C.: Child's Play: A Comparison of Desktop and Physical Interactive Environments. In: Proceedings of Fourth International Conference for Interaction Design and Children, pp. 48–55. ACM, New York (2005)
14. Takken, T., Net, J., Kuis, W., Helders, J.M.P.: Physical activity and health related physical fitness in children with juvenile idiopathic arthritis. In: Annals of Rehumatic Diseases 2003, vol. 62, pp. 885–889. BMJ Publishing Group Ltd & European League Against Rheumatism (2003)

15. Miki, B.: Kids and the Internet: A Developmental Summary. In: ACM Computers in Entertainment, vol. 1(1), pp. 1–10. ACM, New York (2003)
16. Douglas, H.E.H., Beverly, W.A., Sarah, H.C., David, M.R.: Age-Related Improvements in Auditory Backward and Simultaneous Masking in 6- to 10-Year-Old. Children Journal of Speech, Language, and Hearing Research 43(6), 1402–1415 (2000)
17. Takaragi, K., Usami, M., Imura, R., Itsuki, R., Satoh, T.: An Ultra Small Individual Recognition Security Chip. In: IEEE Micro, November 2001, pp. 43–49. IEEE Computer Society Press, Los Alamitos (2001)
18. Gumstix, http://www.gumstix.com
19. Ueno Zoological Gardens (Japanese), http://www.tokyo-zoo.net/

A Comparison between Drill-Based and Game-Based Typing Software

Chun-Hung Lin and Eric Zhi-Feng Liu

Graduate Institute of Learning and Instruction
National Central University
No. 300, Jhongda Rd., Jhongli City, Taoyuan County 32001
Taiwan
sjohn1202@gmail.com, totem@cc.ncu.edu.tw

Abstract. Typing skill is a very important skill for students now, and it's a critical issue about how to train and improve students' typing skill. In the past, it was a common strategy to design software for students to practice their typing skill. Because of the differences in the design approaches, different types of typing software, drill-based and game-based software show up. This study compared the learning genres and the effect on typing speed. Experimental design was used to verify the statistical hypothesis in this study. The experimental group used game-based typing software, and the control group used drill-based typing software. The results of pre-test and post-test were compared to evaluate the effect of different types of typing software. The result showed that both game-based and drill-based typing software could improve students' English typing speed. Besides, different types of typing software had different advantages and disadvantages. Finally, some suggestions were proposed for typing software design.

Keywords: Computer-assisted instruction, typing speed, drill-based typing software, game-based typing software.

1 Introduction

In 21st century, the development of information technologies has mass impact on different aspects of human life. Computers called the greatest invention in 21st century become powerful enough to change education, and because of the popularity of computers, typing skill becomes a basic skill. Improving typing skill can help students to use computers to deal with different kinds of tasks more efficiently. In the past, typing software was commonly used to train students' typing skill, and they usually did not have much attractive multimedia effect. The students just typed according to the letters shown on screen, and improved their typing skill by practicing again and again. Recently, games become more and more popular, and one of the reasons is that games have lots of attractive elements, like lots of multimedia effect and interesting scripts. About the educational effect of typing games, games are more interesting than traditional instruction, and that is the reason why people use typing games to train their typing skill. Many typing software were designed according the motivational

Z. Pan et al. (Eds.): Transactions on Edutainment III, LNCS 5940, pp. 48–58, 2009.

principle, and were expected to help improve students' typing skill. This study tried to realize the effect on typing skill of drill-based and game-based typing software, and proposed possible design direction for typing software.

2 Literature Review

2.1 Game-Based Learning

Because of the development of information technologies, a variety of games show up, and the content of games becomes more and more attractive. Prensky (2001) mentioned that the 21st century is a generation of game-based learning, and he called the people who were born after 1975 as the G generation [1]. Due to the coming of G generation and the development of personal computer, digital simulation games become more and more popular. Actually, game was seen as a natural and important element in students' learning, and it should be integrated into the educational context to increase the learning motivation in the classroom. Many researchers found that when adolescents played games, the learning activities they engaged were more complex and challenging [2-5], and games became powerful tools to improve students' learning [6]. Recently, many researchers also confirmed the learning effect from game-based learning [1, 7-8] and suggested some empirical-based evaluative indicators for computer games [9]. Malone (1980) concluded that the reasons why games can increase motivation were because four elements like fantasy, challenge, curiosity, and control were included in games [10]. Similarly, Prensky (2001) thought that "fun" is why digital games can increase students' learning motivation [1]. Besides, unpredictability and competitions in games can fascinate students, increase their curiosity and motivation, and improve their learning [11-12].

Different from the games in the past which strengthened the importance of multimedia effect and entertainment, recently, some researchers proposed the concept of serious games. Serious games refer to software developed with game technology and game design principle for educational or training purpose, not only for entertainment [13]. Serious game is a type of edutainment software. In the past, the design of games usually focused on entertainment, and tried to increase users' motivation through attractive multimedia effect and scripts. Because a serious game is designed for certain purpose, the educational objective is considered first. Moreover, the need of the learners is also taken into consideration to achieve the learning goal. Under this point of view, entertainment is not the most important consideration, but learners' learning. Because serious games were designed for certain purposes, both educational and game-design professionals were required to design serious games. Two design principles are usually applied in game design: game design and backward design. Game design focused on the entertainment in the games, but backward design focused on learners' learning [14]. Repenning and Lewis (2005) taught undergraduate students how to design educational games, and they found the balance between entertainment and learning is very important [15]. Besides, they also found that it would be more difficult to design an educational game if the designers didn't have enough knowledge about teaching and learning.

2.2 Different Types of Typing Softwares

The typing games can approximately be divided into two different types: drill-based and game-based software. Drill-based software usually doesn't have amazing animation or multimedia effect, and they usually ask users to type according to the letters shown on screen (Fig.1). The more letters users type correctly, the higher score they get. Drill-based software usually shows a virtual keyboard on screen to assist the users to learn typing. The change of color and sound are also used to confirm if the users type correctly or not.

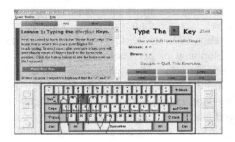

Fig. 1. Letter chase typing tutor (from http://www.letterchase.com/)

Game-based software usually has attractive multimedia effect and scripts, and they are easier for users to engage in using the software. In order to complete the missions in the game, the only strategy the users can use is to type as fast as they can (Fig. 2 and Fig. 3).

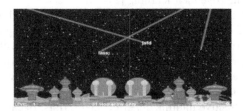

Fig. 2. Martian city defender (from http://freetypinggame.net/play.asp)

Fig. 3. KeyMan typing game (from http://www.typingtest.com/games/default.asp?m=1)

3 Methodology

3.1 Research Questions

1. What are the differences in the characteristics of learning between drill-based and game-based typing software?
2. What are the differences in the effect on typing speed between drill-based and game-based typing software?

3.2 Experimental Design

There were 160 second year junior high school students participating in this study. The students studied in a junior high school in middle Taiwan, and they came from five different classes. 82 students were males (53.2%) and 72 students were females (46.8). Experimental design was used in this study. The independent variable was different types of typing software. There were 96 students in the control group, and they used drill-based typing software to learn typing, and there are 64 students used game-based typing software to learn typing. The dependent variable was typing speed, and the difference of typing speed between pre-test and post-test and the effect on typing speed of different software would be compared. The instructional content and schedule of both groups were the same, and the two groups were taught by the same teacher. The educational experiment was last for four weeks, one time a week, and twenty minutes for each time.

In order to make sure the participants' typing speed before the experiment, a pre-test was applied to control group and experimental group. Then, do the educational experiment for four weeks. The schedule of instruction was: 1. Set the instructional goal. 2. Instruction of learning content. 3. Individual practice with typing software. 4. Feedback from the instructor. Finally, a post-test was applied to both groups to realize the participants' learning outcome.

After excluding six invalid samples, the total number of valid samples in this study is 154. 62 students were in experimental group, and 92 students were in control group. From the comparison of pre-test between control and experimental group, the result showed that the mean of pre-test was 13.68 and the mean of post-test was 13.61. The Levene's test didn't reach significant difference ($F=.020\ P=.887>.05$), and it showed that the deviation of both groups was the same. The typing speed between control group and experiment group didn't reach significant difference ($t = .071$, $p>.05$) (Table 1). It showed that before the instructional experiment, the typing speed of two groups was the same.

Table 1. The descriptive statistics and independent-sample t test of pre-test

Group	N	M	SD	df	t
Control group	92	13.68	6.19		
Experimental group	62	13.61	6.07	152	$0.07^{\text{n.s.}}$

3.3 Instrument

3.3.1 Win WTS (for Pre-test and for Post-test)

WinWTS was free typing software. In this study, WinWTS was used in the pre-test and the post-test to evaluate students' typing speed (Fig. 4). This software provided Chinese and English typing practice and test. Besides, users could decide the length and the difficulty of the test in the software.

Fig. 4. Screenshot of WinWTS from http://www.happyreading.com.tw/

3.3.2 Drill-Based Typing Software

This drill-based typing software was provided by the website - happyreading book-worm (http://www.happyreading.com.tw/) (Fig. 5). This typing software fitted the educational objective. The interface of the software was simple and clear, and the size of text in the software was suitable. Besides, the software fitted the need for students to learn typing skill by drill and practice.

Fig. 5. Drill-based software from http://www.happyreading.com.tw/

3.3.3 Game-Based Typing Software

The game-based typing software chosen in this study was Ozawa-ken for Windows (Fig. 5). The software was interesting and challenging. In this software, the users defeated their opponents by typing correctly and fast. Although the interface was in Japanese, but students would not have trouble in using the software because the interface was clear and simple.

Fig. 6. Game-based typing software from http://www.vector.co.jp/soft/dl/win95/edu/se111693.html

4 Result

4.1 Features of Software and Learning of Different Types of Typing Software

4.1.1 Features of Software

In order to realize the characteristics of different types of typing software, the software was analyzed from three dimensions: characteristics of multimedia, challenge, and game script (Table 2).

About characteristics of multimedia, the drill-based typing software didn't have much multimedia effect, and only simple sound effect and simple interface were designed in it. In the game-based typing software, much multimedia effect and attractive animation were designed in it.

About challenge, both the drill-based typing software and the game-based typing software created the challenge mainly through the length of letter strings, time limit, and scoring. Furthermore, increasing speed, and amount of missions were designed in the game-based typing software.

About the game script, in drill-based typing software, no script was designed. However, in game-based typing software, some attractive script was designed, and it would make the learners more willing to use the software.

Table 2. The comparison of software features between different types of typing software

Software features	Types of software	
	Drill-based typing software	Game-based tying software
Multimedia	Simple sound effect	attractive animation and sound effect
Challenge	length of letter strings, time limit, and scoring	length of letter strings, time limit, scoring, increasing speed, and amount of missions
Game script	no	yes

4.1.2 Features of Learning

When students used the drill-based typing software, they already kept a clear learning goal in mind --- learning typing. Through the instruction of the drill-based typing software, students practiced typing again and again to improve their typing speed. This kind of learning was called explicit learning (Table 3).

Differently, the learning happened in game-based typing software was implicit learning. Students used game-based typing software not because they wanted to practice typing but wanted to enjoy the game. In order to complete the missions in the game, students must type according the requests of the game. In this context, students improved their typing speed gradually during playing the game.

Table 3. The comparison of learning features between different types of typing software

Learning features	Types of software	
	Drill-based typing software	Game-based typing software
Mechanism of learning assistance	Provided a virtual keyboard in the software to assist students in typing	No assistance mechanism
Learning genres	Explicit learning	Implicit learning

4.2 The Effect on Typing Speed of Typing Software

4.2.1 The Comparison of Pre-test and Post-test of Experimental Group

Before the educational experiment, a pre-test was applied to the experimental group to make sure the typing ability of the group, and after the experiment, a post-test was applied to the group. In order to realize effect on students typing speed of game-based typing software, the paired-sample t test was used in this study. The independent variable was the type of test, and the dependent variable was the typing speed.

Table 4. The descriptive statistics and paired-sample t test of experimental group

Test	N	M	SD	df	t
Pre-test	62	13.61	6.07	61	11.04***
Post-test	62	18.53	6.54		

***$p < .001$.

The result showed that the mean of pre-test is 13.61 and the mean of post-test is 18.53. The typing speed between pre-test and post-test reached significant difference ($t = 11.04$, $p<.001$) (Table 4). It showed that game-based typing software can improve the students' typing speed. The possible reason why game-based typing software can improve students' typing speed is that the attractive multimedia effect increases students' learning motivation. In order to complete the missions, the students must type faster and faster. In this context, the typing speed was improved.

4.2.2 The Comparison of Pre-test and Post-test of Control Group

Before the educational experiment, a pre-test was applied to the control group to make sure the typing ability of the group, and after the experiment, a post-test was applied to the group. In order to realize effect on students typing speed of drill-based typing software, the paired-sample t test was used in this study. The independent variable was the type of test, and the dependent variable was the typing speed.

Table 5. The descriptive statistics and paired-sample t test of control group

Test	N	M	SD	df	t
Pre-test	92	13.68	6.19	91	13.83***
Post-test	92	19.15	6.49		

***p< .001.

The result showed that the mean of pre-test was 13.68 and the mean of post-test was 19.15. The typing speed between pre-test and post-test reached significant difference (t = 13.83, p<.001) (Table 5). It showed that drill-based typing software can improve the students' typing speed. Because typing is a kind of motion skill, drill-and-practice is a very useful strategy for this kind of motion skill. In drill-based typing software, students improved their typing speed through practice continually.

4.2.3 The Comparison of Pre-test and Post-test of All Participants

The result showed that the mean of pre-test was 13.66 and the mean of post-test was 18.9. The typing speed between pre-test and post-test reached significant difference (t = 17.7, p<.001) (Table 6). In general, students improved their typing speed after they using typing software, and it showed that both kinds of typing software could improve the students' typing speed.

Table 6. The descriptive statistics and paired-sample t test of all participants

Test	N	M	SD	df	t
Pre-test	154	13.66	6.12	153	17.7***
Post-test	154	18.9	6.49		

***p< .001.

4.3 The Effect on Typing Speed between Drill-Based and Game-Based Typing Software

In order to compare the effect on students typing speed between different kinds of typing software, an independent sample t test was used in this study.

The result showed that the mean of pre-test was 19.15 and the mean of post-test was 18.53. The Levene's test did not reach significant difference ($F=.030$, $P=.862>.05$), and it showed that the deviations of both groups were the same. The typing speed between control group and experimental group did not reach significant difference ($t = .580$, $p>.05$) (Table 7). It showed that the post-test result of control group and experimental group had no difference. This result indicated that the learning effect of typing speed was the same no matter the students used drill-based typing software or game-based typing software. In this study, although the drill-based typing software did not have attractive multimedia effect, but it fitted the students' learning need. That was why the drill-based typing software could improve the students' typing speed. Differently, game-based typing software focused on the entertainment. Because of the multimedia effect and attractive script, students would more engage in using the software than drill-based typing software. However, the result showed that both kinds of typing software could improve students' typing speed, but no one is better than the other. It showed that the single direction design approach could not bring out better learning effect.

Table 7. The descriptive statistics and independent-sample t test of post-test between control group and experimental group

Group	N	M	SD	df	t
Control group	92	19.15	6.49	152	$0.58^{n.s.}$
Experimental group	62	18.53	6.54		

5 Conclusion

In the past, multimedia effect was seen as a very important element in game design [9]. Many researchers focused on the issue about how to make games attractive, and to increase students' motivation by games. However, in this study, the result showed that both drill-based and game-based typing software could improve students' typing speed. This result indicated that the educational element and entertainment element in typing software were beneficial for learning. In drill-based typing software, the design focused on the learning objective and the learning need of students, and improved the students' typing speed through continual practice. In game-based typing software, differently, the students didn't focus on learning typing but just played the game. The students' typing speed was improved indirectly during playing the game. Although both drill-based and game-based typing software could improve students' typing speed, but obviously the characteristics of learning in the two kinds of typing software were different.

In this study, the effect on typing speed of drill-based and game-based typing software was compared. The result showed that the effect on typing speed of the two kinds of software was the same. Repenning and Lewis indicated that entertainment and learning were two aspects needed to be considered when design educational games, and the balance of the two aspects would decide the game was successful or not [15]. In this study, the result showed that only design the software in a single direction would not show better learning result. From leaning direction, like drill-based typing software, although the software fitted the learning objective and the need of students, but because of lack of entrainment elements, the students weren't easy to engage in using the software. In the observation, students finished their assigned typing work they usually stop using this software. Contrarily, from entertainment direction, like game-based typing software, the attractive multimedia effect and script made the students engage in using the software. However, because this kind of software ignored the design for learning objective, the learning effect of game-based typing software was not better than the learning effect of drill-based typing software.

When designing typing software, entertainment and learning are aspects need to be considered [9]. Both entertainment and learning design direction were beneficial for learning typing skill, but different kinds of design also showed different disadvantages and limitations. Therefore, it is better to consider the two aspects at the same time when design edutainment software, and try to keep the balance between the two elements to produce the optimal learning effect [16-17]. The future studies may confirm if the learning effect from both learning element and entertainment element is better than the learning effect only from learning element or entertainment element.

Acknowledgments

The authors would like to thank the National Science Council of the Republic of China for financially supporting this research under Contract No. NSC 97-2631-S-008-003.

References

1. Prensky, M.: Digital Game-Based Learning. McGraw-Hill, New York (2001)
2. Gee, J.P.: What Video Games Have to Teach Us About Learning and Literacy? ACM Computers in Entertainment 1(1), 1–4 (2003)
3. Gee, J.P.: Game-Like Learning: An Example of Situated Learning and Implications for Opportunity to Learn (2005),
   http://www.academiccolab.org/resources/documents/
   Game-LikeLearning.rev.pdf
4. Becker, K.: How Are Games Educational? Learning Theories Embodied in Games. In: DiGRA 2005 Conference, Burnaby, Canada (2005)

5. Kattenbelt, C., Raessens, J.: Computer Games and the Complexity of Experience. In: Di-GRA 2003 Level Up Conference, Utrecht, Netherlands (2003)
6. Hsiao, H.C.: A Brief Review of Digital Games and Learning. In: The First IEEE International Workshop on Digital Game and Intelligent Toy Enhanced Learning, Jhongli, Taiwan (2007)
7. Prensky, M.: Digital Game-based Learning. Computer in Entertainment 1(1), 21–21 (2003)
8. Asgari, M., Kaufman, D.: Relationships Among Computer Games, Fantasy, and Learning. In: The 2nd International Conference on Imagination and Education (2004)
9. Liu, E.Z.F., Lin, C.H.: Developing Evaluative Indicators for Educational Computer Games. British Journal of Educational Technology 40(1), 174–178 (2009)
10. Malone, T.: What Makes Things Fun to Learn? A Study of Intrinsically Motivating Computer Games. Palo Alto Research Center, CA (1980)
11. Jenkins, H.: Game Theory. Technology Review 29, 1–3 (2002)
12. McFarlane, A., Sparrowhawk, A., Heald, Y.: Report on the Educational Use of Games: An Exploration by TEEM of the Contribution Which Games Can Make to the Education Process (2002), http://reservoir.cent.uji.es/canals/octeto/es/440
13. Wikipedia: Serious Game. FL: Wikimedia Foundation, Inc. (2009), http://www.wikipedia.org
14. Wiggins, G., McTighe, J.: Understanding by Design. Prentice-Hall, Englewood Cliffs (2000)
15. Repenning, A., Lewis, C.: Playing a Game: The Ecology of Designing, Building and Testing Games as Educational Activities. In: Proceedings of ED-MEDIA: World Conference on Educational Multimedia, Hypermedia & Telecommunications, Montreal, Canada (2005)
16. Liu, E.Z.F., Kou, C.H., Lin, C.H., Cheng, S.S., Chen, W.T.: Developing Multimedia Instructional Material for Robotics Education. WSEAS Transactions on Communications 7(11), 1102–1111 (2008)
17. Liu, E.Z.F., Cheng, S.S., Lin, C.H., Chang, Y.F., Chen, W.T.: The Development of Evaluation Indicators for LEGO Multimedia Instructional Material. WSEAS Transactions on Computers 7(10), 1782–1791 (2008)

Widget-Based Simulator for Testing Smart Space[*]

Changgu Kang, Yoosoo Oh, and Woontack Woo

GIST U-VR Lab.
Gwangju 500-712, S. Korea
{ckang,yoh,wwoo}@gist.ac.kr

Abstract. In this paper, we propose a widget-based simulator for testing smart space by using virtual space. It is especially useful within this simulation field, because virtual space alleviates limited constraints such as time, space, technique, and cost. Researchers within this ubiquitous computing field use virtual space to simulate entities such as sensors, actuators, and services. Previous works focus more on systematic functions rather than simulation space configurations, and they consider only single service unit simulations. However, our proposed simulator focuses on the easy configuration of simulation space, which users want, and the simulation of entities such as detailed units (e.g., actuators, sensors, and context-awareness). Our simulator supports the set up of a variety of services by using dynamic links. For the design of our simulator, we consider widget-based virtual entities and plug-in techniques. We configure a virtual smart home in order to test our proposed simulation. We also evaluate the robustness of our proposed simulation. Finally, the proposed simulator is expected to provide a simulation environment in which simulation space and testing are made more effective for users.

Keywords: Simulation, virtual reality, smart space, context-awareness.

1 Introduction

A variety of services using virtual space, such as *World of Warcraft*, *Google Earth*, *Virtual Earth*, and *Second Life* has been recently released due primarily to an increase in the interest of virtual space. As a result of various constraints within real space, (e.g., cost, time, and space) virtual space is now viewed as more effective because of the space it provides for indirect experiences and useful information [1]. Specifically, since virtual space utilizes an environment which is not restricted by time and cost, virtual space is more useful for simulations environment. Since 3D virtual space creates realistic visuals, simulation space which uses the virtual space seems more realistic, and users receive realistic visual feedback from such a system. Because of these benefits, the ubiquitous computing research field has used virtual space to test smart services, or smart spaces [5,6,7,8].

---

[*] This research is supported by Korea Creative Content Agency (KOCCA), Ministry of culture, Sports and Tourism (MCST), under the Culture Technology (CT) Research & Development Program 2009.

Z. Pan et al. (Eds.): Transactions on Edutainment III, LNCS 5940, pp. 59–69, 2009.

The process by which a smart space provides vital services is as follows: First, sensor data is collected within a smart space. Secondly, sensor data is interpreted to generate context information. Thirdly, context information is applied to service actuators to provide services for users. Services provided in the smart space consists of sensors, context-awareness, and actuators and most researches work independently during this process to create these entities [2,3,4]. Therefore, when designing such simulators for the testing of smart space, consideration has to be given to simulation environments in respect to each entity (e.g., sensor, context-awareness, and actuator). Moreover, simulators have to be flexible in order to be applied within various simulation scenarios. To satisfy these requirements, simulators must be modified in order for simulation space to become detailed units. It must also be able easily to add new entities to simulation space for various simulation scenarios.

There are several previous works, CAST [5], UbiREAL [6], CASS [7], C@SA [8], etc., which have tested smart space by using virtual space. Most of these works deal with context-awareness for simulations because of its importance in the field of ubiquitous computing. Particularly, UbiREAL was designed for realistic simulation and systematic testing. Moreover, C@SA used intelligent agents for managing and simulating virtual services within virtual smart space. As we mentioned, smart service consists of actuators, sensors, and context-awareness. Therefore, simulators must be able to change each entity within simulation space. To adopt diverse scenarios, simulators must be able to provide new, easily-made virtual entities, and then be able to apply newly developed entities within simulation space. However, previous works usually exclude such these points.

To address these points, we propose a widget-based simulator to test smart space. First, we adopt a widget concept so that the simulator can provide flexible simulation space. Our proposed widget-based simulator provides independent implementation of widgets, and users can configure virtual services by using dynamic links between widgets. Second, we consider plug-ins as appropriate methods to register new widgets. Users can apply developed widgets to simulation space by moving new widgets to a fixed folder. Not only can users create a variety of virtual services by using shared widgets with our proposals, they can also more easily share widgets among themselves. Previous works depended on smart home scenarios within smart space in ubiquitous computing. Our proposed simulator is more general in design than previous works because our target domain not only includes smart homes but also diverse smart spaces.

The rest of this paper is organized as follows: Section 2 contains the design of our widget-based simulator. Section 3 contains the implementation of our simulator. Section 4 contains the evaluation of our proposed simulator. Section 5 contains the conclusion and a discussion of future works.

2 Architectural Design

2.1 Design Goals

In this paper, we consider the following two points as being vital for the design of our proposed simulator:

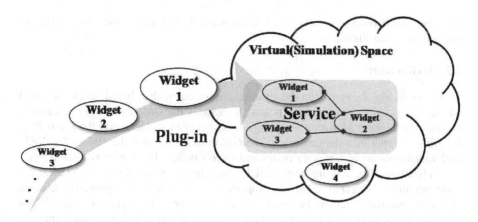

Fig. 1. Concept of widget-based Simulator

1)Widget-based virtual entities
2)Plug-in techniques to register new widgets

1) Widget-based virtual entities. The concept for our proposed simulator is based on the implementation of virtual entities in the form of widgets. This concept is considered in order that the simulation spaces are configured as smaller than service unit. Services should not be determined before simulation programs are enacted, but rather during operation. It is possible to configure services at real-time. Basically, connectivity between widgets is important because new services are generated through the connection of widgets. We define interface based on formal and primitive information (actuator-command) or on the data (sensor-raw data) of entities. Eventually, a context-aware widget must be implemented with input gates from sensor widgets, and output gates must be connected to actuator widgets. Because widgets are connected by context-aware widgets, dependency exists between context-aware widgets, and sensors or actuators. We discover similar points when considering the simulation of actuators and sensors in previous works. The simulation space of previous works includes all actuators and sensors, and only one context-aware module exists. By defining rules of operation for context-aware modules, services can be established. Although these simulators provide new simulation entity configurations for sensors and actuators, they do not support new context-awareness configurations. Also, because rules which control input interface in context-awareness are dependent on simulators and context-aware entities, it is difficult to independently configure context-aware entities within simulation space.

2) Plug-in techniques to register new widgets. Plug-in techniques should be used to register new widgets. When applied to simulators, this technique can assist users in the registration of widgets within simulators. Most previous works don't include precise methods which implement virtual services. Furthermore, there is no way for users to register new virtual services. However, when users share widgets by using our proposed simulator, they can easily register them without much difficulty. Also, our proposed simulator supports the registration of widgets during operation. Our two key points enable users dynamically to configure services by selecting sensors, actuators, and context-awareness widgets which users want. Fig. 1 shows the concept behind our widget-based simulator.

2.2 Architecture

As shown in Fig. 2, we design the architecture for our widget-based simulator based on our two previously mentioned points. It includes the *Object Manager* to manage objects, the *Linking Manager* to manage links between widgets, and the *Input Rule Interface* to input user-defined rules. The *Object Manager* uses the *Object Tree* (oTree) which consists of *Category* nodes and *Object* nodes. The *Category* node doesn't have objective data, and are only used for the classification of objects. The *Object* node can utilize *Widget* or *3D Model* properties to visualize virtual space. The *Linking Manager* manages relations between widgets in order to configure services. When users establish a connection between two widgets, our proposed simulator generates *Link* nodes to the *Link Group* node. Fig. 3 shows the structures for the *Object Manager* and the *Linking Manager*.

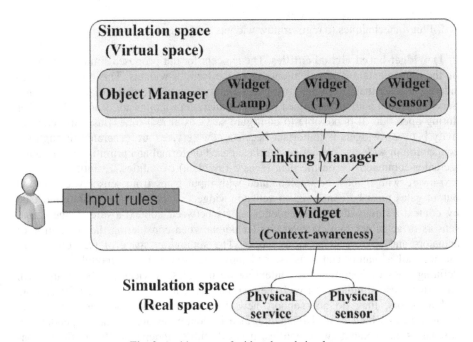

Fig. 2. Architecture of widget-based simulator

We consider two interfaces in order to use a variety of context-aware widgets. First interface is an interface to input user-defined rules. Second interface is an interface between context-awareness widgets and other widgets. Sensor widgets automatically send data to context-aware widgets, including a command by which input actuator widgets are activated. Commands for actuator widgets are deduced by user-defined rules and context information through the conditional matching of context-aware widgets.

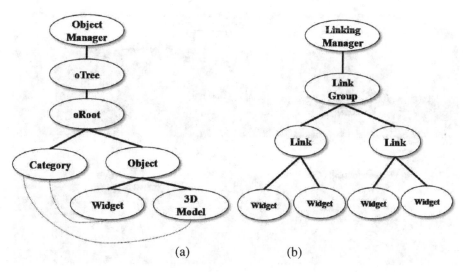

Fig. 3. The structure of (a) The *Object Manager* and (b) The *Linking Manager*

3 Implementation

We implement a widget-based simulator, actuator widgets and a context-aware widget. Actuator widgets are based on a lamp actuator and an air conditioner widget. We use OpenSceneGraph [11] for 3D visualization and 3D Studio MAX 9 [12] for 3D models. We develop our proposed simulator with the use of the visual studio 2005(MFC).

3.1 Widget-Based Simulator

Our simulator includes manipulation functions for configuring simulation space such as translation, rotation, and scale. After exporting our model, or the widgets which users want, users can then use the manipulation functions by clicking on exported widgets or models, and selecting manipulation menus. Fig. 4 shows object manipulation and configured simulation space with the use of the manipulation functions.

Also Fig. 4 (b) shows other interfaces used for simulation. Our simulator supports three interfaces in order to configure virtual (simulation) space: the **Object List**, **Rule Input**, and **Controller**. The **Object List** enumerates widgets and 3d models. Our simulator adds widgets and 3d models to the **Object List** when our simulator starts. Added objects appear in simulation space through the *Export Function* of the **Object List** interface. In addition, users can add objects to the **Object List** by using the *Add Function*. The **Rule Input** Interface saves inputted rules according to the context formulation for context-aware widgets. The **Controller** interface provides control buttons to save and load simulation space as well as some functions for simulation.

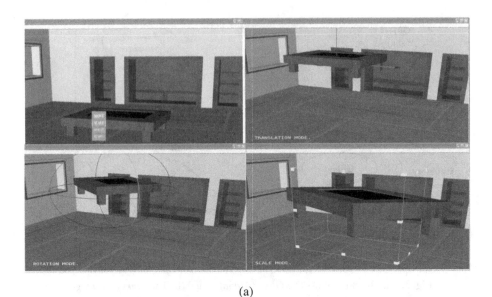

(a)

(b)

Fig. 4. (a) Manipulation functions (e.g., translation, rotation, and scale) and (b) configured simulation space and simulation interface

We implement the SimLib.lib to develop widgets. Users are able to handle events by some functions in the SimLib.lib. Table 1 shows the functions of the SimLib.lib. Additionally, widget developers can establish widget properties such as categories, names, and commands. As we mentioned, our proposed simulator manages widgets and 3D models by using the categories within the tree structure. The Object Manipulator exists to position each 3D model in our simulator. Users can change position, rotation, and scale of 3D models to configure simulation space. Also, users can save and read simulation configuration files in the form of XML. Fig 5 shows the XML format.

Table 1. Functions of SimLib.lib

Type	Function	Description
Required	SetNameObj	Set the name of a widget
	SetCategory	Set the category of a widget
	CreateModel	Register a 3D model for a widget
Optional	DoActionHandle	Set a behavior according to itself commands
	KeyEventHandle	Set a behavior for key input
	MouseEventHandle	Set a behavior for mouse input
	RefreshModel	Change a 3D model

```xml
<?xml version="1.0" encoding="utf-8" ?>
- <VirtualSpace>
  - <VEntities>
    - <AUDIO Trans="0.00000 25.73100 0.00000" Rotate="0.00000 0.00000 0.0
        <Category>MODELLIST</Category>
      </AUDIO>
    - <CUSHION Trans="0.00000 0.00000 0.00000" Rotate="0.00000 0.00000 0.
        <Category>MODELLIST</Category>
      </CUSHION>
    - <ROOFFRAME Trans="0.00000 3.66970 25.91607" Rotate="0.00000 0.000(
        NodeMask="2147483647">
        <Category>MODELLIST</Category>
      </ROOFFRAME>
    - <ROOM Trans="0.00000 0.00000 0.00000" Rotate="0.00000 0.00000 0.00
        <Category>MODELLIST</Category>
```

Fig. 5. The XML format saving and loading simulation space

3.2 Widgets

We develop a context-aware widget, as well as lamp and air conditioner widgets for simulation. The context-aware widget is based on the Unified Context-aware Application Model (UCAM) [3]. Existing UCAM consists of a service and a sensor. We modify that it becomes one unified UCAM. Likewise, we develop context-aware widgets by using modified UCAMs. We implement rule parsing and condition matching modules to modify UCAMs in order to apply user-defined rules from the Rule Input Interface to express UCAMs. Fig. 6 shows the formula for the context-aware widget.

IF WHO:PUBLIC:NAME:STRING:NULL:CKANG [CONDITION]
IF WHERE:PUBLIC:SymbolicLocation:STRING:NULL:ubiHome [CONDITION]
THEN HOW:PUBLIC:Lamp:STRING:NULL:BLUE [ACTION]

Fig. 6. Rule formula of context-aware widget

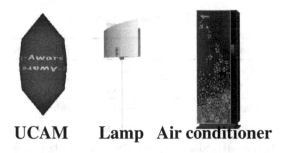

UCAM   Lamp   Air conditioner

Fig. 7. 3D models of implemented widgets

Lamp and air conditioner widgets are developed from the form of actuator widgets. Each widget possesses the 3D model. Fig. 7 shows the 3D model for the implementation of widgets. The lamp widget has command properties by the following colors: WHITE, RED, GREEN, and BLUE. The air conditioner widget has ON, and OFF.

4 Simulation and Evaluation

Fig. 8 shows a simulation model using implemented widgets. Users can simultaneously use physical sensors and virtual services for simulation within virtual and real space by using implemented context-aware widget. We configure virtual smart homes based on the simulation model in Fig. 8 and simulate lamp services by using sensor data inputted from particle sensors [13] such as those found in physical sensors. Fig. 9 shows the simulation of lamp and air conditioner services. We define the rules in Fig. 10. Virtual smart homes are based on the ubiHome [9] as shown in Fig. 11.

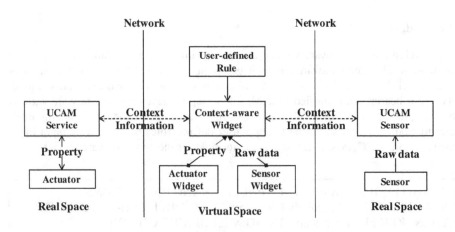

Fig. 8. Simulation model using implemented widgets

Fig. 9. Simulation of lamp and air conditioner

IF HOW:PUBLIC:LightLevel:STRING:NULL:LOW [CONDITION]
THEN HOW:PUBLIC:Lamp:STRING:NULL:RED [RESULT]
IF HOW:PUBLIC:TemperatureLevel:STRING:NULL:HIGH [CONDITION]
THEN HOW:PUBLIC:Aircon:STRING:NULL:ON [RESULT]

Fig. 10. User-defined rules for simulation

Fig. 11. Real ubiHome and virtual ubiHome

We measure the robustness of our application within evaluation areas. Measured items include system error rates, adaptation time, and simulation time. The setup for the measurement of the system error rate is the same as in Fig 10. We use the following conditions to conduct our experiment: Intel® Core™2 Duo 1.66GHz, 2GB RAM, and nVidia GeForce 8400. We measure the resulting error rate by comparing user-defined rules with data inputted from outside UCAM sensors. The adaptation time equals the duration from the time when user change rules to the time when changed rules are applied to simulation environment. Finally, we measure simulation time according to the number of services. The purpose of simulation time also includes whether real time simulation is possible or not. When users add services to simulation space at real time, we measure the time it takes all services to become active. For this measurement, we assume that the data which are for all services to be active always input from a sensor.

As the result of our first experiment, user-defined rules and context information from UCAM sensors were successfully matched without error by using condition matching. The duration for adaptation time averages 8.2 ms. The frame rate for 3D rendering is about 60fps within our experiment environment. The result shows that our modified rules can be applied to simulation environments in less time than the time it takes for 1 frame. The result shows that the number of services does not influence simulation time. In conclusion, even if users add services to simulation space, most simulation time almost does not increase. Table 2 shows the experimental results for adaptation time and simulation time.

Table 2. Experimental results for adaptation time and simulation time

	Adaptation Time	Simulation time according to the number of services					
		1	2	3	4	5	6
Time(ms)	8.2	9.8	8.1	10.5	7.3	9.9	8.2

5 Conclusion

In this paper, we proposed a widget-based simulator for the testing of smart space. Also, we focused our attention on two points in the design of our proposed simulator. Firstly, we focused our research on implementation of widget-based virtual entities. Secondly, we focused on plug in techniques. Users can not only independently implement widget-based virtual sensors, context-awareness, and actuators, but can also configure services with the use of dynamic linking. Users can also configure a variety of services by using and sharing other widgets which other users have developed.

We measured error rates, adaptation time and simulation time according to the quantity of services in order to reveal the application robustness for our proposed simulator. The results show that there are no errors involved in rule matching, and furthermore, it is possible to change and simulate services at real time. In our future, we are considering the simultaneous connection and simulation of services within augment reality (AR), virtual reality (VR), and real space. We have referred to it as the U-VR environment [10]. By implementing our application, users can not only configure U-VR services, but also simulate their own services.

References

1. Kock, N.: E-Collaboration and E-Commerce in Virtual Worlds: The Potential of Second Life and World of Warcraft. International Journal of e-Collaboration 4(3), 01–13 (2008)
2. Choi, A., Oh, Y., Park, G., Woo, W.: Stone type Physiological Sensing Device for Daily Monitoring in an Ambient Intelligence Environment. In: Aarts, E., Crowley, J.L., de Ruyter, B., Gerhäuser, H., Pflaum, A., Schmidt, J., Wichert, R. (eds.) AmI 2008. LNCS, vol. 5355, pp. 343–359. Springer, Heidelberg (2008)
3. Oh, Y., Woo, W.: How to build a Context-aware Architecture for Ubiquitous VR. In: IEEE ISUVR, CEUR-WS, pp. 032–033 (2007)
4. Shin, C., Woo, W.: Socially aware TV Program Recommender for Multiple Viewers. IEEE Transaction on Consumer Electronics 55(2), 927–932 (2009)
5. Kim, I., Park, H., Lee, Y., Lee, S., Lee, H., Noh, B.: Design and Implementation of Context-Awareness Simulation Toolkit for Context learning. In: IEEE SUTC, pp. 96–103 (2006)
6. Nishikawa, H., Yamamoto, S., Tamai, M., Nishigaki, K., Kitani, T., Shibata, N., Yasumoto, K., Ito, M.: UbiREAL: Realistic Smartspace Simulator for Systematic Testing. In: Dourish, P., Friday, A. (eds.) UbiComp 2006. LNCS, vol. 4206, pp. 322–331. Springer, Heidelberg (2006)
7. Park, J., Moon, M., Hwang, S., Yeon, K.: CASS: A Context-Aware Simulation System for Smart Home. In: 5th International Conference on Software Engineering Research Management and Applications, pp. 461–467. IEEE CS, Los Alamitos (2007)
8. De Carolis, B., Cozzolongo, G., Pizzutilo, S., Plantamura, V.L.: Agent-based home simulation and control. In: Hacid, M.-S., Murray, N.V., Raś, Z.W., Tsumoto, S. (eds.) ISMIS 2005. LNCS (LNAI), vol. 3488, pp. 404–412. Springer, Heidelberg (2005)
9. Jang, S., Shin, C., Oh, Y., Woo, W.: Introduction of "UbiHome" Testbed. IPSJ SIG Technical Reports (60), pp. 215–218 (2005)
10. Lee, Y., Oh, S., Shin, C., Woo, W.: Recent Trends in Ubiquitous Virtual Reality. In: International Symposium on Ubiquitous Virtual Reality, pp. 33–36 (2008)
11. OpenSceneGraph, http://www.openscenegraph.org/
12. Autodesk 3D StudioMax9, http://usa.autodesk.com/adsk
13. Particle (TECO), http://particle.Teco.edu/

Entertaining Education – Using Games-Based and Service-Oriented Learning to Improve STEM Education

Jon Preston and Briana Morrison

Southern Polytechnic State University, 1100 S Marietta Parkway
Marietta, GA 30060, USA
{jpreston,bmorriso}@spsu.edu

Abstract. This paper addresses the development of a computer game design and development curriculum at the authors' institution. The basis for curriculum decisions, as well as comparison to the other institutions' curricula is covered. In situating the curriculum within the current degree programs, games-based versions of existing courses are also being offered. The experience of the authors with the initial offering of a games-based introductory programming course is also explained, along with the initial assessment of results from the experience. Our experience of using games-based learning in an introductory laboratory is presented. Finally, we demonstrate how games-based learning can be extended beyond the classroom as we work to promote science, technology, engineering, and mathematics (STEM) with local elementary schools; our current project develops an ocean ecosystem exploration game that teaches oceanography and ecological sustainability.

Keywords: Curriculum, games-based, learning, programming, motivation, STEM, K12, development, sustainability.

1 Introduction

Gaming education has become a hot topic for students and educators. Students are drawn to digital gaming for pleasure and this extends to career choices. Educators view digital gaming as an avenue to increase enrollment in the computing discipline and as a motivation tool.

This paper presents our encompassing vision of incorporating gaming at our institution. This includes defining a new game design and development curriculum, incorporating game-based learning into existing courses, and extending games-based learning beyond the classroom with the effect of promoting science, technology, engineering, and mathematics (STEM) education within our local community. We believe that games-based learning offers an opportunity to motivate students in existing disciplines as well as expand the educational opportunities within universities.

1.1 Game Development Curriculum – Motivation and Development

We became interested in incorporating gaming at our institution for many reasons. There is a wide, fascinating, and growing field of research in the use of computer games in education [9]. Video games are a significant cultural influence [9] and are

Z. Pan et al. (Eds.): Transactions on Edutainment III, LNCS 5940, pp. 70–81, 2009.

useful in improving design strategies [5][7], enhancing and motivating learning [4][12], and increasing the success of job skills training [6]. While traditional educational environments and institutions may fail to properly motivate and situate learning, utilizing best practices of psychology and motivation theory, games-centric learning environments offer potential to meet the needs of competence, autonomy, and relatedness to enable students' success [4]. Research also shows that video game players achieve better scores in critical thinking, strategy development, and problem solving tests than non-players [9].

As we explored adding gaming, we were guided by the motivation theory associated with games in education and how this influences learning. While many debate the meaning of the idea of "fun," we are inspired by Malone's assertion that challenge, fantasy, and curiosity are the keys to making a game fun [9]; further, we see a significant corollary between these ideas of what makes a game fun and what makes a motivating, empowering, and successful games-based curriculum of study.

Challenge: like a game, a program of study must present students with clear (and multi-level) goals and provide feedback as to the progress toward achieving the goals.

Fantasy: student achievement and learning can be motivated by intrinsic and extrinsic settings ranging from mastering new topics/content and achieving good grades, and as Malone points out, these fantasies/settings vary by student.

Curiosity: providing learning environments of an "optimal level of complexity" can inspire students to expand their view of the subject matter such that their "existing knowledge seems incomplete, inconsistent, or unparsimonious" and deep learning can occur.

If, as Malone puts it, "computer programming itself is one of the best computer games of all," [9] then why not adopt computer game design techniques to the process of learning in a game design and development curriculum and within programming courses? This would not only create a new program of study to meet growing demand but also serve our current students to improve retention, motivation, and learning. These ideas led to our overall vision, which has three components. First, we have developed a computer game design and development curriculum based in part on these three keys. We have infused new games-based courses into our existing computing programs, and we have expanded the learning to outside the classroom with service opportunities for games-based learning.

1.2 Games-Based Laboratory Learning

In an effort to improve performance, retention, and motivation in our computing programs (computer science, information technology, and software engineering) and better serve our non-majors, our school began offering a games-based flavour of our introduction to programming course in the Fall of 2008. This has been extended in Spring of 2009 into two courses (introductory programming and intermediate programming). To compliment the lecture content of the course, we designed a series of games-based labs that bolstered the typical content of an introductory course. Our initial foray into games-based programming and the methodology used to assess our efforts may be valuable for others. Our empirical results of our study on student motivation and learning success indicate that students find games-based learning motivating, though there are some interesting challenges to overcome in their perceptions of their ability to create "real" programs.

We describe the physical space created with computer and console setups to support our lab and how this space is used beyond the gaming courses. Further, we present how the concepts of the course were mapped to games-based labs to support core course concepts while all the time using motivating games-based learning. The students' response to the labs and the projects that they were able to develop are positive and in general, while they often felt overwhelmed with the magnitude of the complexity of developing games, they were successful in their development and were ultimately quite satisfied and took ownership of their creations.

1.3 Grassroots, Service-Based Game Development

Game studies are of growing importance and the focus of ever-expanding undergraduate programs throughout the United States and beyond [10]. In addition to programs that study game development, games and simulations have been utilized to motivate learning and allow students to explore educational content; such a constructivist approach to learning has shown promise [1][11], but often educational games ("edutainment") lack the polish and in fact sometimes have a detrimental effect as students are turned off from "lame games" [4]. We have developed a sustainable and low-cost approach to developing compelling, fun, and educational games by tapping into the creative energies of our university students; this group works with a local elementary school and a local non-profit group to build these games and enhance the learning of our university students and the students playing our games. This service-centered approach to game design and development shows much promise, and as an added benefit, the group promotes science, technology, engineering, and mathematics (STEM) education.

We created a game play and development group of students and faculty to create community within our program and extended our game lab and development group to serve our local community. We present details of how our play/design group was able to provide valuable service to a local elementary school as we designed a learning game. Finally, we offer conclusions and discuss our future goals and activities for using games- and service-based learning to promote the education of our students as well as elementary students within our community.

2 Curriculum Development

Initially, we conducted a study of other universities that offered game related programs and courses; through this study, we sought to identify trends in other programs' curricula and learn from past successes so that we could adopt best practices from the inception of our program. Further, we wanted to ascertain how other programs incorporated the IGDA curriculum guidelines.

While hundreds of programs exist, we chose to locate comparable university programs by analyzing various computing education publication venues spanning the

Table 1. Program Course Categorization

Category	Course Type
Game-related	Game design, level design, game business, game analysis, game engine development
Computing	Traditional CS courses such as data structures, operating systems, graphics, HCI, algorithms, software engineering
Arts/Humanities	2D and 3D modeling, art, animation, sound/audio engineering

past four years. This identified 44 institutions. Of these, 22 offered full degrees, 16 offered a select few courses as special topics to existing, non-game degrees, and 6 offered certificates or concentrations/specializations in game design and development.

We categorized the programs' content into three groups: art/humanities, computing (i.e., traditional computer science), and game specific. Each program's upper-division content was examined to determine which course hours fell into each of these three categories. Capstone, studio, and senior project courses were placed within the category that was most closely related to the program's description, but more often than not, these courses were categorized as game-related since the intent of these programs was game focused. Table 1 provides examples of our categorization.

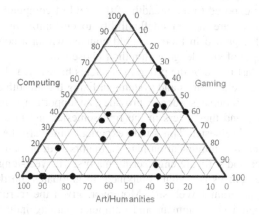

Fig. 1. Full Game Program Emphasis – Games-based programs from around the US offer varying emphasis on game development, traditional computing, and arts/humanities

Figure 1 shows a ternary (triangle) plot of the 21 full degree programs and their relative (%) emphases on gaming, computing, and arts (one program was excluded because it was completely customizable and thus didn't lend itself to our analysis). For example, if a point resides in the lower left corner, this program would emphasis arts with little or no computing or gaming; if a point resides in the top corner, this program would emphasize computing with little or no arts or gaming; and if a point resides in the lower right, this program would emphasize gaming with little or no arts or computing.

From this analysis, we observe that program emphases in gaming range from 9% to 67%, emphases in computing range from 0% to 67%, and emphases in arts range from 0% to 96%. Clearly there is a wide range of approaches in offering game-related curricula.

2.1 Supporting the New Degree

What courses are necessary for a computer game design and development program? As our background research into undergraduate games-related programs revealed, there are a myriad of solutions to this question – all of which serve different student constituencies. Within our new program, the students are exposed to the breadth of the field of computer game design and development, including digital media, human-computer interaction, the history and theory of gaming, game design, 2D and 3D graphics, simulation, modeling, software engineering, artificial intelligence, data structures, and algorithms. Current and emerging domains including online games and massively multiplayer games (MMOG), casual games, mobile games, and serious/educational games are also explored.

Mindful that the IGDA Curriculum Framework [3] does not prescribe specific courses but rather emphasizes core topics, we adopt the same approach in allowing flexibility within our program. Our program supports all but one of the IGDA Curriculum Framework's core areas (we are missing Audio Design, though this could be taught as a special topics course in the future). The required courses in the degree ensure students are exposed to the breadth of the field of computer game design and development. Students are also given flexibility to customize their experience and apply the knowledge gained in their required courses within a concentration where they may gain a depth of knowledge within their chosen area.

Finally, in their last phase of the program, students have a year-long studio experience wherein they develop games and systems utilizing the breadth and depth of their knowledge. This two-course sequence provides an opportunity for students to be mentored by faculty and their peers in the first semester and in turn mentor fellow students in the second semester. This studio experience may also be inter-disciplinary incorporating technical communication majors, majors with domain expertise as well as computer science and software engineering majors. The year-long capstone project developed in these courses is a vital component in graduates' portfolios and will be showcased on the program's Web site. Moreover, given the recruitment and hiring practices in the digital entertainment and computer gaming industry portfolios are crucial in helping graduates secure employment.

Figure 2 shows the core courses that constitute our computer game design and development curriculum. In total, 11 new courses were developed for the new program and we were able to make use of eight existing courses.

The structure of this degree allows for Malone's 3 components: the curriculum itself is challenging with feedback during each course, multiple types of "fantasy" can be explored in many different courses including the studio experience, and the concentrations allow for the students to fulfill their own "curiosity".

2.2 Infusing the Game Development Courses into the Existing Programs

Another motivation in developing the new computer game design and development degree was to provide options for existing computing majors. Our school currently

Fig. 2. Course Development – existing courses are shown in red, new courses design specifically for gaming are shown in green, and newly-created games-based elective and capstone courses are shown in blue

offers three Bachelors of Science degrees in Computer Science, Information Technology, and Software Engineering, a Bachelor of Arts in Computer Science, and three Masters of Science degrees in Computer Science, Information Technology, and Software Engineering. Consequently, the new program needed to fit in well with the existing courses, but we were mindful of the IGDA curriculum suggestion that any new games-based degree needs to go beyond simply adding a few courses to an existing program; our setting would have made such a plan easy given the volume of existing courses, but while the easiest route, this would not have been the best long-term approach for a successful games-based degree.

Core courses such as necessary math, introductory programming, and data structures were available and appropriate to incorporate into the new program. Upper-division courses critical to game development such as Artificial Intelligence, Software Engineering, and Graphics were also currently being taught and were adopted into our new game curriculum, although some additional learning outcomes specific to gaming have been added into the courses. Utilizing these existing courses proved to be vital in the program's success due to budget limitations, and we were thus able to avoid creating an inordinate number of new courses for the new program; additionally, using these current courses ensures that we are able to offer them frequently as they serve students in as many as four different degree programs. Thus we avoid the problem of courses not being offered enough for students to schedule them and graduate in a reasonable amount of time.

While we will try to dispel any misconceptions during orientation sessions for prospective and incoming students and advising of existing students, it seems likely that at least some students will eventually transfer out of the game design and development program into one of our other programs in computing. By building a curriculum that has a large number of lower-division courses in common with our other computing programs we afford such students the opportunity to shift majors without losing credits.

A final benefit of this approach is that we were also able to create a Minor in Computer Game Design and Development; this set of courses allows our current students to explore the field of game design and development while retaining their current major. They are exposed to the "overview" courses and then can choose three other upper-division game courses; additionally, students in the minor may elect to participate in the studio experience to add to the inter-disciplinary teams for a rich experience.

3 Games-Based Laboratory

Within our current curriculum, our three course programming sequence (introductory, intermediate, and data structures) all have a closed lab component. Students attend lecture for 3 hours each week and are required to attend a 2 hour lab to practice the concepts discussed in class. When we introduced the gaming based flavor of the introductory programming course, we recognized the need for a gaming based lab as well. We thus created our "game hive."

The gaming lab occupies a dedicated room that consists of 14 Xbox 360s connected to development computers with Visual Studio 2005 and 2008 as well as the XNA Framework 2.0 and 3.0. Each development space can accommodate up to two students working side-by-side, so the space (and many of the labs) support a paired-programming model of XP (extreme programming), though this is not required and students can work alone.

Each development machine is bound to a different Xbox 360 with an XNA Creators Club Subscription. This allows the PCs to easily deploy to the Xbox 360s via Visual Studio and allows the students to play their games on the console. While the games run completely on the PCs, students were visibly and highly motivated when seeing their creations run on the Xbox 360.

Further, we have made many free audio and graphics editing toolkits available to the students. These tools include Audacity, Sony's free Acid Express, Paint.NET, and the GIMP. Such tools allow students to generate the graphics and audio for their games, and since the tools are free, the costs are minimized for the university and the students (if they choose to install these tools on their personal computers). Similarly, there are free editions of Visual Studio 2005 and 2008 as well as the XNA Framework, so students can replicate the lab set up in their personal computers for free if they desire.

To maximize usage of the space, the other half of the room contains a couch, two 46" wall-mounted plasma televisions and two Wii consoles, one PS3, and another Xbox360 Elite. This "play" area is used by students to play one of the games from our library of over 50 titles. This allows for research of existing games as well as creating community among our large population of commuter students. Additionally, we utilize our game development lab to support local schools and to promote STEM education. We want to encourage students to see computing and gaming as viable educational pursuits. We have had numerous visits as "field trips" to the university; these visits increase the ties between K-12 education and higher education that we have extended into a collaborative game development project. (See section 4.)

3.1 The Lab Exercises

When adding the games flavored introductory programming course, the closed lab assignments needed to be created. The labs have been designed to allow students to learn the programming concepts while implementing games. Our approach utilizes C#

and XNA as the language and API for game development, but our pedagogical approach is language-agnostic and any modern programming language with a sufficient graphics API could be adopted.

Initially the core programming concepts were mapped to the lectures: data types, arithmetic operations, using classes, writing classes, selection structures, repetition structures, and arrays. We created a lab for each concept and added a lab for the introduction to the IDE. Each lab was based on an existing game and clearly identified the learning objectives and grading rubric. Each lab provides background as to the motivation of the lab, and then enumerates the directions that the students are to follow. Typically, students downloaded a "starter project" that contains much of the program already implemented and commented sections indicating the portions that the students had to complete.

3.2 Assessment

In assessing the results of the using the game-based flavor of the introductory programming course, we collected both quantitative and qualitative data. At the conclusion of the course, students were asked to provide anonymous feedback through a survey. The survey was given to students in the games-based section of the course as well as students who were taking the traditional, non-games-focused section of the course. A total of 91 students responded to the survey, yielding a 75.8% response rate. Forty of the gaming students (75%) responded and 51 students (76%) in the traditional offering responded. Students in each of the groups were similar: approximately 73% of each group planned to major in computing, 15% of the gaming students were female (n=6) while 21.6% of the traditional students were female (n=11), and grade expectations for both groups were similar, with the majority of both groups expecting Bs. None of the respondents expected to fail the class, and only 1 respondent from the traditional offering expected a D.

The responses from the gaming section were overwhelming positive. While many felt the course was difficult (as many students feel about their first programming course), they felt they had accomplished something of value. Over half of the students report that they continued to work on their assignments even "after they were working," which indicates that the students were motivated by the content. Nearly two thirds of the students also reported that they showed their assignments to friends. During the closed labs, we noticed that many students customized their games and tried out novel graphics and extended the game play.

Quantitative data collected comparing performance between the games and traditional sections will be reported in a future publication.

3.3 Student Reflection on Their Ability

It is particularly interesting to note that our study finds that more students taking a games-based section of the programming course thought that they had less ability than their counterparts in a non-games-based section. For the gaming students, a majority (52.5%) thought they could not yet write an interesting or meaningful program while only 41.18% of the traditional offering students believed this.

We believe that this is because of the nature of the development programs and the complexity of the labs and assignments in the games-based course. The complexity of the programs they were exposed to was considerably higher than those in a typical introductory programming course. The typical introductory programming assignment is approximately 100 lines of code or less. The game programs utilized in our course consisted of 200 or more lines of code, some of them reached into the thousands. Instead of considering a single class, most programs had four or more classes that the students were to be concerned with.

The overhead of the XNA framework forces students to use additional abstraction skills. The XNA framework requires that the game is initialized and assets (audio, sprites, etc.) are loaded, then the main game loop begins - wherein the update and draw methods are repeatedly called. This event- and loop-driven model of execution may be more difficult to grasp than a top-down model of execution (which is what is used in console-based programs that dominated the non-games-based section of the course).

The gaming students' final assignment was team based--to design and implement their own game. By asking the students to create from scratch their own game, the authors believe the students have a clearer picture of all the skills necessary to create a large scale project and that this is reflected in their answers to the survey question. They may not be able to write a program *alone* that is interesting or meaningful, but they can with a team. This was reflected not only in the final projects created (which were complex and required asset creation and game development) but also in the responses to the survey. Most gaming students were most proud of their final project which can be seen in the following sample of responses that capture the tone of the students' feelings about what they were most proud of and like most about the course:

"The final project where we got into groups and created a game. It was meaningful to me because it was something we all came up with and created, not simply a game we added code to so that it would work."

"That I got the tank assignment working without any help. (It seemed -so- much harder than it was.)"

"1301 Gaming was really fun. Learning how a game actually works was probably the best part, and the time and effort it took for a game to be made. Making my own games was fun also."

"CSE 1301 was fun because I was learning new things. It was also fun to make games with other people that became friends."

"I was really proud of the tank game, because it was the first homework assignment that we had to add code to, to make it work. At first it seemed extremely out of my league, but once I took the time to look at it and tinker with it, I finished it."

4   Service-Oriented Game Development

Beginning in the Fall of 2008, we created a game play and development group at our university. This group was extracurricular and completely voluntary. The group met weekly and alternated between playing games and developing/critiquing games, but soon we realized that having meetings twice a week would allow for more "serious" progress. We wanted to create an atmosphere that allowed students to meet new friends, support their learning via impromptu peer-tutoring, and provide a vehicle by which they could apply their design and development skills in a fun way via game development. This group began with four students and has grown to over a dozen from various majors ranging from computer science to fashion design. We have even had students switch majors into our program as a result of this group.

This cross-discipline game group allows students to incorporate and practice their learning from various computing fields such as usability and HCI, graphics, and algorithms. Non-computing majors are also involved and add perspectives concerning design, playability, fun, and narrative.

4.1 Service to the Community

One of the key elements of our new computer game design and development program is service and partnerships with local businesses and non-profits. In the final year of our program, student teams are to work on long-term (2-semester) projects with real customers such that they are developing games with a purpose (as well as for their portfolios). To this end, we view entrepreneurialism and service as central to our program.

To jump start the service aspect of our vision, we asked our game play and development group of students explore the possibility of creating an educational game for a local elementary school. With the help of a local non-profit group, the university students met with a group of elementary school students to begin exploring a game about oceanography.

4.2 Collaborative Game Design

Similar to [5] and [7], our game design group sought to incorporate the input of the elementary students that would be playing the game. While this could be considered typical "listen to your customers early in the design process," we consider this step important to this project specifically as we wanted to not only incorporate the elementary school students' suggestions into the design of the game, but we also wanted to motivate their STEM learning; it was critical that the elementary students gain insight into the design and development process so that they aren't just learning about oceanography but also learning what goes into the design and development of the simulation.

As Figure 3 shows, the students (both elementary and university) that worked with us on the design really got involved and took ownership of the process. They had many creative ideas and also confirmed some of our original design elements such as submarine customization, achievements and trophies, and mini-games. Some ideas, such as adding a popcorn maker in the ocean research base, were surprises to us, but are easily added to the game and we hope that such Easter eggs will make the students feel they had a strong impact on the development of the game.

The current oceanography game that we developed contains three main components: a submersible builder (fully customizable with lights, textures, measurement instrumentation, etc.), an ocean environment exploration game, and a system to adjust and "fish out" certain species. By utilizing all three of these pieces, the elementary students can learn about design trade-offs, exploration, and ecosystems. Our game components support the learning objectives of the teachers, who were very pleased and supportive.

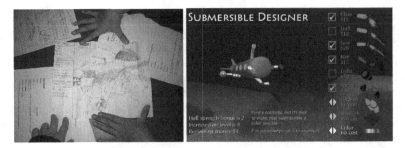

Fig. 3. Collaborative learning and game development projects can enhance the learning experience of elementary and university students. The completed submersible design game allows students to make choices that affect their ocean ecosystem exploration.

5 Conclusion and Future Work

It has been exciting to see how motivated students at our university have been with the addition of gaming education at our institution. The degree program has received very favorable reviews from students and has generated interest from perspective students. The gaming based versions of the software development courses have proven so popular that additional sections have had to be added to the course schedule. The community that our play and development group of students has developed is also impressive, and it is inspiring to see our university students making connections with and motivating the elementary students. In an era where student interest in STEM education seems to be waning, we hope that we have had a long-term impact on students to see that science, mathematics, and computer science are all interesting fields where creativity and imagination are key elements of success.

For the future, we will fully implement the degree program and expand the games flavor of course offerings to additional courses (specifically data structures). We expect to extend the process of game design as service into other areas. These include partnering with a non-profit group at Emory University to work on a game in the field of medicine for a mobile/handheld platform. We would like to extend the current oceanography game and make it available at aquariums such as the Tennessee and Georgia aquariums so others can explore and learn while playing. We have also proposed our sustainable service-based game development process into the field of engineering education to help students learn by completing virtual labs that take the place of difficult-to-obtain or hazardous laboratories. We look forward to developing these partnerships as well as others.

References

1. Aguilera, M., Mendiz, A.: Video Games and Education (Education in the Face of a "Parallel School"). ACM Computers in Entertainment 1(1), 1–14 (2003)
2. Bennedsen, J., Caspersen, M.E.: Failure rates in introductory programming. SIGCSE Bull. 39(2), 32–36 (2007)

3. Church, D., et al.: IGDA Curriculum Framework: The Study of Games and Game Development (beta 2.3) (February 2003),
http://www.igda.org/academia/curriculum_framework.php
4. Denis, G., Jouvelot, P.: Motivation-Driven Educational Game Design: Applying Best Practices to Music Education. In: Proceedings of the 2005 ACM SIGCHI International Conference on Advances in Computer Entertainment Technology, Valencia, Spain, pp. 462–465 (2005)
5. Good, J., Robertson, J.: Computer Games Authored by Children: A Multi-Perspective Evaluation. In: IDC 2004, College Park, MD, June 2004, pp. 123–124 (2004)
6. Greitzer, F., Kuchar, O., Huston, K.: Cognitive Science Implications for Enhancing Training Effectiveness in a Serious Gaming Context. ACM Journal of Educational Resources in Computing 7(3), art. 2 (November 2007)
7. Knudtzon, K., et al.: Starting an Intergenerational Technology Design Team: A Case Study. In: IDC2003, Preston, UK, July 2003, pp. 51–58 (2003)
8. Lewis, J.: C# Software Solutions: Foundations of Program Design. Addison-Wesley, Reading (2007)
9. Malone, T.: What Makes Things Fun to Learn? Heuristics for Designing Instructional Computer Games. In: Proceedings of the 3rd ACM SIGSMALL symposium and the first SIGPC symposium on Small systems, Palo Alto, CA, pp. 162–169 (1980)
10. Morrison, B., Preston, J.: Engagement: Gaming throughout the Curriculum. In: Proceedings of the 2009 ACM SIGCSE Conference, Chattanooga, TN (2009)
11. Prensky, M.: Digital Game-Based Learning. Computers in Education (CIE) 1(1), 21–24 (2003)
12. Steiner, B., Kaplan, N., Moulthrop, S.: When Play Works: Turning Game-Playing into Learning. In: IDC 2006, Tamperte, Finland, June 2006, pp. 137–140 (2006)

Learning English through Serious Games – Reflections on Teacher and Learner Performance

Bente Meyer

Associate Professor, Department of Curriculum Research, Danish School of Education, University of Aarhus, (+45) 8888 9509
bm@dpu.dk

Abstract. In this paper I shall discuss the potential of educational games (Serious Games) for teaching and learning English online focusing on user engagement, performance and design. The paper builds on data from a research project, *Serious Games on a Global Market Place* in which a platform for learning English as a foreign language in primary school (www.Mingoville.com) has been studied in the context of English as a foreign language in Denmark. On the basis of the initial research results from the project I am proposing that performance and engagement through Serious Games for language learning should be understood in the context of gaming and learning as both separate and interconnected processes. In this connection the mediating role of the teacher is particularly significant.

Keywords: Serious games, Computer Assisted Language Learning (CALL), teacher-learner roles, design for teaching and learning.

1 Introduction

Recently, a fair amount of attention has been given to the role of games in e-learning [10, 14, 31]. Academic literature on game-based learning generally argues that games provide better learning, new forms of knowledge and added motivation to learning [16, 20, 29]. In addition to this games are understood to appeal to new generations of learners, and as challenging traditional ways of schooling [15, 30, 34]. This has implications for e-learning, as suggested by Ang and Rao [1] "game theories provide a better framework for designing E-learning, making the experience of learning more immersive and engaging". Game-based learning and design may in this way provide the claimed 'missing link' in e-learning between technology and meaningful, learner-centred learning.

In this paper I shall explore the challenges of designing game-based material for language learning as a specific field of competence. The empirical context of the paper is a project on *Serious Games on a Global Market Place* (2007-10)[1] in which academics work with companies to explore, build and implement game prototypes, using the products and experience of commercial game designers to develop knowledge about serious game challenges, educational design, and assessment with the aim

---

[1] The project is funded by The Danish Council for Strategic Research under The Programme on *Creativity, Innovation, New Production Forms and the Experience Economy*.

Z. Pan et al. (Eds.): Transactions on Edutainment III, LNCS 5940, pp. 82–92, 2009.

of innovation. One aspect of this research consists in analysing and developing a design for learning English through serious games as well as exploring how this design is used and implemented in classroom teaching and learning.

In the paper my focus will be on the performance and practice of teachers and learners in classroom based sessions that involve game-based material for language learning. As suggested by de Castell & Jenson [9] recent research on the educational significance of gaming has generally overlooked the significance of the cultural and contextual aspects of gaming, forgetting that "there is a politics, an economy, a history, social structure and function, and an everyday, lived experience of a game". Thus, games and game activity take on meaning from the educational as well as general cultural context in which they exist and 'act'. I shall argue that in defining game-based language learning as an aspect of serious games studies both platform design and teacher-learner interaction are significant in defining how learners can be players and players can be learners.

1.1 Designing Serious Games for Language Learning – A Framework for Analysis

Designing game-based material for learning can be understood as a process that involves three levels: a practice level, an organisation level and a theoretical reflection level [7, 8]. According to Cobb et.al. [4] design experiments in learning involve both a pragmatic approach, understood as the "engineering" of specific forms of learning, and a theoretical approach, i.e. a study of the forms of learning used within the context in question.

In the *Serious Games* project it is our aim to work respectively with engineering game-based language learning and with what Katrin Becker describes as "a reverse engineering process" [3], i.e. a process of uncovering instructional design principles in existing educational games. This double strategy of analysing existing games and generating theoretical concepts and practical methods for innovative product development, has provided a framework for the ways in which our research may predict the potential, benefits and learning outcomes of serious games locally as well as globally.

In the Serious Games project we understand serious games as digital games and equipment with an agenda of educational design and beyond entertainment [25]. This approach is consistent with the argument, made by game theorist James Paul Gee that "Good commercial video games are by no means trivial phenomena. They are deep technologies for recruiting learning as a form of profound pleasure" [14]. Gee's contention addresses the fact, often discussed in educational game theory, that gaming is understood to be inimical to school culture as educational cultures rest on the "dominant cultural (op)positioning of play and education" [9]. Consequently, play and gaming are understood to represent childish activities that are potentially disruptive and antithetical to schooling where 'real' and 'serious' learning is supposed to be the aim of the activities. Gaming is, as claimed by for instance de Castell and Jenson, a fundamentally unpopular culture in schools, a fact that influences teachers' views on gaming as well as their practice [9].

1.2   Defining Learning Games – Entertainment, Edutainment or Serious Game?

If we look at the educational use of games in general we see a number of game types that all affect the understanding and design of serious games. These educational uses of games can, I propose, be divided into three main categories [33] 1) *Edutainment and learning games*. Edutainment can be described as the earliest example of a game-based learning type and can be understood broadly as a concept where entertainment is used to facilitate learning. Games of the edutainment type are generally designs to be used without teacher intervention. In addition to this edutainment may be associated with developmental and learning theories that do not correspond to contemporary ideas of learning and schooling [11] 2) *Research based educational games* are made for educational use e.g. in schools and involve teacher intervention. In this category we place serious games. Serious games can be understood as the second generation of learning games in which educational design has been adjusted to the learning theories of modern schooling. 3) *Games for entertainment* are not designed for educational use but are sometimes used in the educational system to facilitate learning in different subjects e.g. the games Civilization and SimCity which have been used to facilitate respectively history and social studies [12, 31].

In the case of Mingoville.com, the platform studied in the *Serious Games on a Global Market Place* project, the platform can be understood as game-based material of the edutainment type in the sense that it combines entertainment and learning, as well as conceptualises play as an activity that teaches children something in order to convince parents and teachers that learning can be fun [12, 17, 32]. In an earlier paper I have identified the Mingoville platform as an example of what Ang & Zaphiris have named an extrinsic game type, i.e. "a structured series of puzzles or tasks embedded in a game or narrative structure with which they have only the most slender connection" [2, 26]. In Mingoville children of 9-11 years meet the Pinkeltons, who are citizens of the simulated

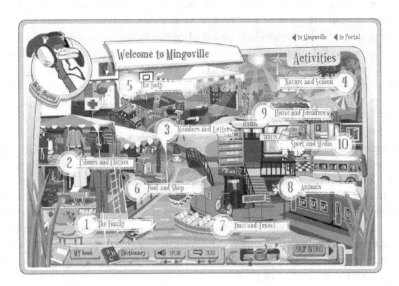

Fig. 1. The Mingoville Universe

world Mingoville – a city inhabited by flamingos. The Mingoville platform can be described not as a full game in itself, but rather as a web-based learning environment that capitalises on the mini-games and other entertainment activities that children engage in in their spare time outside school.

1.3 Gaming and Language Learning – A Communicative Approach

Games may have a number of potentials for foreign or second language learning. Most of these potentials are associated with the ability of games to provide learning environments that contextualise knowledge and provide immersive experiences for learners. As suggested by a recent review in *Languages, technology and learning* [27] learning a language is different from any other subject in the curriculum as it combines explicit learning of vocabulary and language rules with unconscious skill development in the fluent application of both these things. For language learners this implies that they should be able to master both grammatical knowledge and fluency, the latter being often difficult to provide in classrooms where a couple of lessons a week may fail to provide the meaningful exposure to the foreign language required for learning.

One of the major challenges of foreign language learning is thus thinking about how technology can mediate or create connections between the teaching's formal and more informal learning environments, ie. how for instance games can provide meaningful examples of the type of language environments learners will encounter in their new speech community. Unfortunately, much language instruction is still based on drill and exercise principles, leaving fluency and the development of communicative language competence to out of school practices. The role of technology in schools may to some extent support these practices as "gap-fill and drill lend themselves easily to programming" [27].

However, games and simulations have been part of language learning for decades, and have had a role in supporting communicative approaches to language learning, i.e. in providing authentic and meaningful opportunities for language production and use. Game-based language learning has for instance supported fluency and communicative competence by letting learners simulate or play real life situations, drama or narrative [5, 6, 22]. In addition to this puzzles and minigames such as Hangman have been used to enhance vocabulary acquisition and use. In this sense games have been associated with a move from the teaching of discrete grammatical structures to the promotion of communicative ability [36]. According to Macedonia [23] games may serve to preceduralise foreign language knowledge, i.e. to encourage and support fluency against the generally rule-based, declarative approach to foreign language teaching.

An additional perspective in designing and developing game-based material for language learning is the role of English in children's online gaming activities outside school. In the *Serious Games on a Global Market Place* project the use of English online has been understood to be a significant aspect of children's engagement in games as a socially valued way of performing. Language learning is in this context involved in children's use of games as a social practice primarily out of school [24]. For many of the children that we interviewed in the research project mentioned above English was the language that they were expecting to use for communication in online gaming out of school, and for some children it was not always possible to remember which language they had actually used in gaming, their first language or English. In this sense language learning and language use was for the children a natural aspect of acting in meaningful social contexts online, among them game communities.

2 Studying Performance and Learning in the Classroom – The Mingoville Study

As described above it has been the intention of the research project to develop the initial design of the Mingoville.com platform by testing and revising ideas about game-based language learning and teaching through an ongoing analysis of the platform itself, its genesis as well as pupils' interaction and learning with the platform. The focus of the research has been both on pupils' language acquisition and use and the roles of teachers and pupils in the classroom in connection with game-based language learning.

Following the analysis of the Mingoville platform in the autumn of 2007, the second phase of research in Mingoville.com was piloted in the spring of 2008 through two classroom studies, both in suburban schools near Copenhagen. Additional studies have been made in the spring of 2009 to develop the initial results and to focus on 3rd form users' (beginners') interaction with the platform. The data from the most recent study will be analysed during the spring and summer of 2009.

The purpose of the studies was to observe user performance and response to the platform and to compare these with the learning theories and educational design principles embedded in the platform. Educational design is to some extent largely a conceptual matrix that must be tested against the real work and learning done by users [4]. In this sense gaming was conceptualised as a contextually embedded activity, i.e. an activity that involved "a social structure and function, and an everyday, lived experience of a game" [9].

2.1 Conceptualising Teacher and Learner Roles in the Classroom

In the pilot study we sought mainly to understand classroom interaction, including pupils' and teachers' interaction with the platform, as a performative practice, i.e. as a practice defined by the roles and functions given to and negotiated by teachers and learners through the educational context and learning culture of the individual school.

Traditionally, the roles given to teachers and learners in school are defined by relationships of power determined by age, professional position and knowledge. This relationship is often described as asymmetrical, and is assumed to be challenged when digital media are involved [19, 28, 35]. When gaming is involved these roles are often challenged in the sense that "games have the potential to offer an inquiry-based, constructivist approach that allows learners to engage with the material in an authentic, yet safe environment" [3]. One particularly interesting aspect of studying the teacher-learner relationship would therefore be to investigate the role of the teacher afforded by the game-based learning environment, as game environments are often predominantly player- and learner-centred and the role of the teacher thus remains unclear. The study of serious games in classroom environments should in this connection focus not only on the role of learners as players but also on the interventionary role of the teacher and on the significance of the teacher's role in transforming user behaviour, i.e. in aligning player activity with learner activity.

As our study aimed to understand the performance and role of the teacher and learners in the classroom during game-based teaching and learning, we had suggested to teachers that they use the platform in the ways that they found most relevant for their teaching. This approach allowed us to see how teachers managed, negotiated, and conceptualised gaming in the classroom as an aspect of teaching English as a foreign language. Comparison and analysis of the two classroom studies would therefore be based on an understanding of how teachers contextualised the platform as part of their individual instructional strategy rather than on the similarity or sameness of instructional approaches, as a more controlled study would prefer. As the examples below will show, teachers intuitively chose two very different approaches to using the platform, one being exploratory and the other directed.

In the first classroom we visited, which was a fifth form class (11 year age group) the children had been advised by the teacher to use Mingoville.com in the ways that they found interesting and that reflected the individual pupil's need to work with specific aspects of the language (for instance vocabulary, grammar, spelling). This approach can be described as exploratory, and is associated with the idea that gaming is an experimental and engagement-driven activity.

In the second classroom, a fourth form class (10 year age group), the teacher had selected a specific set of tasks for the pupils to work on. In this class the teacher's approach to teaching with the platform was directed, i.e. she conceptualised the platform as a serious learning material that required the intervention of an instructor or supervisor. The tasks chosen were related to the mission *Animals* which aims to teach children a basic vocabulary related to this theme.

2.2   Gaming and Learning in the 5th form Classroom

In the classroom sessions with Mingoville.com the extrinsic design of the platform, i.e. the mixture of tasks and exercises available on the platform became extremely significant in the learning activities and in the pace and rhythm of interaction and learning exhibited by learners. The extrinsic platform design for instance generally inspired learners, if they found the opportunity, to choose the most playful and game-like activities rather than activities that were more obviously school related. The playful and game-like activities chosen by learners would generally be activities that most clearly resembled the mini-games played by children on free websites in their spare time. This choice was made possible by the direct reference to these out of school activities in the platform and was most obvious in the 5th form class where the teacher had allowed the pupils to choose freely between the activities in the platform. In the 4th form class where pupil activities were generally structured and supervised by the teacher this was less obvious, though still observable.

One example of a game activity chosen by children was a Pacman spelling game in which the learner leads the Pacman through a labyrinth to select and 'eat' the exact letters that make up a certain word (for instance "parrot", or "cat"). The Pacman game is used in several of the platform missions, and was hugely popular with the children in both of the classes that we observed, however only the 5th formers were allowed to choose this task freely. Also, this was the task that almost all children would complete and play several times, even though they had obviously 'learned' the spelling of the words in question. In the interviews almost all children (including the 4th formers) said that they felt they learned to spell English words from playing this game, and that they chose it because it was great fun to play.

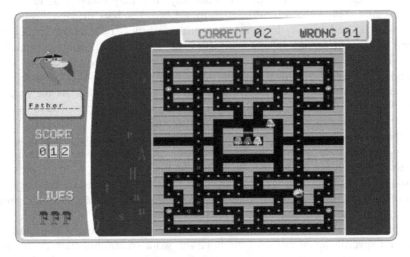

Fig. 2. The Pacman game

In the 5th form class, gaming was observable as a central classroom activity as pupils generally chose to interact with the Pacman game and other game-based activities in the platform. In the 5th form class, students to a larger extent than in the 4th form class used the platform selectively and in exploratory ways, largely to identify and try out the game activities in the individual missions. Rather than exploring the platform in accordance with the linear framework suggested by the platform missions and tasks, the 5th form students would skip from one mission to the other in order to seek out the gaming interest that they found challenging and entertaining. The 5th formers did not feel that they had to finish tasks or do them in any specific order. Finally, in the 5th form class, children quickly tired of the platform, after little more than 30 minutes most of them had moved on to search for their favourite songs and music videos in YouTube.

In the 5th form class, pupils were understood by teachers to be doing language learning, but they were also to some extent understood to be exercising their out of school identities as players and gamers while interacting with the platform, and thereby to some extent bringing unsolicited and unwanted entertainment into the classroom. On the one hand teachers acknowledged that gaming, including the Pacman activity, could facilitate vocabulary acquisition and spelling, on the other hand the role of the teacher was often to slow down the pace of playing and interacting and to encourage pupils to concentrate, repeat and persist. Often teachers would insist, when they were guiding or supervising individual pupils, that pupils should engage in introductions to tasks and other kinds of preparatory work that children were more likely to skip in order to move on to 'real' task interaction. In this sense teachers were trying to reconceptualise gaming as a profound or 'serious' learning activity based on concentration and perseverance, in which a linear process of solving and understanding tasks should generally be observed.

2.3 Gaming and Learning in the 4th Form Classroom

In the 4th form classroom gaming was from the beginning conceptualised as a learning activity by the teacher which allowed the children to understand gaming as a teacher controlled activity from the outset. In the 4th form class where the teacher had pre-selected the tasks, pupils were much more likely to work through the tasks and to do this in the order suggested by the teacher, though some of the children also chose to do the tasks in the order that seemed interesting to them. In the 4th form class pupils generally did a variety of tasks because they were asked to do so by the teacher, however, game and play-like activities such as *Painting the animals* and *In Jonathan's House* were clearly the most popular. One of the most frustrating tasks was according to pupils a storybook task, *How Jon lost his legs* where children after listening to the text had to place text fragments in the right order. This task was understood by children to be too elaborate and lengthy.

The attention span of the fourth formers was generally longer than that of the 5th formers, also their pace of learning and interacting with the platform was much more relaxed than the 5th formers, who would typically move quickly through the tasks, and often skipped from the platform menu to individual tasks as described above. Whereas it may be argued that these differences in attention span and platform response could be due to age differences, 4th formers were also observed to prefer the most playful tasks and to have little patience with tasks that were too 'bookish'. In addition to this, some 4th formers would do 'entertaining' tasks (for instance the Pacman task) that they were not asked to do, in these cases the teacher said that they we allowed to work on tasks of their own choice when they had finished what they had been asked to do. Gaming in this sense often worked as a reward after 'learning'.

2.4 Teachers' Roles in the Classroom

The empirical studies show that teachers were open to using games as an aspect of language teaching, but also that teachers felt that gaming should be understood as learning primarily through the intervention of the teacher. As suggested by de Castell and Jenson [9], it is generally the role of the teacher and the school to establish boundaries and define 'no go' zones for learners, often with the result that learners' freedom of movement in physical and virtual space is restricted. As argued by de Castell and Jenson this may prevent learners from becoming 'full participants' [21] in a game-based learning culture that is often designed and conceptualised as immersive. In the pilot study described above, it was obvious that teachers aimed at restricting and disciplining learner behaviour, however, they did so precisely because they felt that gaming had to be managed to become an activity that involved school-based learning and acquisition. In this way the schooling and the gaming cultures were found to be at odds as originally indicated by the platform design itself, i.e. in the split between 'educational' and 'entertaining' activities.

In general the teachers succeeded in communicating to the pupils that gaming in an educational context could and should be focused, paced and persistent, however, teachers also vented their frustration at pupil behaviour understood as superficial and unwarranted gaming and out of school behaviour. Gaming was in this sense understood both as an in school, formal activity with a potential for language acquisition, and an out of school, informal entertainment activity that could potentially disrupt school learning. The extrinsic design of the platform as well as teachers' approaches to game behaviour and learning both contributed to defining the ways in which serious games were conceptualised and used in the classroom.

3 Conclusions

In this paper I have argued, based on the observations made in the two classrooms as well as interviews with teachers and children during and after the Mingoville sessions, that the Mingoville platform and its learning activities were differently negotiated in the two classes described, mainly because the intervention (or non-intervention) of the teacher defined the ways in which learners could be players and players could be learners. In addition to this, I have suggested that the extrinsic design of the platform [2] has affected the ways in which Mingoville.com can be conceptualised and used by learners and educators in classroom settings. This has implications for foreign language learning as the flow and intrinsic structure of gaming needed for developing fluency to some extent is missing in Mingoville. However, Mingoville does provide opportunity for the repetition of vocabulary and spelling in a playful way, which seems to engage some learners, though not all.

As mentioned above the activities of the children in the classrooms showed that children were generally attracted to the most game- and play-like activities in the platform and that whenever possible, they would often choose these activities instead of activities that were more recognizable as traditional learning activities, for instance spelling exercises. In the 5th form class the exploratory approach to the platform quickly inspired children to identify the platform with gaming activities and to explore challenges and playful activities rather than persevering for the sake of learning content. In the 4th form class pupils would also choose gaming activities if allowed, however, pupils were generally directed by teacher guidance and intervention to complete tasks and persevere in order to learn. These differences in platform use and performance suggest not only that pupils prefer to be players rather than learners if these roles are not integrated in serious game design, but also that the ontological perspectives on games often discussed in game theory are not sufficient to understand how games work in education [10]. Rather than asking "what is a game?" we should therefore explore the performative and social aspects of gaming in and out of classrooms, i.e. the context of playing should be significant in understanding how language games work as both dynamic and serious environments for learning. Exploratory and directed approaches to using games in the classroom are in this sense not outside perspectives added to the core of the game itself, but integrated aspects of the game understood as an actor in teaching and learning English in a formal learning context in Denmark.

Following this argument, it should be underlined that in doing gaming in school the teacher is an extremely significant actor in mediating between the 'fun' and the 'serious' aspects of gaming mentioned above. In school gaming is understood as an activity that sometimes bridges the gap between entertainment and learning as well as the gap between formal and informal learning. In the Mingoville sessions, teachers in their different ways attempted to bridge the mixture of activities and learning approaches suggested by the platform design by insisting that school learning is a profound activity, even when this includes gaming. This highlights not only the role of the teacher as someone who might be sceptical of game-based activities, but also as someone who mediates between game performance as an in school and an out of school learning activity. In this sense the teacher is central to the transformation of first generation edutainment types of games to second or even third generations of serious games, although the seriousness of gaming proposed by teachers may not correspond to the seriousness of games understood by game theory to go beyond edutainment.

References

1. Ang, C.S., Rao, R.K.: E-learning as computer games: Designing immersive and experiential learning. In: Aizawa, K., Nakamura, Y., Satoh, S. (eds.) PCM 2004. LNCS, vol. 3333. Springer, Heidelberg (2004)
2. Ang, C.S., Zaphiris, P.: Developing Enjoyable Second Language Learning Software Tools: A Computer Game Paradigm. In: Zaphiris, P. (ed.) User-Centered Computer Aided Language Learning, Science Publishing (2006)
3. Becker, K.: Digital game-based learning once removed: teaching teachers. British Journal of Educational Technology 38(3) (2007)
4. Cobb, et al.: Design Experiments in Educational Research. Educational Researcher 32(1) (2003)
5. Crookall, D., Oxford, R.L.: Simulation, Gaming, and Language Learning. Newbury House Publishers (1990)
6. Crookall, D.: Second language acquisition and simulation. Simulation & Gaming 38(6) (2007)
7. Dale, E.L.: Pedagogisk Profesjionalitet [Pedagogic Professionalism] Gyldendal, Oslo (1989)
8. Dale, E.L.: Professionalisering og læring i organisationer (Professionalism and Learning in Organisations). In: Andersen, P., Frederiksen, P. (eds.) Innovation, kompetence, læring (Innovation, Competence, Learning). Dafolo, Frederiksberg (2000)
9. de Castell, S., Jenson, J.: Serious Play. Journal of Curriculum Studies 35(6) (2003)
10. de Castell, S., Jenson, J.: Video games and Digital Game Play – The New Field of Educational Game Studies. Orbit 35(2) (2005)
11. Egenfeldt-Nielsen, S.: Beyond Edutainment: exploring the educational potential of computer games. Unpublished Phd. IT University of Copenhagen (2005)
12. Egenfeldt-Nielsen, S., et al.: Understanding Video Games: The Essential Introduction. Routledge, New York (2008)
13. Garcia-Carbonell, A., Rising, B., Montero, B., Watts, F.: Simulation/gaming and the acquisition of communicative competence in another language. Simulation and gaming 32(4) (2001)
14. Gee, J.P.: What Video Games have to Teach us about Learning and Literacy. Palgrave/Macmillan, New York (2003)
15. Gee, J.P.: Situated Language and Learning. A Critique of Traditional Schooling. Rouledge, New York (2004)

16. Gee, J. P.: Pleasure, Learning, Video Games, and Life: the projective stance. E-Learning 2(3) (2005)
17. Johannesen, J.: Mingoville.dk – et eksempel på sproglige muligheder inden for it (Mingoville.dk – an example of language learning with ICT). Sprogforum Tidsskrift for sprog- og kulturpædagogik (Journal of language and culture education) 38 (2006)
18. Kirriemur, J., McFarlane, A.: Literature Review in Games and Learning. Futurelab (2006)
19. Kimber, K., et al.: Reclaiming Teacher Agency in a Student-Centred Digital World. Asia-Pacific Journal of Teacher Education vol 30(2) (2002)
20. Kirriemur, J., McFarlane, A.: Literature Review in Games and Learning. Futurelab (2006)
21. Lave, J., Wenger, E.: Situated Learning. Legitimate Peripheral Participation. Cambridge UP, Cambridge (1991)
22. Li, R.-C., Topolewski, D.: ZIP & TERRY: a new attempt at designing language learning simulation. Simulation and gaming 33(2) (2002)
23. Macedonia, M.: Games and foreign language teaching. Support for Learning 20(3) (2005)
24. Meyer, B.: Languages with ICTs – ICTs with Languages. In: Buhl, M., Holm Sørensen, B., Meyer, B. (eds.) Medier og It - Læringspotentialer (Media and ICT – Learning Potentials), Danish University of Education Press (2006)
25. Meyer, B., Sørensen, B.H.: Serious Games in language learning and teaching – a theoretical perspective. In: Proceedings of DIGRA, Tokyo, Japan (2007)
26. Meyer, B., Sørensen, B.H.: Designing e-learning through games – reconceptualising the 'fun' and the 'serious' in computer assisted language learning. In: Proceedings of ICEL, University of Cape Town, South Africa (2008)
27. Milton, J.: Literature review in languages, technology and learning. Futurelab Series (2006), http://www.futurelab.org.uk/research/lit_reviews.htm
28. Prensky, M.: Digital Game-based Learning. McGraw-Hill, New York (2001)
29. Shaffer, D.W.: Pedagogical praxis: The professions as models for post-industrial education. Teachers College Record (2004)
30. Sefton-Green, J.: Digital Diversions. Youth Culture in the Age of Multimedia. UCL Press, London (1998)
31. Squire, K.: Gameplay in Context: Learning Through Participation in Communities of Civilization III Players. Unpublished PhD thesis. Instructional Systems Technology Department, Indiana University (2003)
32. Sutton-Smith, B., Kelly-Byrne, D.: The idealization of play. In: Smith, P.K. (ed.) Play in Animals and Humans, Basil Blackwell Inc., Oxford (1984)
33. Sørensen, B.H.: Didaktisk design for serious games (Didactic design for serious games). In: Selander, S., Svärdemo-Åberg, E. (eds.) Didaktisk design i digital miljö – om lärende, multimodalitet och spel., Liber AB (2008)
34. Walkerdine, V.: Children, Gender, Video Games. Towards a relational Approach to Multimedia. Palgrave Macmillian, Oxford (2007)
35. Warschauer, M.: Technological change and the future of CALL. In: Fotos, S., Browne, C.M. (eds.) New Perspectives on CALL for Second Language Classrooms, Lawrence Erlbaum Associates, Mahwah (2004)
36. Warschauer, M., Kern, R.: Introduction. In: Warschauer, Kern (eds.) Network-based Language Teaching: Concepts and Practice. Cambridge UP, Cambridge (2000)

Motivational Factors in Educational MMORPGs: Some Implications for Education

Kuo-Hsun Hung, Charles Kinzer, and Cheng-Ling Alice Chen

Box 8, 525 W 120th Street, New York, New York 10027-6696
Location: 322 Thompson Hall
kh2203@columbia.edu, kinzer@tc.columbia.edu, cc2550@columbia.edu

Abstract. Studies have shown that motivation is an important factor positively related to learning outcomes. Thus, educators have tried to combine digital games with teaching materials to motivate students participating in learning activities for the past two decades. However, most studies so far view games as universally motivating rather than acknowledging that several factors may be at work within games to influence motivation. We feel it is important to understand the various factors in educational games that motivate students. Twenty 5th grade students in KaoHsiung, Taiwan participated in a study. Each participant completed a motivation and overall attitude questionnaire after playing educational MMORPGs. Results suggest that four factors motivated students to play the game provided, and allow extension to other educational MMORPGs: achievement (desire for competition with a standard of excellence), social (collaboration with others and building social networks), immersion, and the completeness of instructional mechanisms. Implications for both educators and educational game designers are provided.

Keywords: MMORPG, educational MMORPG, motivation.

1 Introduction

> *"The fundamental deficiency of the school system is its failure
> to motivate the youth of the country to want to learn."* [1]

During the past two decades, digital games have been acknowledged as motivational and have become a source of study for educational researchers and instructional designers who wish to maximize motivation in educational materials [2]. Studies indicate that educational games are effective for increasing motivation because they generate enthusiasm, excitement, and enjoyment [3] [4]. However, early research on video games and motivation has viewed digital games as a universally motivating factor for education. Very few research studies further analyzed specific factors within games in attempts to discover how games with educational features motivate.

Among different types of digital games, massively multiplayer online role playing games (MMORPGs) continue to grow in popularity. These games allow thousands of gamers to play simultaneously in the game's persistent virtual world via the Internet. Recently, researchers have started to explore the possibilities of using MMORPGs in

Z. Pan et al. (Eds.): Transactions on Edutainment III, LNCS 5940, pp. 93–104, 2009.

education [5]. For example, Beedle and Wright (2007) indicate that playing MMORPGs can inspire creativity, motivation, problem solving skills, and communication skills [6]. Dickey (2007) also argues that playing MMORPGs can foster learning while requiring players to think, plan, and act critically and strategically [7]. He further indicated that different types of quests in MMORPGs could facilitate different knowledge domains (e.g. declarative knowledge, procedural knowledge, strategic knowledge, and metacognitive knowledge). Many research institutes also are building their own virtual worlds or MMORPGs for education, such as Quest Atlantis (at Indiana State University, by Sasha Barab and colleagues), River City (at Harvard University, led by Chris Dede), Learning Village (at The Chinese University of Hong Kong, led by Junjie Shang), MMOG for Photography (at the National Taiwan Normal University, by Kuang-Chao Yu and colleagues), Whyville (by Numedeon, Inc.), and Zon (at Michigan State Unviersity, led by Yong Zhao). While MMORPGs have been proven to be a tool that can strengthen students' learning, to enhance their efforts educational game designers need to know more about how educational MMORPGs motivate students. Studying specific motivational factors in educational MMORPGs will help ensure that they do not simply become, as Brody (1993) has said, "not-very-entertaining learning activities" or a "not-very-educational game" [8].

To address the above need, we set out the following two objectives for the study briefly reported herein: To examine the motivational factors of playing educational MMORPGs; To discuss how educators and educational game designers could use motivational factors in designing learning activities and educational experiences within MMORPGs.

The remaining sections of this paper will continue to discuss the conceptual framework, research methodology, major findings and implications related to the above goals.

2 Conceptual Framework

Martin and Briggs (1986) indicated that "motivation is a hypothetical construct" and differs among academicians noting that it is important to define motivation in research studies related to motivation [9]. In this study, we follow Tuzun's (2004) definition of motivation and define motivation as "individuals' showing their willingness to initiate and sustain participation in educational MMORPGs" (p. 7) [10].

Our conceptual framework is based on Yee's (2007) theory that indicates players are motivated to play MMORPGs by achievement, social, and immersion factors [11]. His theory extended Bartle's Player Types of Multi-User Dungeon (MUD) (Bartle, 1996) and also used qualitative information from surveys of over 3000 commercial MMORPG players [12]. Here we briefly discuss Yee's factors of achievement, social, and immersion.

2.1 Achievement

McClelland and associates (1953) defined achievement motivation as involving "competition with a standard of excellence" [13]. This definition allows a myriad of activities to be considered to be achievement motivated, the crucial point being a concern with doing those activities well, better than others, or best of all. Achievement goals can affect the way a person performs a task and represent a desire to show competence [14].

An MMORPG is a virtual place for people to seek achievement [11]. Different players may try to achieve different "standards of excellence" such as advancing in level, gaining power, surpassing others, or getting prestige and abilities while they are playing in the MMORPG world. They may also want to acquire special items for their characters in a variety of ways, such as defeating monsters, doing quests, buying things, or by gathering raw materials and then fashioning them into desired items. The acquisition of these items allows players to level up faster, which in turn adds to their in-game prestige [15]. In addition, many MMORPGs provide player rankings and also allow competition between players, and rankings also plays a fundamental role on motivation [16]. In this sense, MMOPRGs can motivate those who are competitive or simply want a quantitative descriptor of their achievement in the game world.

2.2 Social

Maslow (1943) stated that when people have gratified their physiological and the safety needs they will hunger for relations with other people [17]. They want to become a part of family, friends, or society. Research has shown that the motives regulating social life in groups also derive from evolved structures forming the genetic framework upon which later developments were based [18]. These social motives include various forms of social bonding, such as: (1) filial love, (2) parental love, (3) conjugal love, (4) friendship, and (5) seeking and maintaining positive relationships with unfamiliar others of both sexes and a similar age. There is no doubt that these motives form the basis for humans who are "social beings." An important reason that people play MMORPGs appears to be that their friends are playing [11]. That is, players often want to bring real-life friendships to MMORPGs. Moreover, players may want to make new friends in MMORPGs. Ways that some MMORGs have facilitated friendship and gratify player's social needs are through Guilds and Groups. Guilds are groups of players who come together for social reasons or to facilitate advancement in the game. As a result, guilds provide an opportunity for players to collaborate and progress to higher levels. Groups are formed when a player finds a task to be greater than what his/her current skill is able to conquer. Guilds are more continuously long-term, while groups often form to meet specific goal and advance. A group even within a guild will proceed within a given quest to overcome an obstacle.

2.3 Immersion

Immersion is the sense that a player has of being in a virtual world [12]. Yee (2007) stated that one important reason for players to get immersed in the MMORPGs is to escape from real life problems and to allow a transportive, fantasy experience. Immersion is related to the concept of presence [11]. In virtual world terms, although presence is an aid to immersion, it is not sufficient to cause immersion. For virtual worlds, immersion takes longer to develop than most players suppose. Bartle (1996) indicated three situations, forming possible cycles, that influence players' tendency to feel immersed in a virtual world [12]:

(1) If they are playing and feel as if they are in the virtual world, they are immersed;

(2) If, while immersed, they are interrupted, they are no longer immersed.

(3) If, having been interrupted, they return and pick up where they left off, they are again immersed.

3 Ed-Wonderland

In this study, we used a self-developed educational MMORPG called Ed-Wonderland to explore the two objectives noted earlier. In this section we will introduce the instructional goals, game zones, game values, and educational theories of Ed-Wonderland, and discuss the educational theories we utilized to design Ed-Wonderland.

The instructional goal of Ed-Wonderland is to increase English-language learners' vocabulary proficiency while playing, learning, sharing, collaborating, competing, chatting, and completing quests in its virtual environment. Its aim is to provide a content-rich English learning environment reflective of the target language (in this case, English), and to form an online English learning community through game-play and learning.

Ed-Wonderland has five game areas: Welcome Island—where first time users acquire information needed to play Ed-Wonderland. Community Island—where all residents of Wonderland live. Educational Island—where most educational content/activities are presented. Forest Island —where players compete with creatures around vocabulary knowledge to "level up" (see Fig. 1). Carnival Island—where individual or multiplayer educational games are provided. Fig. 2 shows a screen of a game called "Happy Runner" in Carnival Island.

Players can gain four types of "value" in the game (Intelligence, Experience, Money, and Energy), earned by defeating monsters, playing sub-games, completing quests, or helping others, respectively. The Intelligence value indicates the learners' academic achievements. The Experience value represents level of engagement, measured by the number of activities completed (games, vocabulary, quests). The Money value allows players to virtually buy items including clothes, furniture, houses, and so on while the Energy value relates to a player's speed and health status. These game values help players monitor their game status and learning.

Fig. 1. Players are defeating monsters in the Forest Island

Fig. 2. A game called "Happy Runner" provided in Carnival Island

Ed-Wonderland was designed to incorporate socio-cultural, metacognitive, and multiple context theories of education, which have been shown to have positive influences in teaching and learning. Briefly, a socio-cultural theory of learning avers that human intelligence originates in a society or culture, and individual learning results from interaction with one's social environment [19]. Learning results from the accretion and reorganization of individual knowledge structures and the conversations and collaborations that groups of learners conduct. Thus, like most MMORPGs, Ed-Wonderland provides graphical chat functions, competition, collaborative activities and embedded games to address social factors, and official websites for asynchronous communication.

Metacognitive theory indicates that the ability to monitor one's learning is linked to better performance [20]. Educational MMORPGs can facilitate metacognitive strategies, as they are permanent platforms where players' achievements are not erased and can be thought about strategically over time. Ed-Wonderland records students' learning histories automatically so that students can always have chances to track their own learning. In addition, students can understand their overall learning status by checking their own game values on demand.

While metacognitive theory addresses the benefits of monitoring one's learning, multiple context theory indicates that knowledge taught in a single context is less likely to support transfer than knowledge taught in multiple contexts [21]. Educational MMORPGs can embed multiple contexts within an environment; thus designers can provide different contexts to support a given concept's learning. In Ed-Wonderland, vocabulary knowledge is taught or used via scenes, games tasks, or sub-games in mini-environments and across different "Islands" so that students are learning vocabulary knowledge in various contexts.

4   Research Methodology

4.1   Participants and Setting

The research was conducted in a computer lab of a primary school in KaoHsiung, Taiwan in January, 2009. The primary school is one of the largest primary schools in the Kushan district of KaoHsiung city, with approximately 1600 students and 100 teachers. We asked one of the two computer teachers in the school to select one 5th grade class that was representative of the school's 5th grade students' academic performance. Twenty 5th grade students (female=10, male=10) agreed to participate. Eleven of the twenty participants went to after school English classes (female=4, male=7); ten were interested in learning English vocabulary words (female=3, male=7); and ten had MMORPG playing experience (female=2, male=8).

We first conducted a twenty-minute session to introduce Ed-Wonderland and its game world, rules, and functions. This was followed by a 1-hour play session. During the play session, an Applied Linguistics master's student, fluent in both Mandarin and English, served as an online assistant to help the participants with English-related questions. After the play session, each participant completed a motivation questionnaire and overall attitude questionnaire. The two questionnaires are described in the next section.

4.2 Instruments

Motivation Questionnaire. To see if Yee's (2007) factors were salient, and whether or not additional factors might be present in educational MMPORGs, we began with a pilot study in November, 2008 [22]. Participants were interviewed about what motivated them in Ed-Wonderland. Pilot study results indicated that besides the achievement, social, and immersion factors, the completeness of the *instruction mechanism*, including the teaching materials and tools that support learning, was an additional factor for students in choosing whether or not to play educational MMORPGs. Based on the pilot study results, we then designed a 32-item questionnaire to explore four factors related to students' motivation of playing educational MMORPGs such as Ed-Wonderland. The four factors are: achievement, social, immersion, and the instruction mechanism.

Overall Attitude Questionnaire. We also designed an overall attitude questionnaire. The first part of this questionnaire investigates participants' attitudes toward Ed-Wonderland. An interesting finding in our pilot study was that even though participants agreed that playing educational MMORPGs could make learning more motivating, they tended to choose commercial MMORPGs with entertainment goals rather than educational MMORPGs during their leisure time. Thus, the second part of this questionnaire investigates this area.

5   Results

5.1   Participants Are Motivated by Achievement, Social, Immersion, and Instructional Mechanism Factors

The mean score of the achievement factor (1=low / 5=high) is high (M=4.53, SD=.79). This indicates that the participants agreed the achievement factor motivates them to play educational MMORPGs such as Ed-Wonderland. Dividing the achievement factor into its components questions indicates that participants indicate that getting high scores, and adding to their intelligence value (M=4.45, SD=.83), experience value (M=4.60, SD=.68), energy (M=4.45, SD=.76), and virtual money (M=4.55, SD=.89) is motivational. They also want to challenge others (M=4.35, SD=.93) and are more likely to be motivated if educational MMORPGs provide "high score" boards (M=4.45, SD=.83). A t-test to examine whether the mean overall achievement-factor score of males and females indicates no significant difference by gender on the achievement factor; the difference between mean achievement score of males (4.58) and females (4.47) is not large enough to be statistically significant (p=.709) (see Table 2). Therefore, the achievement factor is equally high and important for both males and females in terms of motivation.

The mean score of the social factor (1=low / 5=high) is high (M=4.37, SD=.88). This indicates that the participants agreed the social factor motivates them to play educational MMORPGs such as Ed-Wonderland. Participants want to know/meet other players (M=4.45, SD=.83), and chat with their real life friends (M=4.55, SD=.76) or new friends they make in the game (M=4.55, SD=.76). The difference between mean social score of males (4.43) and that of females (4.31) are not large enough to be statistically significant (p=.703). Therefore, the social factor appears equally high in importance to both males' and females' motivation to play educational MMORPGs such as Ed-Wonderland.

The Immersion factor was also listed as an important motivational factor important (M=4.44, SD=1.00) for participants deciding to play educational MMORPGs. With regard to component questions within this factor, our results indicate that participants want to explore new game scenes (M=4.50, SD=1.05) and use different personalities when playing (M=4.45, SD=.76). They also want to buy new things such as clothes (M=4.60, SD=.75), furniture (M=4.60, SD=.75), and houses (M=4.70, SD=.66). The difference between mean immersion score of males (4.43) and that females (4.46) are not large enough to be statistically significant (p=.902). Thus, the immersion factor appears to be equally high and important across males and females.

The mean score of the instructional mechanism factor (1=low / 5=high) is high (M=4.47, SD=.78), indicating that instructional mechanisms motivates players to play educational MMORPGs such as Ed-Wonderland. There was no statistically significant difference between the mean instructional mechanism scores of males (4.49) and females (4.46) (p=.924). As for the other factors noted above, the instructional mechanism factor is equally high in motivational value across males and females.

In summary, the participants indicate that achievement, social, immersion, and instructional mechanism factors are important with regard to motivating them to play educational MMORPGs such as Ed-Wonderland. This finding is in line with Yee's factors of achievement, social and immersion, but extends those to add "instructional mechanism." Independent t-tests to examine differences between males and females found no statistically significant differences in any of the four factors, indicating that males and females are influenced equally by these factors as they relate to motivation to play MMORPGs such as Ed-Wonderland.

5.2 Attitudes toward Ed-Wonderland is positive

The mean score of overall attitude toward Ed-Wonderland is high (M=4.47, SD=.78). This indicates that participants have positive attitudes toward Ed-Wonderland. When asked whether they would rather play a commercial MMORPG or an educational MMORPG such as Ed-Wonderland, however, responses were essentially neutral (M=3.55, SD=1.32). The high standard deviation indicates that fairly strong feelings about this, in either direction, existed in our group of participants. This area is one that would be fruitful for further investigation, as biases toward commercial, or "non-educational" MMORPGs could ultimately be an important, perhaps even an overriding consideration in determining motivation to play. Students are biased against games that are educational because they don't view such items as true games, thus educational game designers have a significant hurdle to overcome. Our sample is, of course, small, and our results should be taken as indicators of areas that require further, more stringent research, but we feel that taken together, the trends in the data are consistent and point toward important possibilities that should be explored.

Table 1. Means scores and standard deviations of motivational factors (1=low, 5=high)

		M	SD
	Achievement	4.53	0.79
1.	Getting a higher intelligence value	4.45	0.83
2.	Getting a higher experience value	4.60	0.68
3.	Getting a higher energy value (walk faster)	4.45	0.76
4.	Getting more virtual money	4.55	0.89
5.	Making my avatar more powerful	4.55	0.95
6.	Getting more special items	4.65	0.67
7.	Learning more English vocabulary words	4.45	0.83
8.	Challenging Others (e.g., playing vocabulary tic-tac-toe game with others)	4.35	0.93
9.	Understanding the game more (e.g. knowing more hidden areas and hidden characters)	4.75	0.55
10.	Achieving a high score board	4.45	0.83
	Social	4.37	0.88
11.	Knowing more players	4.55	0.69
12.	Helping other players	4.15	1.18
13.	Chatting with real life friends	4.55	0.76
14.	Chatting with friends in the game	4.55	0.76
15.	Participating in a guild	4.10	0.91
16.	Collaborating with others to complete tasks (e.g. defeating monsters together)	4.25	0.97
17.	Learning with others (e.g., learning English vocabulary words)	4.45	0.83
	Immersion	4.44	1.00
18.	Exploring new game scenes	4.50	1.05
19.	Using different personalities to play the game	4.45	0.76
20.	Immersion in the virtual world	3.80	1.58
21.	Buying clothes	4.60	0.75
22.	Buying furniture	4.60	0.75
23.	Buying houses	4.70	0.66
24.	Relaxing	4.75	0.55
25.	Forgetting real life problems	4.15	1.31
	Instructional Mechanism	4.47	0.78
26.	Updating educational scenes (e.g. coffee shop or bus)	4.50	1.00
27.	Providing everyday readings	4.45	0.69
28.	Recording my actions in the game	4.50	0.69
29.	Recording answer result	4.15	1.04
30.	Having complete educational content	4.60	0.68
31.	Having systemtic educational content (from easy to hard)	4.50	0.61
32.	Having experts online to answer questions	4.60	0.68

Table 2. T-Test of achievement, social, immersion, and instructional mechanism score based on gender

	Female (n=10)		Male (n=10)		Comparing means	
	M	SD	M	SD	T	p
Achievement	4.47	.60	4.58	.69	.379	.709
Social	4.31	.58	4.43	.73	.388	.703
Immersion	4.46	.45	4.43	.83	-.125	.902
Instructional Mechanism	4.46	.45	4.49	.81	.097	.924

6 Implication for Education

Given the caveats mentioned above in terms of our sample size, our findings, point to the following implications for both educators and educational game designers:

6.1 For Educators

Educational MMORPGs such as Ed-Wonderland could be used to motivate students to learn. Not all students succeed in the school system. We believe that this is less a function of a given students' capability, and more a function of mismatches between teaching methods, materials, and procedures and students' motivation and variable strengths. We also believe that educational games may provide a way to address issues of motivation and could benefit educators' efforts to engage students in learning activities. If students are motivated, they will spend more time on the task that motivates them, and if educational games are motivational they can increase time within educational activities. Research has shown that time is an important factor that is positively related to learning outcomes. For example, learners need time to rehearse information in order for it to go into long-term memory. Ericsson et al. (1993) reviewed a many fields where time spent practicing is critical to success [23], and Singley and Anderson (1989) also stated that the development of expertise is only possible with major investments of time [24]. In this study, we found participants showed positive attitudes toward Ed-Wonderland and were willing to use Ed-Wonderland to learn English vocabulary words. In addition, at least four motivational factors motivated our participants to use Ed-Wonderland, indicating that using educational MMORPGs such as Ed-Wonderland may be an engaging way for users to learn.

Educational MMORPGs such as Ed-Wonderland could be a social learning platform for after class usage. According to our findings, the social factor is important for motivating participants to play educational MMORPGs such as Ed-Wonderland. Thus, educational MMORPGs may be valuable platforms for building out-of-classroom social networks. In addition, Goldstein (1994) pointed out that playing video games is a social activity that often involves cooperation between and among players [4]. Therefore, educational MMORPGs may serve as an environment where more able partners can assist with scaffolding and coaching, and also assist teachers in supporting learning via appropriate communication technologies.

Educators could utilize the four motivational factors in their learning activities. That games are motivating is widely accepted. In our study, we found four motivational factors that educators could use to design "game-like" learning activities, either together or separately. For example, educators could use score systems, high score boards (both individual and group), or competitions as part of their learning activities to motivate students to achieve "standards of excellence". The test scores in schools system could be accumulated like the game scores in MMORPGs. These may let students know not only their performances on a particular test, but also all their previous performances on previous tests. Furthermore, study groups structured like guilds in MMORPGs could be encouraged. Group members should be heterogeneous, with high performers encouraged to help low performers, as occurs in most MMORPGs. Teachers could also facilitate collaboration within a study group by setting group goals or through appropriate competition with other study groups. While many of these aspects are things teachers do intuitively, looking at these factors and how they positively affect game play in MMPORGs can be informative in traditional classrooms situations as well.

6.2 For Educational Game Designers

The instructional materials and tools should be thorough. Unlike most traditional single player educational games that usually teach only a few concepts in a game, MMORPGs are ideal platforms to carry systematic and thorough teaching materials. It is important to develop systematic and thorough teaching material so that students will feel they are systematically developing their knowledge, not just learning something "randomly." Besides, educational game designers should provide tools to support metacognitive strategies such as recording students' learning histories to help them track their own learning, and incorporate ways to encourage reflection on their learning, gameplay and learning/playing histories.

Educational games could be accompanied with other materials. Of course, educational games are is not the only option for students during their leisure time or in classrooms. Even though students may have positive attitudes toward educational MMORPGs, they may choose commercial MMORPGs to play in leisure time, rather than educational MMORPGs. Our results, however, suggest that this may be true for some people and not others, and that there may be a bias against things termed "educational" rather than "entertaining" games. We believe however, that taking into account the motivational factors shown to be important by the participants in our study may mitigate negative bias toward educational games and place them on an equal footing with entertainment. In effect, motivational factors may serve to blend education and entertainment, resulting in a satisfying game experience and learning outcomes as well.

References

1. Gordan, A.K.: Game for Growth. Science Research Association, Inc., Palo Alto (1970)
2. Chang, M., Wu, S., Heh, J.-S.: Making the Real World as a Game World to Learners by Applying Game-Based Learning Scenes into Ubiquitous Learning Environment. In: Pan, Z., Cheok, D.A.D., Müller, W., El Rhalibi, A. (eds.) Transactions on Edutainment I. LNCS, vol. 5080, pp. 261–277. Springer, Heidelberg (2008)
3. Gee, J.: What Video Games Have to Teach Us About Learning and Literacy. Longman, New York (2003)
4. Goldstein, J.: Handbook of Computer Game Studies. The MIT Press, Cambridge (2005)
5. Dickey, M.D.: Three-dimensional Virtual Worlds and Distance Learning: Two Case Studies of Active Worlds as a Medium for Distance Education. British Journal of Educational Technology 36, 439–461 (2005)
6. Beedle, J.B., Wright, V.H.: Games and Simulation in Online Learning: Perspectives from Multiplayer Video Games, ch. 7. Idea Group Inc., NY (2007)
7. Dickey, M.D.: Game Design and Learning: A Conjectural Analysis of How Massvely Multiple Online Role-Playing Games (MMORPGs) Foster Intrinsic Motivation. Educational Technology Research and Development, 253–273 (2007)
8. Brody, H.: Video Games that Teach? Technology Review, 51–57 (1993)
9. Martin, B.L., Briggs, L.J.: The Affective and Cognitive Domains: Integration for Instruction and Research. Educational Technology Publications, Englewood Cliffs (1986)
10. Tuzun, H.: Motivating Learners in Educational Computer Games. Unpublished doctoral dissertation, Indiana University, Bloomington (2004)
11. Yee, N.: Motivations of Play in Online Games. Journal of CyberPsychology & Behavior 9, 772–775 (2007)
12. Bartle, R.: Hearts, Clubs, Diamonds, Spades: Players Who Suit MUDs. The Journal of Virtual Environments 1 (1996)
13. McClelland, D.C., Atkinson, J.W., Clark, R.A., Lowell, E.L.: The Achievement Motive. Appleton-Century-Crofts, New York (1953)
14. Harackiewicz, J., Barron, K., Carter, S., Lehto, A., Elliot, A.: Predictors and Consequences of Achievement Goals in the College Classroom: Maintaining Interest and Making the Grade. Journal of Personality and Social Psychology 73, 1284–1295 (1997)
15. Riegle, R.P., Matejka, W.A.: The Learning Guild: MMORPGs as Educational Environments. In: 22nd Annual Conference on Distance Teaching and Learning, the Board of Regents of the University of Wisconsin System (2006)
16. Garcia-Mateos, G., Fernandez-Aleman, J.L.: Make Learning Fun with Programming Contests. In: Pan, Z., Cheok, D.A.D., Müller, W., El, R. (eds.) Transactions on Edutainment II. LNCS, vol. 5660, pp. 246–257. Springer, Heidelberg (2009)
17. Maslow, A.H.: A Theory of Human Motivation. Psychological Review 50, 370–396 (1943)
18. Bischof-Kohler, D.: Zur Phylogenese menschlicher Motivation. In: Eckensberger, L.H., Lantermann, E.-D. (eds.) Emotion und Reflexivität, pp. 3–47. Urban und Schwarzenberg, Wien (1985)
19. Vygotsky, L.S.: Mind in Society: The Development of Higher Psychological Processes. Harvard University Press, Cambridge (1978)
20. Mayer, R.E., Wittrock, M.C.: Problem-solving Transfer. In: Berliner, D.C., Calfee, R.C. (eds.) Handbook of Educational Psychology, pp. 47–62. Simon & Schuster Macmillan, New York (1996)

21. Bransford, J., Brown, A., Cocking, R.: How People Learn: Brain, Mind, Experience, and School. National Academy Press, Washington (2000)
22. Hung, K.H.: A Study of Motivation for Playing MMORPGs and an Educational MMORPG: Ed-Wonderland. Unpublished pilot study (2008)
23. Ericsson, K.A., Krampe, R.T., Tesch-Romer, C.: The Role of Deliberate Practice in the Acquisition of Expert Performance. Psychological Review 100, 363–406 (1993)
24. Singley, M.K., Anderson, J.R.: The transfer of cognitive skill. Harvard University Press, Cambridge (1989)

A Distributed Multi-agent Architecture in Simulation Based Medical Training

Jun Hu and Loe Feijs

Department of Industrial Design
Eindhoven University of Technology
5600MB Eindhoven, The Netherlands
{j.hu, l.m.g.feijs}@tue.nl

Abstract. This paper addresses the issues of distributed interactions in a simulation based medial training environment, where a team of doctors, nurses and assistants are trained for handling difficult delivery situations using simulations. A scripting language is proposed, using a metaphor of play, with which the timing and mapping issues in distributed presentations are covered. A generic architecture for the systems is also presented, which covers the timing and mapping issues of conducting such a script in a medical training environment. The difference between playing a medical training scenario and playing a multimedia entertainment scenario is discussed, based on which the future research and development are proposed.

Keywords: Distribution, multi-agent, delivery simulator, medical training.

1 Introduction

In the United States as many as 98,000 people die each year from medical errors that occur in hospitals, according to a book with the title *To Err is Human*[1]. It was found that in America 75 percent of the failures in rescue were caused by either the diagnosis or the treatment being too late. Many of these deaths could have been avoided by improved the communication and coordination with in the medical teams.

In medical education, how to act in emergency situations is often trained on an individual basis. In practice, patients are however handled by a team from multiple disciplines, hence the training must target on the entire team. A British study shows that regular team training leads to 50 percent less brain damage caused by lack of oxygen during birth [2]. In the last three years, Máxima Medical Center in Veldhoven has been providing such multidisciplinary team training with the help of medical simulation. The team training is given by a gynecologist and an experienced midwife, taking place in a fully equipped delivery room that tries to reproduce the real lift situation (fig. 1). The training uses a patient simulator that is the most advanced up to date. The aim is to increase the skills of a multidisciplinary group of employees in the delivery room and especially to prevent inadequate communication in critical obstetric situations.

Z. Pan et al. (Eds.): Transactions on Edutainment III, LNCS 5940, pp. 105–115, 2009.
© Springer-Verlag Berlin Heidelberg 2009

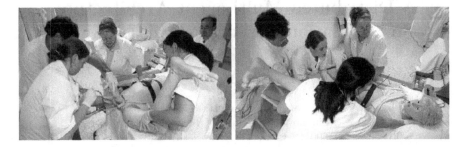

Fig. 1. Team training with delivery simulators in MMC

Patient simulators are already commercially available from several suppliers (for example the patient simulator "Noelle", a product of Gaumard Miami, Florida. Fig. 2). Although technically advanced, the level of realism is not particularly high. Next to the toy like external appearance, it is also the not really flexible material applied which has the effect that the training experience is still quite remote from the reality. Especially, most of the commercial products today are designed as a stand alone system that does not really take the team training aspects into account. These team training aspects are for example the communication among team members, the position of every member, the monitoring and analysis of the team performance and so forth. Hence a 10 year cooperation plan has been set up between Eindhoven University of Technology and Máxima Medical Center to develop the next generation simulation based training facilities, involving several departments from both institutes as weel as external partners.

For a more realistic experience and an optimal training result it is necessary to involve as many different senses as possible: vision, sound, smell and also importantly a realistic touch experience (moistness, warmth, friction). To realize the technology should allow mixing things that are real and things that appear to be real, and augmented reality seems to be promising. Augmented reality is already applied at present for several training goals where the real experience is

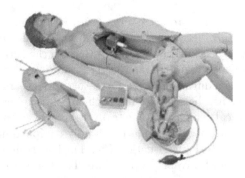

Fig. 2. Noelle from Gaumard

too dangerous or too expensive [3]. Examples are training firemen (judging risks for collapsing of a building or the probability of an explosion with a tanker truck overturn), or military personnel (training with realistic impacts of shells).

Next to patient simulators there are also additional possibilities and requirements for visualizing a realistic environment (virtual reality). One can think of adding objects in the background (walls, doors, windows, equipment, but also persons walking by). The advantage of virtual reality is that the very same training room can be used for very different training scenarios with little effort, changing from a delivery room to an emergency room or a mobile situation in an ambulance.

For team performance monitoring and analysis, video based techniques such as 3-D visual signal processing [4] and video content analysis [5] can be applied. D-D Depth map generation techniques create the depth map from a non-calibrated video sequence using the "structure-from-motion" algorithm. This technique facilitates the creation of a 3-D model of a scene from any view angle, which is an essential component in human body and behavior simulation. Human behavior analysis and simulation can be started by the analysis of human motion, since motion reflects the behavior, focusing not only on the global motion estimation, such as human segmentation and tracking, but also on the feature-based motion analysis. Further, human modeling techniques including a 2-D or 3-D human geometry (skeleton) model and a fitting algorithm link the detected motion to the model, generating a reliable human model that tracks the motion with sufficient accuracy. It enables fast semantic analysis of human behaviors. Based on these technologies, combining with sound and facial expression analysis, it is possible to couple emotional state recognition to the imposed conditions of the delivery simulator.

The aforementioned concepts brings more software and hardware devices and components into the training room than a single patient simulator. We also aim at an open system architecture that is flexible and extensible enough for the industry to introduce further development and future technologies into simulation based team training. This paper presents the concepts of such an architecture. First the notion of "Play" is introduced as a metaphor for scripting the training scenarios, then the main architectural constructs needed for bringing a "Play" to live are described, followed by a discussion of the difference between playing a medical training scenario and playing a multimedia entertainment scenario, and its implication for future research and development.

2   Scenario Based Scripting: Play Metaphor

In the delivery room, a team of experts must work together, reacting to each other on expected and unexpected situations at right and sometimes critical moments. For a successful training session with certain focused training purposes, the communication, the situations, the reactions and the timing must be planned in advance for a optimal training result. At the moment this is often done by manually preparing a training scenario and carrying out under the supervision of a leading gynecologist. Observing this team training practice, we find the Play metaphor proposed by Hu (2006) to be applicable, although it is originally designed for distributed interactive multimedia [6].

A *play* is a common literary form, referring both to the written works of dramatists and to the complete theatrical *performance* of such. Plays are generally performed in a *theater* by *actors*. To better communicate a unified interpretation of the text in question, productions are usually overseen by a *director*, who often puts his or her own unique interpretation on the production by providing the actors and other stage people with a *script*. A script is a written set of directions that tell each actor what to say (*lines*) or do (*actions*) and when to say or do it (*timing*). If a play is to be performed by the actors without a director and a script from the director, the results are unpredictable, if not chaotic. Here we use the word "play" for both its written form of a script, and the stage performance form of this script.

There are obvious similarities between a theater play and a training session, and the metaphor can be directly used by taking a training room as a theater. The trainees, the simulators and other hardware and software devices are actors, and the training room is their performing theater. The script describes the training scenario, where actions must be taken with right timing. One might also argue why a "Play" metaphor is needed and why the training scenarios can not be directly used. There are two reasons for this. First, we are not only aiming at the delivery simulations, but also other medical training simulations such as newborn babies, a more generic set of terms are necessary to keep the system flexible for extensions. Second, we need a striping language that imposes timing and communication among the trainees, the simulators and other system components. A stricter definition is necessary when the machines are included in interaction loops.

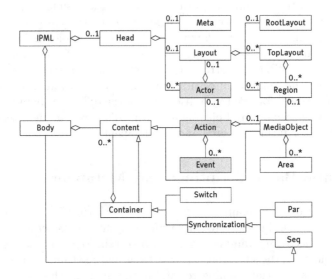

Fig. 3. Scripting language extends SMIL

We propose an extension to SMIL (Synchronized Multimedia Integration Language) [7] for scripting the scenarios, by introducing the metaphor of play, adding event-based linking elements and keeping timing and synchronization elements [6]. Fig. 3 shows an object-oriented view on the structure of the language IPML.

3 Actors: Distributed PAC Agents

Many interactive architectures have been developed along the lines of the object-oriented and the event driven paradigms. Model-View-Controller (MVC) [8] and Presentation-Abstraction-Control (PAC) [9] are the most popular and often used ones [10].

The MVC model divides an interactive agent into three components: model, view and controller, which respectively denotes processing, output and input. The model component encapsulates core data and functionality. View components display information to the user. A View obtains the data from the model. There can be multiple views, each of which has an associated controller component. Controllers receive input, usually as events that encode hardware signals from input devices.

Coutaz (1987) proposed a structure called Presentation-Abstraction-Control [9], which maps roughly to the notions of View-Controller pair, Model, and the Mediator pattern [11]. It is referenced and organized in a pattern form by Buschmann et al. [10]: the PAC pattern "defines a structure for interactive software systems in the form of a hierarchy of cooperating agents. Every agent is responsible for a specific aspect of the application's functionality and consists of three components: presentation, abstraction, and control. This subdivision separates the human-computer interaction of the agent from its functional core and its communication with other agents."

In the design of the simulation based training system, PAC is selected as the overall system architecture, and the actors are implemented as PAC agents that are managed by the scheduling agents in a PAC hierarchy, connected with the channels, and performing the actions.

This structure separates the user interface from the application logic and data with both top-down and bottom-up approaches (fig. 4). The entire system is regarded as a *top-level* agent and it is first decomposed into three components: an *Abstraction* component that defines the system function core and maintains the system data repository, a *Presentation* component that presents the system level interface to the user and accepts the user input, and in between, a *Control* component that mediates the abstract component and the presentation component. All the communications among them have to be done through the control components.

At the *bottom-level* of a PAC architecture are the smallest self-contained units which the user can interact with and perform operations on. Such a unit maintains its local states with its own *Abstraction* component, and presents its own state and certain aspects of the system state with a *Presentation* component. The communication between the presentation and the abstraction components is again through a dedicated *Control* component.

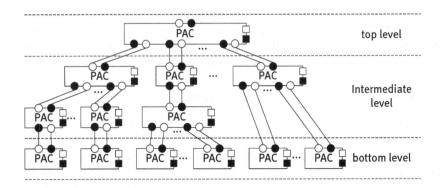

Fig. 4. Distributed PAC in a hierarchy

Between the top-level and bottom level agents are *intermediate-level* agents. These agents combine or coordinate lower level agents, for example, arranging them into a certain layout, or synchronizing their presentations if they are about the same data. The intermediate-level may also have its interface *Presentation* to allow the user to operate the combination and coordination, and have an *Abstraction* component to maintain the state of these operations. Again, with the same structure, there is a control component in between to mediate the presentation and the abstraction.

The entire system is then built up as a PAC hierarchy: the higher-level agents coordinate the lower level agents through their *Control* components; the lower level agents provide input and get the state information and data from the higher level agents again through the *Control* components. This approach is believed more suitable for distributed applications and has better stability than MVC, and it has been used in many distributed systems and applications, such as CSCW [12], distributed real-time systems [13] , web-based applications [14,15], mobile robotics [16,17], distributed co-design platforms [18] and wireless services [19].

To a large degree the PAC agents are self-contained. The user interface component (Presentation), the processing logic (Abstraction) and the component for communication and mediation (Control) are tightly coupled together, acting as one. Separations of these components are possible, but these distributed components would then be regarded as PAC agents completed with minimum implementation of the missing parts. Thus the distribution boundaries remain only among the PAC agents instead of composing components.

Based on this observation, each component is formally described by Hu (2006) [6], modeling the communication among PAC agents with push style channels from the Channel pattern. In fig. 4, a "●" indicates a data supplier component, a "○" indicates a data consumer component and a connecting line in between indicates the channel. The symbol "■" indicates that the attaching component has a function of physically presenting data to the user, and the symbol "□" indicates the function of capturing input from the user interface or the environment.

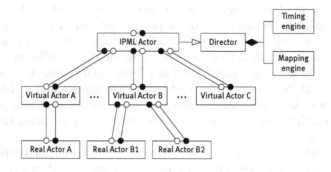

Fig. 5. IPML system: an IPML actor

An actor is then basically a PAC agent. It reacts on the user input events and scheduling commands, and takes corresponding actions. The final system is simply an IPML actor, or in other words, an *Actor* implementation that is capable of presenting the IPML scripts. The IPML actor implements the role of a *Director*, which has a mapping engine [20], creates, manages and connects the virtual actors, and has a timing engine which schedules the timed actions for the delegating virtual actors (fig. 5). Depending on the physical configuration of the "theater" – the presenting environment, the mapping engine may also connect appropriate "real actors" to virtual actors, where the virtual actors keep the role of software drivers for the "real actors". The mapping engine may make use of distributed lookup and registration services such as UPNP [21] and JINI [22] to locate and maintain a list of "real actors", but this architecture leaves these possibilities open to the implementation of the mapping engine. The timing engine takes the timing relations defined using the SMIL timing module, translates them into an internal representation (based on Peri Nets [23,24] and OCPN [25], see also a detailed description in [6]), and schedules the actions for the actors, no matter whether the actors are distributed over the network.

4   Discussions

When comparing the requirements to playing a medical training scenario and the requirements to playing a multimedia entertainment scenarios, the following differences and points of attention appear:

A. In the medical training scenario the need for explicit control of timing aspects is even more important than in entertainment applications.
B. In the medical training scenario the need for team training is very essential. Whereas many entertainment applications nowadays under development are still geared towards and individual experience, team training is the most important issue in present day medical training.
C. In the medical training scenario there will be variations among the capabilities of the various manikins and instrumentations of the training rooms.

At present most training rooms are pioneering the role of team training anyhow and the scenarios are developed locally and tuned to the available manikins and instruments. But as to the training centers and the manikin industry manufactures, there will be more and more different versions of the manikins with formalized capability lists. Then it must be possible that the IPML plays execute in different training rooms without elaborate manual adaptation or rewriting. Automated mapping software as a part of the software architecture can run the same scenario's by adapting them to the manikins at hand.

D. In the medical training scenario there is a larger need for evaluating the performance of the users. It is not enough to optimize their experience according to certain dramatic, physical and emotional goals. Each session will be followed by a debriefing session in which the actions performed, their timing, their precise locations, the forces used, are essential. When the session is part of a qualification or examination this becomes even more obvious.

These points are easily illustrated by examples from obstetrics, notably breech deliveries, which is precisely the field in which our group cooperates with Prof G. Oei MD and others of the MMC (Máxima Medisch Centrum), Veldhoven, The Netherlands together with the Máxima Academie, the training center.

A. the timing of the various phases of the delivery and the various degrees of oxygen shortage associated will determine whether or not the baby will suffer brain damage. Particularly when the umbilical cord is blocked, every second counts.

B. we just give a very simple example of a team aspect. From the instructions for Lovset's maneuver we quote "Grasp his thighs and pelvis with both hands (if he is slippery use a gauze swab or small towel), your thumbs along his sacrum, your forefingers on his symphysis, and your remaining fingers round his thighs" [26]. Clearly the doctor's assistent has to anticipate and it is essential that the doctor communicates his strategy. Only then can the assistant make sure the gauze swab or the small towel is at hand precisely when the doctor needs it.

C. Different manufacturers of manikins have their own product lines. Important examples are Gaumard, Laerdal, Limbs and Things and Meti. These companies each have their own strengths and weaknesses. For example Meti excels in physio-pharmacological models, Laerdal excels in matters of circulation and respiration, and so on. Moreover they release new versions every few years. In view of the costs, a training center cannot have them all.

D. A very clear example of the need to record and check quantitative performance data is the problem of shoulder dystocia. When the fetus is in breech position, the legs will be delivered first, instead of the head. Then it can happen that the shoulders get stuck in which case the doctor has to perform very specific maneuvers such as the Van Deventer maneuver or the Lovset maneuver. The latter maneuver involves rotating the baby in a certain manners of 180 degreesOnly after that it is allowed to pull. Measuring the leftward and rightward rotations in degrees and the subsequent force in Newton is essential because in real life these parameters will determine the fait and the health of the baby. If the manoeuvres have not been done correctly, the higher force needed will have caused damages such as partial paralysis.

IPML satisfies the needs of A perfectly and it is well-prepared for B in the sense that the play for the actors is already organized as a team effort, not as a single actor. IPML is also perfectly prepared to cope with the demands of C because of the mapping structure and mechanisms [6, Chapter 9]. For D, however, it is necessary to extend IPML with Logging and Verification constructs. We propose an extended language version IPML/V, with V for verification. Because the language is XML based this presents no difficulties at the syntactic level. Moreover, the original play is still written in IPML. But during execution it is transformed into an IPML/V file, essentially a structured logging file. Semantically this is what happens: whenever a play is executed, the execution engine keeps track of which alternative actions have been chosen and at which time the events have actually happened. The result is not just a sequential log, but a log in which the events and the time stamps appear as annotations in their original structured setting. Checking any logical condition φ written in a logical formalism, against a given IPML/V model M can be done either in run-time or by postprocessing. Logically it amounts to checking the truth or falsehood of a formula in a model, usually written as $M \vDash \varphi$.

A further development in the description of the training scenarios is providing a graphical WYSIWYG authoring and analyzing tool on top of the IPML and IPML/V. IPML is a scripting language that is based on XML, which is designed to satisfy the needs of a strict definition of the timing and mapping strategies and relations in a scenario. The primary purpose of XML or any XML based language is to facilitate the sharing of structured data across different information systems and to encode documents and serialize data. It can be read and written using a plain text editor however the process can be cumbersome and trivial. Visualizing the interactive components and defining the timing and mapping relations among them graphically would help the doctors and the trainers to concentrate on the training scenarios instead of a scripting hassle.

5   Conclusions

The concepts of the Play metaphor, the IMPL scripting language and the Distributed PAC based multi-agent architecture are found to be applicable in simulation based medical training, because of the similar requirements on timing and mapping in applications of both distributed multimedia entertainment and simulation based medial training. However there are also clear differences between these two application areas. Further research and development need to be done to deal with the issues such as multiple participants in team training and the verification of the actual performance of a training session.

References

1. Kohn, L.T., Corrigan, J., Donaldson, M.S.: To Err Is Human: Building a Safer Health System. National Academies Press (2000)
2. Draycott, T., Sibanda, T., Owen, L., Akande, V., Winter, C., Reading, S., Whitelaw, A.: Does training in obstetric emergencies improve neonatal outcome? BJOG: An International Journal of Obstetrics and Gynaecology 113, 177–182 (2006)
3. Azuma, R.T.: A survey of augmented reality. Presence: Teleoperators and Virtual Environments 6(4), 355–385 (1997)
4. Lao, W., Han, J., de With, P.H.N.: 3d modeling for capturing human motion from monocular video. In: Proc. Int. Symp. On Information Theory in the Benelux (WIC), Noordwijkerhout (NL), pp. 299–306 (2006)
5. Han, J., Farin, D., de With, P.H.N., Lao, W.: Real-time video content analysis tool for consumer media storage system. IEEE Transactions on Consumer Electronics 52(3), 870–878 (2006)
6. Hu, J.: Design of a Distributed Architecture for Enriching Media Experience in Home Theaters. Technische Universiteit Eindhoven (2006)
7. Ayars, J., Bulterman, D., Cohen, A., Day, K., Hodge, E., Hoschka, P., Hyche, E., Jourdan, M., Kim, M., Kubota, K., Lanphier, R., Layaïda, N., Michel, T., Newman, D., van Ossenbruggen, J., Rutledge, L., Saccocio, B., Schmitz, P., ten Kate, W., Michel, T.: Synchronized multimedia integration language (SMIL 2.0), 2nd edn. W3C recommendation (2005)
8. Krasner, G.E., Pope, S.T.: A cookbook for using the model-view controller user interface paradigm in smalltalk-80. Journal of Object Oriented Program 1(3), 26–49 (1988)
9. Coutaz, J.: PAC, an implementation model for dialog design. In: Interact 1987, Stuttgart, pp. 431–436 (1987)
10. Buschmann, F., Meunier, R., Rohnert, H., Sommerlad, P., Stal, M.: Pattern-Oriented Software Architecture, A System of Patterns, vol. 1. John Wiley & Sons, Inc., Chichester (1996)
11. Gamma, E., Helm, R., Johnson, R., Vlissides, J.: Design Patterns – Elements of Reusable Object-oriented Software. Addison-Wesley, Reading (1995)
12. Calvary, G., Coutaz, J., Nigay, L.: From single-user architectural design to PAC*: a generic software architecture model for cscw. In: CHI 1997 Conference, pp. 242–249. Addison-Wesley, Reading (1997)
13. Niemelä, E., Marjeta, J.: Dynamic configuration of distributed software components. In: Demeyer, S., Bosch, J. (eds.) ECOOP 1998 Workshops. LNCS, vol. 1543, pp. 149–150. Springer, Heidelberg (1998)
14. Illmann, T., Weber, M., Martens, A., Seitz, A.: A pattern-oriented design of a web-based and case oriented multimedia training system in medicine. In: The 4th World Conference on Integrated Design and Process Technology, Dallas, US (2000)
15. Zhao, W., Kearney, D.: Deriving architectures of web-based applications. In: Zhou, X., Zhang, Y., Orlowska, M.E. (eds.) APWeb 2003. LNCS, vol. 2642, pp. 301–312. Springer, Heidelberg (2003)
16. Khamis, A., Rivero, D.M., Rodriguez, F., Salichs, M.: Pattern-based architecture for building mobile robotics remote laboratories. In: IEEE International Conference on Robotics and Automation (ICRA 2003), Taiwan, vol. 3, pp. 3284–3289 (2003)
17. Khamis, A.M., Rodriguez, F.J., Salichs, M.A.: Remote interaction with mobile robots. Autonomous Robots 15(3) (2003)

18. Fougeres, A.-J.: Agents to cooperate in distributed design. In: IEEE International Conference on Systems, Man and Cybernetics, vol. 3, pp. 2629–2634 (2004)
19. Niemela, E., Kalaoja, J., Lago, P.: Toward an architectural knowledge base for wireless service engineering. IEEE Transaction on Software Engineering 31(5), 361–379 (2005)
20. Feijs, L., Hu, J.: Component-wise mapping of media-needs to a distributed presentation environment. In: The 28th Annual International Computer Software and Applications Conference (COMPSAC 2004), Hong Kong, China, pp. 250–257. IEEE Computer Society Press, Los Alamitos (2004)
21. Michael Jeronimo, J.W.: UPnP Design by Example: A Software Developer's Guide to Universal Plug and Play. Intel Press (2003)
22. Edwards, W.K.: Core JINI, 2nd edn. Prentice Hall PTR, Englewood Cliffs (2000)
23. Petri, C.A.: Kommunikation mit Automaten. Bonn: Institut für Instrumentelle Mathematik, Schriften des IIM Nr. 2 (1962)
24. Petri, C.A.: Kommunikation mit automaten. New York: Griffiss Air Force Base, Technical Report RADC-TR-65–377 1 (1966); 1–Suppl. 1 English translation
25. Little, T.D.C., Ghafoor, A.: Synchronization and storage models for multimedia objects. IEEE Journal on Selected Areas in Communications 8(3), 413–427 (1990)
26. Awori, N., Bayley, A., Beasley, A., Boland, J., Crawford, M., Driessen, F., Foster, A., Graham, W., Hancock, B., Hancock, B., Hankins, G., Harrison, N., Kennedy, I., Kyambi, J., Nundy, S., Sheperd, J., Stewart, J., Warren, G., Wood, M.: Primary Surgery: Non-trauma, vol. 1. Oxford Medical Publication (1990)

Designing a Trading Card Game
as Educational Reward System
to Improve Students' Learning Motivations

Peayton Chen[1], Rita Kuo[2], Maiga Chang[3], and Jia-Sheng Heh[1]

[1] Dept. of Information and Computer Engineering, Chung-Yuan Christian Univ., Taiwan
[2] Dept. Of Digital Design, Mingdao Univ., Taiwan
[3] School of Computing and Information Systems, Athabasca University, Canada
peayton@hotmail.com, ritakuo924@gmail.com, maiga@ms2.hinet.net,
jsheh@ice.cycu.edu.tw

Abstract. Reward is the simplest way to motivate students in education. It can encourage students to learn and get immediate achievement. Moreover, it is also has potential to construct students' intrinsic motivation. However, traditional rewards are often less valuable thus can't keep motivating students, e.g. symbolic rewards like stars or stickers can't be used by the students after the class; therefore, the values of symbolic rewards are not appreciated by the students. This research designs cards of a self-developed computerized trading card game (TCG) as educational rewards in order to inspire students learning, e.g. higher learning performance a student shows up, higher level cards the student would receive from the teacher. And of course, the student would have higher chances to beat other players in the TCG. Through the TCG, the rewards can hold students' interest for longer.

Keywords: Trading Card Game, Reward, Learning motivation, Competition, Game.

1 Introduction

Rewards are often used as praises by teachers when students behave well. Some researchers argue that reward is positive reinforcement that can improve students' learning motivation [7][14]. On the other hand, some others point out that the usage of rewards might cause negative effects [1][9]. Although the researchers have different opinions about the effect of rewards, rewards can provide short-term incentive immediately to intrinsic motivation [5]. Wu and Elliott (2008) have found that students have different preferences toward to rewards [15] and Winefield, Barnett and Tiggemann (1984) have showed that the reward contingency also affects the learning performance [2]. Teachers need to consider carefully while designing reward dispatching methods. Stars and stickers are widely used as educational rewards in schools. However, the symbolic meanings of the stars and stickers are intrinsically meaningless to students, e.g. the stars and stickers can't be used by the students to buy anything after

Z. Pan et al. (Eds.): Transactions on Edutainment III, LNCS 5940, pp. 116–128, 2009.

the school. Although McNinch (1997) chooses cash as reward and successfully stimulates students to read [7], it is also easily criticized by others as suborning. For these reasons, this research designs different level cards of a self-developed trading card game (TCG) as educational rewards to stimulate students' learning motivation. To students, the cards of the TCG can be collected and played anytime and anywhere after the class.

This research designs a TCG platform and its cards for making the educational rewards be valuable and appropriate to students. Section 2 discusses the game genres and the game-based learning definitions. The TCG elements are analyzed based on three famous commercial TCGs: "Magic: The gathering" [10], "Yu-Gi-Oh!" [22] and "Aquarian Age" [3] in Section 3. Section 4 designs a computerized TCG according to the analysis in Section 3. A prototype TCG is developed in Section 5. At the end, Section 6 gives a brief conclusion and describes possible future works.

2 Games and Learning

According to Vossen's research in 2004, three attributes are used to analyze game category, are competitive, interactive, and physical [6]. Table 1 lists six game subcategories. For example, card games like poker are categorized as an interactive non-physical game which has attributes: competitive, interactive, and non-physical.

Table 1. Game Categories according Vossen's research [6]

Game Subcategory	Competitive vs. Non-competitive	Interactive vs. Non-interactive	Physical vs. Non-physical
Non-competitive Non-physical Games	Non-competitive	Non-interactive	Non-physical
Parallel Non-physical Games	Competitive	Non-interactive	Non-physical
Interactive Non-physical Games	Competitive	Interactive	Non-physical
Non-competitive Sports	Non-competitive	Non-interactive	Physical
Parallel Sports	Competitive	Non-interactive	Physical
Interactive Sports	Competitive	Interactive	Physical

Trading Card Game is a kind of card games but is different from the poker or UNO. First of all, in general, TCGs have more cards than the poker and UNO, poker has only 56 cards and UNO has 108 cards whereas TCGs always have hundreds of cards. Second, cards in TCG are extendable, which means, we can design new cards when we need. Children and adolescents, including students, spend their leisure time on playing games [12]. The game features attract players are fantasy, curiosity, challenge and control [11]. Some researchers point out that playing can hold student attentions and make learning be more interesting [12][17]. For this reason, many studies use commercial games directly or design new education games and have evidences of students can get significant improvement in learning [12][13][16][20].

Besides, researchers point out that if the reward is worthless to student, the effect of motivation improvement will be no significant or even no effect [4][21]. Since the games attract students so much, this research considers using cards in TCG as educational rewards; making the educational rewards become useful and playable to the students; and, aiming to implement a TCG environment on computers for students competing themselves with their classmates with the educational rewards, the different level cards, they have received from the teachers and/or online testing.

Interpersonal motivation is important in learning [18]. Malone and Lepper propose that competition is an approach to create interpersonal motivation [8][19]. For this purpose, this research uses the players' scores and ranks in the TCG to establish a competitive environment. By depleting opponent's cards, students can earn scores for rank promotion. The ranks can intrinsically motivate students. The way to deplete the opponent easier is to get higher level cards, and the students can get higher level cards by accomplishing the task/test their teacher(s) assign/give to them. The students can receive rarer cards from the teacher(s) according to their performance. Thus, the students will keep learning in order to have better performance to get higher level and rarer cards for defeating others and making them hold/get higher ranks among players.

3   TCG Environment Analysis

3.1   Game Flow Analysis

Most modern TCGs are turn-based. Each player acts after the previous player finished his/her actions. When all the players take their turns, the circle will restart again from the first player. The game will stop when one of the players achieved the game goal, e.g. reaching the specific scores or making all other players withdraw from the game. Three well-known TCGs, "Magic: The gathering", "Yu-Gi-Oh!", and "Aquarian Age", are analyzed to find the TCG model.

Because of the TCGs are turn-based, the game flow is the first issue to discuss. Table 2 analyzes the basic unit of the three TCGs. Each TCG has atom action. Taking "Magic: The Gathering" as example, the atom action is "step"; the set of the atom actions is "phase"; and, a player could have several phases before he/she claim him/her is done and the next player is allowed to do actions, the duration of a player's all phases form a "turn".

Table 2. Action analysis of game flow according to three commercial TCGs

	Magic: The Gathering	Yu-Gi-Oh!	Aquarian Age
Atom action	Step	Action	Action
Set of atom actions	Phase	Phase	Phase
The duration of a player's all phases	Turn	Turn	Turn

Based on Table 2, this research defines the TCG flow as five parts with a hierarchical relationship.

- Action: the atom action in TCGs, e.g. drawing a card or going to attack.
- Phase: a collection of atom actions.
- Turn: the duration from a player starts his/her actions to gives the token out to the next player.

- Round: the duration of all the players finished their turn once.
- Game: a set of rounds from the very beginning to someone reached the game goal.

Different TCGs have different definitions to the phases. Table 3 lists the three major phase categories and its definitions and explanations:

- Initial phase: this phase is the first phase of a turn. At this phase, most of TCGs only allow players drawing card(s) from a pack which is also called library or deck. For example, the beginning phase in "Magic: The Gathering" belongs to the initial phase.
- Main phase: this phase allows players doing actions to attack other players or defending himself/herself in the game. Players at this phase could also doing some strategic actions such like putting cards into the game field or using Tool/Magic Card to change other cards' attribute values.
- Final phase: this phase is the last phase of a turn. This phase assesses the player's status to make sure the resources the player currently has comply with the rules. For example, the end phase of "Magic: The Gathering" asks the player discarding the surplus cards if the player has cards on his/her hands more than the rule defined.

Table 3. Three major phase categories in different commercial TCGs

	Magic: The Gathering	Yu-Gi-Oh!	Aquarian Age
Initial Phase	Beginning Phase	Draw Phase, Stand Phase	Draw Phase, Influence Phase
Main Phase	First Main Phase, Combat Phase, Second Main Phase	Main Phase I, Battle Phase, Main Phase II	Main Phase Power Card Phase,
Final Phase	End Phase	End Phase	Discard Phase

3.2 Game Elements Analysis

After we analyzed the TCG flow, the elements of TCG environment are needed to discuss to help us developing a computerized TCG. This research considers three major TCG elements: player, game field, and card.

Table 4. The player attributes in TCG environment according to the three commercial games

	Magic: The Gathering	Yu-Gi-Oh!	Aquarian Age
Life Points	Lose, if life point drops to 0	Lose, if life point drops to 0	Lose, if accumulating damage over to 10
Remaining Cards	Lose, if runs out of cards		

Player

Players are defined as people who can do actions in the game. The player has several attributes for representing the player's status and being used to check whether the player wins or loses. Life points and remaining cards are two attributes which have been widely used for this purpose. As Table 4 lists, two "lose" criteria in "Magic: The Gathering" are: (1) if a player's life point drops down to zero; (2) if a player is required to draw a card while there is no remaining cards in his/her deck.

Table 5. Four areas in the Game Field according to the three commercial TCGs

	Magic: The Gathering	Yu-Gi-Oh!	Aquarian Age
Cards in player's hand	Hand	Hand	Hand
Card set for player drawing	Library	Deck Zone, Extra Deck Zone	Deck
Used or destroyed cards	Graveyard	Graveyard	Graveyard, Damage Zone
Cards in using	In Play	Monster Card Zone, Spell & Trap Zone, Field Card Zone	Field

Game Field

Game field is the area players placing and manipulating cards during they play the game. Table 5 lists four major areas in the game field for different purposes: (1) for players to hold the cards; (2) for storing cards which have not been drawn yet; (3) for collecting the used, destroyed, and defeated cards; and, (4) for placing the cards to attack and/or defend include set traps. For example, the four areas in "Magic: The Gathering" are called (1) Hand; (2) Library; (3) Graveyard; and, (4) In Play.

Cards

Cards are the major tools for players to fight with each others. The cards can be clustered into three categories:

- Avatar Card: these cards can attack or defend for the players, just like soldiers fight according to commander's orders. To win a TCG, player needs to use Avatar Card to defeat opponent's Avatar Card. The creature cards in "Magic: The Gathering" belong to Avatar Card as Table 6 lists.
- Tool Card: these cards can change other cards' attribute values during the game and will be discarded when its duration is expired or when it is attacked by other players. The sorcery card, instant card, enchantment card and artifact card in "Magic: The Gathering" belong to Tool Card.
- Power Card: To restrict player's action in a turn, player usually needs to pay additional resources, the Power Cards, to take specific actions. Land Card in "Magic: The Gathering" belongs to Power Card.

3.3   Game Rules Analysis

Most of the rules in TCGs can be classified into four types. Figure 1 shows the idea of different rule types: "card ↔ card", "card ↔ game field", "card ↔ player", and "game field ↔ player".

Table 6. Three card categories of commercial TCGs

	Magic: The Gathering	**Yu-Gi-Oh!**	**Aquarian Age**
Avatar Card	Creature Card	Monster Card	Avatar Card, Break Card
Tool Card	Sorcery Card, Instant Card, Enchantment Card, Artifact Card	Spell Card, Trap Card	Permanent Card, Project Card, Fast Card
Power Card	Land Card	N/A	Cards with face-down

- Card ↔ Card: Cards in the game field would interact with each others, e.g. Avatar Card can attack other Avatar Card, and also, Tool Card can change Avatar Card's attribute values such as speed and attacking power.
- Card ↔ Game field: The card positions in the game field represent the card status, e.g. a card in the graveyard presents it had been destroyed or discarded.
- Card ↔ Player: If a player's Avatar Card is defeated by attacking, then the attack will cause damage to the player's attribute such as life points and may affect the game results, e.g. the player loses the game.
- Game field ↔ Player: If a player runs out of his/her cards in the deck/library, then the player loses the game.

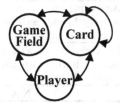

Fig. 1. Four different rules coming from the relations among the TCG elements

4   TCG Design

For constructing a computerized TCG environment as educational reward system, this research designs a TCG according to the analysis in the previous section.

4.1   Environment Design

The computerized TCG has three major parts, which are the cards, the game field, and the player schema.

Cards

According to Table 6, this research designs "Avatar Card", "Magic Card" and "Trap Card" for the computerized TCG. Table 7 shows that each card type's definition and effect, moreover, each card type has different attributes. For example, the attacking power is an attribute of Avatar Card and can be used to calculate the damage this card might cause to other Avatar Card during fighting.

Each card in this computerized TCG has "rank" attribute which is the card level. Using Avatar Card to attack is the major way to defeat opponent's Avatar Card. When an Avatar Card is defeated, the player's life points will be taken based on the avatar card's "size" attribute. The larger avatar will cause the player larger damage when it is defeated. A player thus can use Magic Card to increase opponent's Avatar Card size and then defeat it to make bigger damage to the opponent's life points.

On the other hand, Magic Card and Trap Card are used to create helpful situation to support the player by enhancing the player's Avatar Card or disturbing opponent's Avatar Card. The attributes of Magic Card and Trap Card are almost the same, but the timing of using the two card types are different. Magic Card can be used by the player directly at his/her main phase whereas Trap Card can only react according to the opponent's actions. This research doesn't design Power Card but use "Action Point (AP)" to limit how many atom actions a player can do in a turn to simplify the game rules. Players need to pay specific APs for each atom action.

Table 7. The computerized TCG's card types and its attributes

Card Categories	Card Type	Definition	Related Attributes
Avatar Card	Avatar Card	Fight with other Avatar Card.	Attacking Power, Hit Point, Size, Race, Rank etc.
Tool Card	Magic Card	Active: players can use it actively. Magic Card can alter other cards' attribute values.	Description/Effect, Duration, Rank, Scope etc.
	Trap Card	Passive: players can't use it directly; it will be triggered by opponent's actions.	
Power Card		N/A	

Game Field

Figure 2 shows the game field, which has two sides that this research designed for two players. Each side has four areas based on the analysis in Table 5. The four areas are Hand (H), Deck (D), Graveyard (G), and Field where two kinds of cards, Avatar Card (A) and Tool Card (T), can be placed. Table 8 lists each area's notation, the description, and the card type restriction. For example, A^p_i means the area where player p can place only one of his/her Avatar Cards in his/her hands, H^p_k.

As Figure 2 shows, each player can place his/her Avatar Card into one of six places which are presented in three rows; the first row contains A^p_1; the second row contains A^p_2 and A^p_3; and the third row contains A^p_4, A^p_5 and A^p_6. Each row makes a sense of "distance" to the others. Therefore, if an Avatar Card's "attack range" (the Avatar Card's attribute represents how far the Avatar Card can attack) is shorter than the distance between it and its target, the player must do "move" atom action to make it closer to its target (but, the player can never move or put his/her Avatar Card into the opponent's game field).

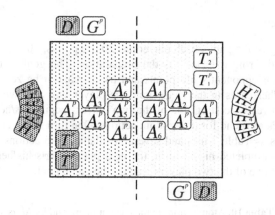

Fig. 2. The Game Field of the two players computerized TCG

Table 8. Four major areas in the Game Field and its notations and descriptions

	Area	Notation	Description
Cards in player's hand	Hand	H^p_k	Cards have been drawn but not used yet. These cards are hold in player's hand.
Card set for player drawing	Deck	D^p	Face-down cards and no one can take a peek to them. Player must draws from the top.
Used or destroyed cards	Graveyard	G^p	Face-up cards and can be checked at anytime.
Cards in using	Field	A^p_i	Places for Avatar Card.
		T^p_j	Places for Tool Card.

Player Schema

As the player analysis mentioned in Section 3, two attributes are designed for the player schema in the computerized TCG:

- Life points: When a player loses his/her Avatar Card, his/her life points would drop down according to the rule and will loses the game if life points $\leqq 0$.
- Remaining Cards: If a player needs to draw a card but cannot accomplish due to he/she has no more cards in the Deck area, then the player loses the game.

Table 9. Phases in one turn and actions in each phase

	Phases in this research	Actions in each phase
Initial Phase	Draw Phase	Draw a card from deck.
Main Phase	Combat Phase	Player can do the following atom actions if still have APs: • Play • Defend • Attack • Move • Magic Table 10 lists detailed descriptions and AP costs.
Final Phase	Discard Phase	Discard cards if needed.

4.2 Rule Design

At the beginning of the game, each player has 20 life points, 40 cards in the Deck and can draw 6 cards from the Deck as the preparation. The goal of the computerized TCG is to reduce opponent's life points and try to make it be zero. If the opponent runs out of his/her cards in the Deck area, the player will also win the game. After both players get ready to start, one of the two players begins his/her first turn. Each player has 3 APs to spend for doing atom actions. One turn in the computerized TCG has three phases as Table 9 lists and several available atom actions as Table 10 lists. When a player completed his/her turn, the next player starts his/her turn. The game will be end until one of the two players reaches the game goal.

Table 10. Atom actions at the combat phase and its AP costs

Atom Action	AP costs	Action description
Play	1	Put a card on the correct place in game field. Avatar Card must be face-up but effect cards must be face-down.
Defend	1	Take defensive pose for the possible incoming attacks.
Attack	1	Attack an opponent's Avatar Card.
Move	1	Move an Avatar Card to another place.
Magic	1	Use a Magic Card in hands.
	0	Use a Magic Card in the game field.

Table 11. Game rules and some examples

Rule Type	Examples
Card↔Card	• Avatar Card can attack opponent's Avatar Card and cause damage based on the following formula: If the opponent's Avatar Card is defending, then: *Damage = Attacker's attacking power – defender's defensive power* Else: *Damage = Attacker's attacking power* • Magic Card can increase or decrease Avatar Card's attribute values; or can destroy opponent's Tool Card. • Trap Card will be triggered and reacted by opponent's attack action or magic action automatically.
Card↔Game Field	• If a card is discarded, defeated, expired or destroyed, then the player needs to remove them into the graveyard.
Card↔Player	• If an Avatar Card is defeated, the player's life points will be taken based on his/her Avatar Card's "size" attribute. For instance, *size* is defined as an integer and its value is from 0 to 3, the larger number means the avatar is bigger (but doesn't mean the avatar is stronger): *Player's Life Point will be taken* $= 2^{size}$
Game Field↔Player	• If the player runs out his/her cards in the deck, then the player loses. • Player can take play action to put cards in the game field.

Phases are order sensitive. For instance, once a player has announced that he/she completed his/her Combat Phase, then the player will be not allowed to go back to either Draw Phase or Combat Phase again. However, the atom actions are order insensitive. Means player can do any atom actions as long as he/she still has APs to spend. Table 11 lists the rules of the computerized TCG developed by this research.

4.3 Cards as Reward

To keep students' motivation of learning, this research provides an environment in which students can use the cards they've got from learning. For instances, the teacher can give the student cards if the student did well in either his/her homework, quiz, or exam; or the teacher can give the student different level cards according to his/her answers to the question the teacher asked; or the learning management system can give the student cards according to his/her learning attitudes and performance. The computerized TCG can increase the rewards (cards) usability and stimulate students' learning motivations because of more they've learned or better they've performed, more and better cards they can get and use to play the game and defeat their fellows.

As Figure 3 shows, teachers can pre-define the relations between the learning and the reward, the system then can give appropriate cards to students automatically.

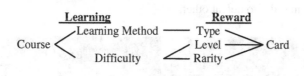

Fig. 3. The relations between the learning and the educational reward

According to Figure 3, different cards may be delivered to the student due to the course difficulty. For example, students could get Tool Card after got good marks for their paper-pencil exam and get Avatar Card after got good marks for their online exam. Also, the card's level or rarity may correlate with the difficulty of the exam. The relations between the learning and the reward make students want to learn and challenge in order to get more valuable cards. Furthermore, because of the cards and the computerized TCG is independent from the courses, teachers can use the same cards as rewards of different courses to let students get cards from all courses.

5 Prototype System

The prototype system of the computerized TCG can be used as educational reward system. Figure 4 illustrates the educational reward system flow. First of all, the teacher created questions and built the relations between cards and the questions (step 1 in Figure 4). Second, the students can start their learning by using either traditional classroom learning or e-learning (includes mobile learning) (step 2). Third, the server then calculates the students' learning performances and delivers cards to the students automatically (step 3). Fourth, the students can use the cards they've collected to play TCG with others just for fun (step 4). Fifth, the game play process could be recorded

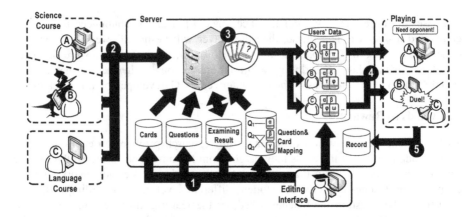

Fig. 4. Computerized TCG System Flow

for future study (step 5). Because of the computerized TCG is a real game, so the students can have fun from it without pressure. Also, the cards are educational rewards, so the students would want to collect the rare and powerful cards via learning and/or practices in order to defeat others.

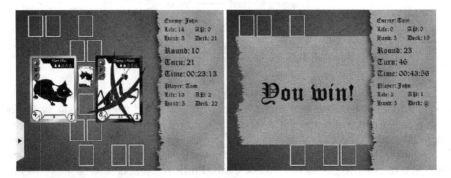

Fig. 5. System snapshot: (left) Tom uses Avatar Card, "Dark Rat", to attack John's Avatar Card, "Praying Mantis"; (right) John wins the game

Figure 5 shows two snapshots of the computerized TCG. Figure 5(left) is Tom's screen shot which shows Tom using his Avatar Card to attack John's. The left part of the screen is the game field and the right part is players' status. The player's status is at the bottom side and the opponent's status is at the upper side. Figure 5(right) is John's screen shot and shows the game result, John wins the game.

6 Conclusion

This research analyzed three famous TCGs and implemented a prototype computerized TCG and educational reward system to increase student's learning motivation.

Students can collect and use cards to play or even show-off, which can really encourage students to learn in order to get new cards. Moreover, because the computerized TCG is real game, it is fun and will not make students feel they are still "learning". The cards and the pre-defined relations between the courses and rewards make the educational reward system can be used in variety disciplines and courses.

There are still several issues needed to discuss to improve this research. The efficiency of using cards in TCG as educational reward should be evaluated via quantitative and qualitative experiment results. How to help teachers dispatching different cards as different educational reward in the traditional classroom settings could be an important issue in practice.

Acknowledgments

This research is supported as part of project "NSC 97-2511-S-033-002-MY3" by National Science Council, Taiwan, Republic of China. The authors also wish to acknowledge the support of iCORE, Xerox and the research related gift funding provided to the Learning Communities Project by Mr. Allan Markin.

References

1. Kohn, A.: Punished by rewards: The trouble with gold stars, incentive plans, A's, praise, and other bribes. Houghton Mifflin, Boston (1999)
2. Winefield, A.H., Barnett, J.A., Tiggemann, M.: Learned helplessness and IQ differences. Personality and Individual Differences 5(5), 493–500 (1984)
3. Aquarian Age Rulebook,
   http://www.aquarian-age.org/rulebook/main.html
4. Marinak, B.A.: Insights about Third-Grade Children's Motivation to Read. College Reading Association Yearbook (28), 54–65 (2007)
5. Witzel, B.S., Mercer, C.D.: Using Rewards to Teach Students with Disabilities. Remedial & Special Education 24(2), 88–97 (2003)
6. Vossen, D.P.: The Nature and Classification of Games. Avante 10(1), 53–68 (2004)
7. McNinch, G.W.: Earning by Learning: Changing Attitudes and Habits in Reading. Reading Horizons 37, 186–194 (1997)
8. Schwabe, G., Göth, C.: Mobile learning with a mobile game: design and motivational effects. Journal of Computer Assisted Learning 21(3), 204–216 (2005)
9. Palardy, J.M.: Principles of learning: A review. Journal of Instructional Psychology 21(4), 308–312 (1994)
10. Magic: The Gathering Rules,
    http://www.wizards.com/Magic/TCG/Resources.aspx?x=magic/rules
11. Pivec, M., Dziabenko, O., Schinnerl, I.: Aspects of Game- Based Learning. In: 3rd International Conference on Knowledge Management, Graz, Austria, pp. 216–225 (2003)
12. Virvou, M., Katsionis, G., Manos, K.: Combining Software Games with Education: Evaluation of its Educational Effectiveness. Educational Technology & Society 8(2), 54–65 (2005)
13. Steinman, R.A., Blastos, M.T.: A trading-card game teaching about host defence. J. Medical Education 32, 1201–1208 (2002)

14. Johnston, R.C.: Speaker Gingrich touts reading program's payoff. Education Week 22, 5 (1995)
15. Wu, S.C., Elliott, R.T.: A Study of Reward Preference in Taiwanese Gifted and Nongifted Students With Differential Locus of Control. Journal for the Education of the Gifted 32(2), 230–244 (2008)
16. Anderson, T.A.F., Reynolds, B.L., Yeh, X.P., Huang, G.Z.: Video Games in the English as a Foreign Language Classroom. In: 2nd IEEE International Conference on Digital Games and Intelligent Toys Based Education, pp. 188–192. IEEE Press, Banff (2008)
17. Boyle, T.: Design for multimedia learning. Prentice Hall, London (1997)
18. Malone, T.W.: Toward a Theory of Intrinsically Motivating Instruction. Cognitive Science: A Multidisciplinary Journal 5(4), 333–369 (1981)
19. Malone, T.W., Lepper, M.R.: Making learning fun: a taxonomic model of intrinsic motivations for learning. In: Snow, R.E., Farr, M.J. (eds.) ptitude, Learning, and Instruction, Conative find Affective Process Analyses, vol. 3, Erlbaum, Hillsdale (1987)
20. Šisler, V., Brom, C.: Designing an educational game: Case study of 'Europe 2045'. In: Pan, Z., et al. (eds.) Transactions on Edutainment I. LNCS, vol. 5080, pp. 1–16. Springer, Heidelberg (2008)
21. Schultz, W., Tremblay, L., Hollerman, J.R.: Reward Processing in Primate Orbitofrontal Cortex and Basal Ganglia. Cerebral Cortex 10(3), 272–283 (2000)
22. Yu-GI-Oh! Rulebook, http://www.yugioh-card.com/en/rulebook/

Sketch Learning Environment with Diagnosis and Drawing Guidance from Rough Form to Detailed Contour Form

Masato Soga[1,*], Shota Kuriyama[2,**], and Hirokazu Taki[1,***]

[1] Faculty of Systems Engineering, Wakayama University
930 Sakaedani, Wakayama 640-8510, Japan
[2] Shima Seiki Mfg., Ltd.
85 Sakata, Wakayama 641-8511, Japan
soga@sys.wakayama-u.ac.jp

Abstract. We developed a sketch learning environment with a diagnosis function and the ability to guide drawing from a rough form to detail a detailed contour form. We use a cup and a dish as motifs. When a learner uses the environment, the system first requires the learner to draw a circumscribed-rectangle of the motif's view on paper. Then, the system diagnoses the circumscribed-rectangle and advises the learner if it has errors. The system guides the learner from a rough form to a detailed contour form by repeatedly drawing circumscribed-rectangles. We evaluated the environment and confirmed a significant learning effect.

Keywords: Sketch, Learning environment, Painting, Drawing, Skill.

1 Introduction

There exist many systems and software that support drawing or painting on computers. For example, Baxter developed an excellent system called DAB that assists a user in painting on a virtual paper on a computer [1]. The user operates a stylus pen on a haptic interface as a brush, and the system paints colors using the virtual brush on the virtual paper. The motion and pressure of the virtual brush reflect those of the stylus pen.

---

* Masato Soga received a doctor's degree from Osaka University in March 1992. He is engaged in research on the skill learning environment including sketch learning environment. He is an associate professor of Faculty of Systems Engineering at Wakayama University.

** Shota Kuriyama received a master's degree from Wakayama University in March 2009. He was engaged in research on the sketch learning environment while he belonged to the graduate school of Systems Engineering at Wakayama University.

*** Hirokazu Taki received a doctor's degree from Osaka University. He was a researcher in Mitsubishi Electric Corporation (1980-1996) and also a researcher in ICOT(1986-1990). He is engaged in research on knowledge engineering. He is a professor of Faculty of Systems Engineering at Wakayama University.

Z. Pan et al. (Eds.): Transactions on Edutainment III, LNCS 5940, pp. 129–140, 2009.
© Springer-Verlag Berlin Heidelberg 2009

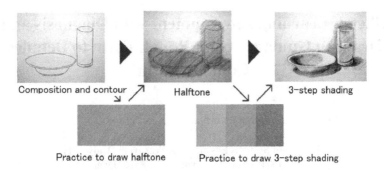

Composition and contour   Halftone   3—step shading

Practice to draw halftone   Practice to draw 3—step shading

Fig. 1. Process for drawing a sketch. This process was proposed by a painter who teaches sketch drawing to novice learners, and therefore, it may not be used by all painting teachers.

Although DAB is an excellent system, it does not have a function for diagnosing the sketches by users. Therefore, novice learners cannot use DAB for self-learning. Learning support for drawing or painting is a task that differs from drawing support or painting support. Functions for diagnosis and advice are required for learning support. Our project was the first learning environment that could diagnose a learner's sketch and then provide advice.

We have previously developed various sketch learning support environments. Our environments are capable of diagnosing sketches drawn on real paper. This function is a unique feature of our environments, and it is important for learners, because drawing on a paper using a real pencil requires a different skill as compared to drawing on a virtual paper using a mouse or a stylus pen.

Our first sketch learning environment is described in [2-4]. This environment could diagnose a sketch drawn by a learner and provide adaptive advice for the correction of errors in the sketches. Figure 1 shows the process for drawing a sketch. The process comprises 3 stages, namely, (1) composition and contour, (2) halftone, and (3) 3-steps shading. This environment could successfully diagnose the learners' sketches after they completed each stage. However, because of this limitation, if a drawn sketch had many errors, the learner had to correct many errors at once or redraw the sketch. Some learners felt overburdened by this and occasionally, some lost the motivation to continue learning how to draw sketches.

To avoid these situations, we developed environments that could diagnose sketches while the learners were still drawing them. These environments were developed based on the cognitive process of a human being's interaction with objects. Human interactions with objects comprises three main stages, namely, recognition, selection (or decision), and action (Fig. 2). This process is explained for the task of drawing a sketch as follows.

In the recognition stage, a learner perceives objects as a motif of drawing, and recognizes them. If the learner recognizes, say, a dish, then he/she moves into the selection (or decision) stage as follows. The learner thinks how to draw the dish. Then, he/she decides to draw the edge of the dish first. The edge of the dish appears elliptical from his/her viewpoint. Then, he/she thinks how to draw the ellipse. He/she

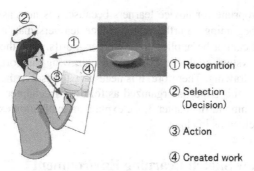

Fig. 2. Interaction between a learner and objects. The interaction comprises 3 stages, namely, (1) recognition, (2) selection (decision), and (3) action. A learner creates his/her work by repeating this process many times.

decides to divide it into two parts. He/she decides to draw the upper half of the ellipse first by moving his/her arm like a compass. Then, he/she decides to draw the lower half of the ellipse in the same manner after putting the paper upside down. Therefore in the selection (or decision) stage, the learner selects (or decides) appropriate actions that he/she will perform in the next stage. Finally, in the action stage, the learner acts in accordance with the actions that he/she selects (or decides) in the selection (or decision) stage.

Based on the human interaction process, we developed a sketch learning support environment that provides adaptive advice in real time. This environment comprises two subsystems - an area-dependent advice system and a hand and arm motion advice system.

The area-dependent advice system [5,7] is designed for supporting the recognition stage. It obtains the learner's drawing position data using the pen tablet. It identifies the area in the motif that the learner is drawing. The system offers advice according to the areas where the learner draws. The system originally has an abstract sketch area map. This map comprises small areas in a sketch. Each area is related to specific advice contained in the advice DB.

The hand and arm motion advice system [5,6] is designed for supporting the action stage. It obtains the learner's arm motion data when he/she installs 3D magnetic position sensors in his/her shoulder, elbow, and wrist. The system compares the learner's arm motion data with the teacher's correct data stored in the system. Specifically, the system compares speeds, arm orientations, and drawing areas by arm motions. If an error occurs, the system offers advice to the learner using the 3D arm model in real time.

The two systems were combined into one environment to support the selection (or decision) stage. The environment could determine where a learner was drawing, and simultaneously determine the hand and arm motion. Therefore, the environment could decide whether the hand and arm motion is appropriate for the area where the learner is drawing.

We evaluated the environment and confirmed the effect of advice. However, there remained two unsolved issues. One is that the area-dependent advice system provides advice on the detailed contour of the motifs from the beginning. However, this method is not appropriate for novice learners because it is not easy to draw detailed contour from the beginning. Furthermore, novice learners may acquire only a few drawing skills that cannot be applied to any other motifs. In other words, the area-dependent advice system could be effective for drawing support, but not for skill learning support in drawing. Therefore, it is necessary to resolve these issues.

The remainder of this paper is organized as follows. In chapter 2, we describe our new learning environment. In chapter 3, we explain an evaluation experiment. Finally, we present the conclusions in chapter 4.

2   Design of New Sketch Learning Environment

To resolve the abovementioned issues, we developed a new sketch learning environment that provides diagnosis and drawing support from a rough drawing to a detailed contour drawing. We use a cup and a dish as motifs. When a learner uses the environment, the environment first requires the learner to draw a circumscribed rectangle of the motifs' view. Then, the environment diagnoses the circumscribed rectangle and advises the learner of errors, if any. The environment guides the learner from a rough form to a detailed contour drawing by repeatedly drawing circumscribed rectangles. Our new learning environment can be used only in the composition and contour stage (Fig. 1), because its objective is to solve the issues in this stage.

2.1   Composition of Sketch Learning Environment

Figure 3 shows a composition of the sketch learning environment and a flow of the procedure. The environment comprises two databases (DBs) and a pen tablet. The DBs are the advice DB and the DB of the motifs' views and auxiliary lines.

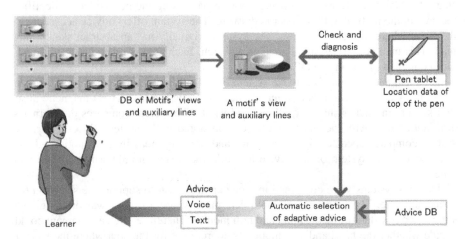

Fig. 3. Composition of sketch learning environment and a flow of the procedure. The environment comprises two DBs and a pen tablet. The DBs are the advice DB and the DB of the motifs' views and auxiliary lines.

2.2 Preparation

We used a dish and a cup as motifs. Advice data in the advice DB and data in the DB of motifs' views and auxiliary lines must correspond to the motifs. Therefore, the motifs are fixed. Learners cannot use their own motifs. Therefore, the environment is motif-dependent. However, the design of the learning environment and the methodology described in this paper can be applied to other motifs.

Motifs are kept on a table at a distance of 1 m from a learner. The comparative position between the dish and the cup is fixed in advance. A learner's viewpoint is also fixed in advance. Therefore, the learner must arrange his/her sitting height by changing the chair height at the beginning.

The learner uses a pen tablet called Intuos 3, 12x19 and a grip pen for Intuos 3 made by Wacom (left-hand side, Fig.4). The tablet's active area size is 12" x 19". The tablet can obtain location data of the grip pen by electromagnetic induction. We improved the grip pen of the tablet Intuos 3 (right-hand side, Fig.4) by attaching a pencil tip to it. The learner places a paper on the tablet, and draws a sketch using the improved grip pen by observing the motifs on the table.

Fig. 4. The left-handed side shows a sketch being drawn on a paper on the tablet Intuos 3 using the improved grip pen by observing motifs on a table. Right-hand side shows the improved grip pen of the tablet Intuos 3. A pencil tip is attached to it.

2.3 Strategy for Learning Support

This environment is designed to resolve the issues in chapter 1. Therefore, the necessary objectives and functions that the environment must support are as follows.

(1) To support the learning of general drawing skills. It is desirable for a learner to learn more general drawing skills that are independent of the motifs.
(2) To support learning by reflection.
(3) To reduce modification load.

To achieve (1), we propose a method in which the environment requires a learner to draw circumscribed rectangles of motifs or parts of motifs at every drawing step. The circumscribed rectangle motif's view reflects not only the size and location but also the aspect ratio of the motif or a part of it. It is easy for a learner to determine the size, location and aspect ratio of motif's view by drawing a circumscribed rectangle.

To achieve (2) and (3), we propose a method in which the environment diagnoses a learner's drawing at every step, and provides advice if the drawing has errors. The learner can reflect on his/her drawing by checking at every step. In this manner, the modification load becomes minimal as well.

On the basis of the abovementioned discussion, the flow of the procedures of the learning environment is as follows. When a learner uses the environment, the environment first requires the learner to draw a circumscribed rectangle of the entire motif's view. Then, the environment diagnoses the circumscribed rectangle and advises the learner if it has errors. The environment guides the learner from a rough form to a detailed contour form by repeatedly drawing circumscribed rectangles (Fig. 5).

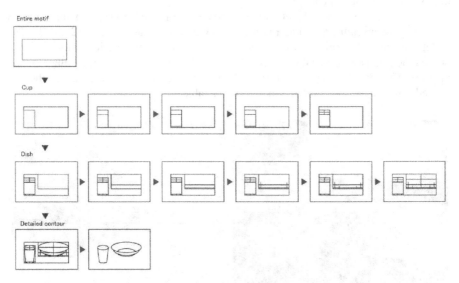

Fig. 5. Flow of guidance from a rough form of the entire motif view to a detailed contour form by repeatedly drawing circumscribed rectangles and auxiliary lines

2.4 GUI and Interaction between a Learner and the Environment

Figure 6 shows the GUI of the learning environment. It can show the motif CG in the DB of the motifs' views and auxiliary lines. A learner can select "Display motif CG" or "Do Not display motif CG" on the GUI. It is recommended that the motif CG is not displayed, since the learner can then draw a sketch by observing only the motif CG without observing the real motifs. The learner is strongly recommended to draw a sketch by recognizing a real motif in the real world. Otherwise, he/she cannot enhance his/her drawing skills. The ability to recognize a real motif and its projection on a paper is an important skill for drawing a sketch.

It is important to draw a sketch by considering the proportions of motifs. Here the proportion is the size ratio between the motifs and their aspect ratios. If a learner can recognize the proportion correctly, he/she can draw a sketch well. Therefore, the environment supports the drawing of auxiliary lines. First, the learner draws the circumscribed rectangle of the entire motif. At this stage, the learner can recognize and learn the entire motifs' proportions carefully.

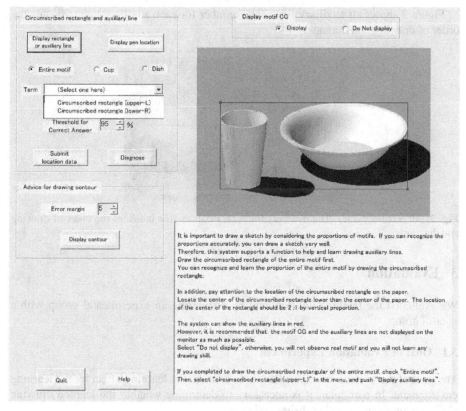

Fig. 6. GUI of the learning environment

At the same time, the environment advises the learner to focus on the location of the circumscribed rectangle drawn on a paper. The environment indicates to the learner that the center of the circumscribed rectangle should be located at a point lower than the center of the paper. In addition, it indicates that the location of the center of the rectangle should be 2:1 by vertical proportion.

The learner checks "Entire motif" at the upper left of the GUI. Then, the learner selects "circumscribed rectangle (upper-L)" in the menu, and selects "Display auxiliary lines." Then, the environment shows a circumscribed rectangle of the entire motif in red. If the learner understands what is to be drawn, he/she draws a circumscribed rectangle of the entire motif on the paper on the tablet. Then, the learner points to the upper-left vertex of the drawn circumscribed rectangle using the improved grip pen and clicks the "Submit location data" button. Similarly, the learner submits location data of the lower-right vertex as well.

The location data of the upper-left and lower-right vertices form a unique rectangle. Therefore, when the learner clicks the "Diagnose" button, the environment calculates the difference between the circumscribed rectangles of the input data and the data in the DB of motifs' views and auxiliary lines. If there is a difference between the two, the environment retrieves adaptive advice sentences from the advice DB and indicates the advice to the learner using voice and text messages.

Figure 7 shows all auxiliary lines. The number for each auxiliary line indicates the order of drawing and diagnosis.

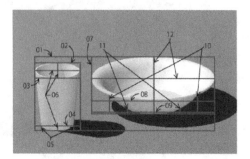

Fig. 7. All auxiliary lines. The numbers for each auxiliary line indicates the order of drawing and diagnosis.

3   Evaluation

We evaluated the learning environment by comparing an experimental group with a control group.

3.1   Goal of Evaluation Experiment

The goal of the evaluation experiment is to confirm the learning effect by the learning environment. In particular, it is necessary to determine whether the learned drawing skills are applicable to other dishes and cups.

3.2   Method of Evaluation Experiment

Figure 8 shows the flow of the evaluation experiment. 20 students from our university participated in this experiment. They were all novices. They were divided into two groups, namely, the experimental group and the control group, each comprising 10 students. The students in the experimental group used the learning environment; those in the control group did not use the learning environment but read instructions on paper. The same dishes and cups are used in the pre-test and in the training and learning stage; however, the layouts are different. The dimensions of the dishes and cups are different in the training and learning and the post-test stages. This is done to determine whether or not the subjects in the experimental group can learn general drawing skills using the learning environment.

In the training and learning stage, subjects in control group read instructions on paper. These instructions are the same as those provided by the learning environment to the experimental group. Therefore, the only difference between the experimental and control groups is that the former trains and learns interactively. The learning environment diagnoses and advises them on drawn auxiliary lines and contours step-by-step. However, the control group trains and learns without any such interaction.

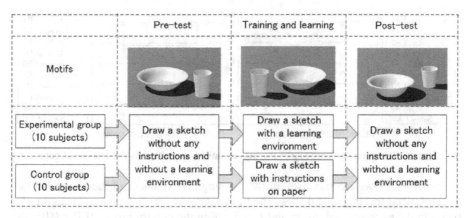

Fig. 8. Flow of evaluation experiment. The same dishes and cups are used in the pre-test and the training and learning stages. Different dishes and cups are used in the training and learning and the post-test stages.

3.3 Results

Figures 9 - 13 show a comparison of the learning performances between the experimental and control groups. In these figures 9 - 13, the horizontal axis indicates time, and the vertical axis indicates the accuracy rate of each subject. If the accuracy rate is increasing, it implies that a subject is exhibiting a learning effect. The accuracy rate is given as the ratio between the subject's drawing and the correct drawing. If the accuracy rate is equal to 1.0, it implies that a subject's drawing is perfectly accurate. Note that the accuracy rate does not imply the ratio of the number of subjects who draw correctly.

Figure 9 shows a comparison of the learning performances of the aspect ratio of circumscribed rectangles of entire motifs. The t-test results of learning performances are P = 0.056 in the experimental group and P = 0.774 in the control group. If P < 0.05, the result is significant. Therefore, the result of the experimental group is close to being significant.

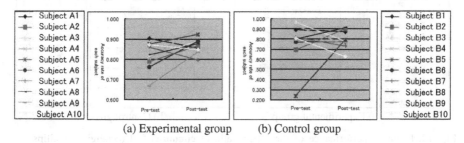

(a) Experimental group   (b) Control group

Fig. 9. Learning performance of the aspect ratio of circumscribed rectangle of entire motif

Figure 10 shows a comparison of the learning performances of the aspect ratio of circumscribed rectangles of cups. The t-test results of learning performances are P = 0.095 in the experimental group and P = 0.440 in the control group. If P < 0.05, the result is significant. Therefore, both results are not significant.

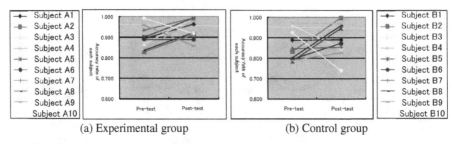

(a) Experimental group   (b) Control group

Fig. 10. Learning performance of the aspect ratio of circumscribed rectangle of cups

Figure 11 shows a comparison of the learning performances of the aspect ratio of circumscribed rectangles of dishes. The t-test results of learning performances are P = 0.003 in the experimental group and P = 0.428 in the control group. If P < 0.05, the result is significant. Therefore, the result of the experimental group is very significant.

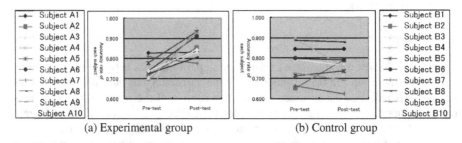

(a) Experimental group   (b) Control group

Fig. 11. Learning performance of the aspect ratio of circumscribed rectangle of dishes

Figure 12 shows a comparison of the learning performances of the aspect ratio of circumscribed rectangles of ellipses of cups. The t-test results of learning perform-ances are P = 0.106 in the experimental group and P = 0.884 in the control group. If P < 0.05, the result is significant. Therefore, both results are not significant.

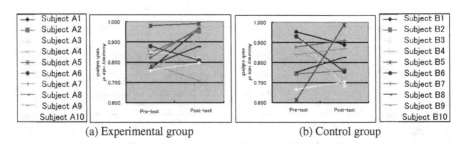

(a) Experimental group   (b) Control group

Fig. 12. Learning performance of the aspect ratio of circumscribed rectangles of ellipses of cups

Figure 13 shows a comparison of the learning performances of the aspect ratio of cir-cumscribed rectangles of ellipses of dishes. The t-test results of learning performances are P = 0.003 in the experimental group and P = 0.996 in the control group. If P < 0.05, the result is significant. Therefore, the result of the experimental group is very significant.

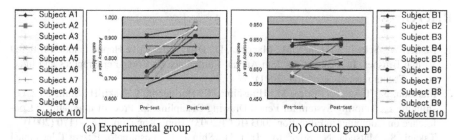

(a) Experimental group   (b) Control group

Fig. 13. Learning performance of the aspect ratio of circumscribed rectangles of ellipses of dishes

3.4 Discussion

The experimental results indicate that the learning environment is effective for learning how to draw accurate circumscribed rectangles of a dish and the ellipse of a dish. A significant learning effect could not be observed in drawing circumscribed rectangles of a cup and the ellipse of a cup. We consider why the results of the experiment exhibit such a difference.

We believe that the result comes from the facts that a dish is larger and it has a shape that differs significantly from a circumscribed rectangle. If a motif is large, it is probably difficult for learners to recognize the aspect ratio correctly since they cannot recognize the entire motif at once. In addition, if the motif has a shape that differs significantly from a circumscribed rectangle, it is probably difficult for learners to recognize the circumscribed rectangle since they have to mentally visualize the circumscribed rectangles.

4 Conclusion

In this paper, we first explained the background of our sketch learning support environment project, and then described the necessity of developing the new sketch learning environment with a diagnosis function and the ability to guide drawing guidance from a rough form to a detailed contour form. We use a cup and a dish as motifs. When a learner uses the environment, the system first requires the learner to draw a circumscribed rectangle of the motif's view on paper. Then, the system diagnoses the circumscribed rectangle and advises the learner if it has errors. The system guides the learner from a rough form to a detailed contour form by repeatedly drawing circumscribed rectangles.

Finally, we evaluated the environment, and confirmed a significant learning effect when learners draw dishes. However, we could not confirm a significant learning effect when learners draw cups. We believe that the result comes from the facts that the dish is larger and it has a shape that differs significantly from circumscribed rectangle.

We conclude that our learning environment is more effective when learners try to draw complicated motifs. In the future, we intend to apply the learning environment to more complicated motifs.

References

1. Baxter, W., Scheib, V., Lin, C.M., Manocha, D.: DAB: Interactive Haptic Painting with 3D Virtual Brushes. In: Proc. of the 28th Annual Conference on Computer Graphics and Interactive Techniques, pp. 461–468 (2001)
2. Matsuda, N., Takagi, S., Soga, M., Hirashima, T., Horiguchi, T., Taki, H., Shima, T., Yoshimoto, F.: Tutoring System for Pencil Drawing Discipline. In: Proc. of International Conference on Computer in Education 2003 (ICCE2003), Hong Kong, pp. 1163–1170 (2003)
3. Takagi, S., Matsuda, N., Soga, M., Taki, H., Shima, T., Yoshimoto, F.: An Educational Tool for Basic Techniques in Beginner's Pencil Drawing. In: Proc. of Computer Graphics International 2003, Tokyo, Japan, pp. 288–293 (2003)
4. Takagi, S., Matsuda, N., Soga, M., Taki, H., Shima, T., Yoshimoto, F.: A Learning Support System for Beginners in Pencil Drawing. In: Proc. of GRAPHTE 2003, Melbourne, Australia, pp. 281–282 (2003)
5. Iwaki, T., Tsuji, T., Maeno, H., Soga, M., Matsuda, N., Takagi, S., Taki, H., Yoshimoto, F.: A Sketch Learning Support System with Automatic Diagnosis and Advice. In: Int. Conf. of Computers in Education 2005 (ICCE 2005), Singapore, pp. 977–979 (2005)
6. Soga, M., Matsuda, N., Takagi, S., Taki, H., Yoshimoto, F.: Sketch Learning Environment Based on Drawing Skill Analysis. In: Apolloni, B., Howlett, R.J., Jain, L. (eds.) KES 2007, Part III. LNCS (LNAI), vol. 4694, pp. 1073–1080. Springer, Heidelberg (2007)
7. Soga, M., Matsuda, N., Taki, H.: Sketch Drawing Support Environment based on Recognition Skill Analysis. In: Proc. of International Symposium on Skill Science 2007 (ISSS 2007), Tokyo, Japan, pp. 61–67 (2007)

Application of Visualization in Virtual Endoscopy System

Yanjun Peng, Rong Hua, Weidong Zhao, and Xinming Lu

College of Information Science and Engineering, Shandong University of Science
and Technology, Qingdao, China, 266510
pengyanjuncn@yahoo.com.cn

Abstract. Application of visualization in virtual endoscopy is researched in this
paper. Boundary model and local feature structure are used to realize tissue
segmentation. A new efficient algorithm based on distance transform is
presented to solve path planning. As to real-time processing, a frame in virtual
endoscopy is divided into near viewpoint part and far viewpoint part based on
volume data characteristics in our method. In the aspect of scene rendering, a
ray casting algorithm based on the boundary voxel is proposed. The voyage
images can be rendered in real time with high quality in virtual endoscopy system by using of these techniques.

Keywords: Virtual endoscopy, path planning, ray casting.

1 Introduction

Virtual endoscopy is one of the important applications of visualization. Image processing, computer graphics, visualization in scientific computing, virtual reality technologies are combined together to simulate conventional technology of endoscopy by
using of medical data. It overcomes the traditional endoscopy's disadvantage which
need to insert the human body, it's a complete non-contact inspection method and
can be applied to medical training[1-4], surgical planning[5,6], achieving surgical
precision positioning[7,8], auxiliary diagnosis[9,10], and etc. It is being taken more
and more seriously since it appeared.

There are three key areas of virtual endoscopy system: tissue segmentation, path
planning, real-time processing.

In recent years, Gordon K. and James W. D. put forward transfering functions including the density gradient and the two-order derivative along the gradient direction
after analyzing a 3D graph, which corresponded separately to the density of a
voxel[11]. Voxels are classified correctly by the eigenvalues of Hessian matrix based
on the two-order derivative of the voxel's density considered the local character structure of 3D volume data, such as the linear structure (vessel, trachea, nerve), sheet
structure (organ, pallium), punctate structure (never cell) in Sato Y and Nakajima S's
articles[12,13].

There are two main methods to extract center path: thinning and distance transform. The basic idea of thinning [14,15] is to iteratively peel off the boundary voxels
layer by layer, and the topological connection in original graphs is kept. In contrast,

Z. Pan et al. (Eds.): Transactions on Edutainment III, LNCS 5940, pp. 141–153, 2009.
© Springer-Verlag Berlin Heidelberg 2009

distance transform method also maintains the topological connection. The Euclidean distance can be substituted with the distance interval among voxels in order to save time[16,17].

Martin L. and Ming W. use consistency of adjacent frames in virtual voyage procedure to accelerate redering speed [18,19].

We use boundary model and local feature structure to realize tissue segmentation. A new efficient algorithm is presented to solve path planning based on distance transform. As for real-time processing, a frame in virtual endoscopy is divided into near viewpoint part and far viewpoint part based on volume data characteristics in our method. In the aspect of scene rendering, a ray casting algorithm based on the boundary voxel is proposed. The voyage images can be rendered in real time with high quality in virtual endoscopy system by using of these techniques.

2 Local Feature Structure Segmentation Based on Boundary Model

2.1 Boundary Model

Definition 1 Boundary voxel set B: Given a data set and an object O defined in the inner of the 3D data set, there is a segmentation function Q. Q can divide the data set into two subsets, one is a subset of the inner of O and the other is a subset of the outer of O. A voxel is called boundary voxel, if some of its contiguous six voxels are in the inner of O and others are in the outer of O.

Definition 2 Special tissue voxels set T: T is defined as all voxels belong to the inner of the certain tissue, including all boundary voxels and inner voxels.

Suppose that the tissues we are concerned are with partial eigenstructures, such as linear structure, point-like structure, Sheet structure, etc, maximum density is Imax , minimum density is Imin, voxel density is I and voxel coordinates is X(x,y,z), $I = f(X)$.

The definition of the boundary model is:

$$I = g(d) = I_{min} + (I_{max} - I_{min}) \frac{1 + h(\frac{d}{\sigma\sqrt{2\pi}})}{2}$$

d stands for the distance along the gradient direction of the voxel's density, h(x)∈[-1,1].

$$g'(d) = \frac{I_{max} - I_{min}}{\sigma\sqrt{2\pi}} \exp(-\frac{d^2}{2\sigma^2}) \tag{1}$$

From the above equation, $g'(0)$ is the maximum of $g'(d)$. Meanwhile $g'(d)$, expresses the one-order directional derivative along the gradient direction. According to the definition of directional derivative, we can deduce the following equation:

$$g'(d) = f'_{\nabla f(X)}(X) = \nabla f(X) \bullet \frac{\nabla f(X)}{\|\nabla f(X)\|} = \|\nabla f(X)\| \tag{2}$$

From Equ. (1) and Equ. (2), if d=±σ, then $g'(d)$ is an inflection point. Hence, $g'(d)$ is the maximum, when d=±σ.

$$g''(d) = -\frac{d(I_{max} - I_{min})}{\sigma^3\sqrt{2\pi}}\exp(-\frac{d^2}{2\sigma^2})$$ (3)

We can also conclude the following equation from Equ. (2)

$$f''_{\nabla f(X)}(X) = \nabla(f''_{\nabla f(X)}(X)) \bullet \frac{\nabla f(X)}{\|\nabla f(X)\|} = \nabla(\|\nabla f(X)\|) \bullet \frac{\nabla f(X)}{\|\nabla f(X)\|}$$

By Taylor expansion, written in matrix as below:

$$g''(d) = f''_{\nabla f(X)}(X) = \frac{1}{\|\nabla f(X)\|^2}(\nabla f(X))^T Hf(X)\nabla f(X)$$

$Hf(X)$is the Hansen matrix of voxel x, and we can also use Laplace's expansion obtain the approximate value of $g''(d)$.

$$g''(d) = f''_{\nabla f(X)}(X) \approx \frac{\partial^2 f(X)}{\partial x^2} + \frac{\partial^2 f(X)}{\partial y^2} + \frac{\partial^2 f(X)}{\partial z^2}$$

From Equ. (1) and Equ. (3),

$$\sigma = \frac{g'(0)}{\sqrt{e}\, g''(-\sigma)} \quad , \quad d = \frac{-\sigma^2 g''(d)}{g'(d)}$$ (4)

Because $\|\nabla f(X)\|$ maybe get 0 in the inner of tissues, Equ. (4) is transformed into the following equation:

$$d \approx \frac{-\sigma^2 g''(d)}{g'(d)+1}$$ (5)

$$\text{For } m(I) = \frac{1}{n}\sum g''(d)$$ (6)

$$l(I) = \frac{1}{n}\sum g'(d)$$ (7)

$$d_I \approx \frac{-\sigma^2 m(I)}{l(I)+1}$$ (8)

m(I) and l(I) correspond the centroid, the density of which is $g''(d)$ and $g'(d)$, which is also the average value, and n is the number of voxel with density value of I ,using (6)and (7) to replace $g''(d)$,and $g'(d)$ in (5), we can obtain Equ. (8).

2.2 Delete the Redundant Voxel Which Does Not Belong to Specific Organization T

In the method of above, it is inevitable to add some voxels which do not belong to this certain tissue into set T. Notice that these voxels have two characteristics: their loca-tions are between the pre-appointed box and this tissue; their densities are equal to densities of the inner voxels of this tissue. Hence, we regard the pre-appointed voxel A in the inner of this tissue as a seed point. Beginning with the voxel A, those voxels having the same densities and not belonging to this tissue are deleted. Then the same operation is done to the contiguous voxels of A and all voxels extended to boundary voxels. The boundary voxels defined as Definition 2 are strict.

Definition 1' Boundary B: According to the gradient value $\| \nabla f(B) \|$ of the pre-appointed boundary voxel B, we can initialize a domain [-v, v]. For the voxels generated from Definition 2, if their gradients are in the domain $[\| \nabla f(B) \| - v, \| \nabla f(B) \| + v]$, these voxels belong to the boundary voxels set B, moreover $B \subset T$.

Define 3 Greatest-span voxel: Among these voxels, the farthest voxel away from C is called the Greatest-span Voxel of C which travels along the path from Z axis to X axis, then to Y, and travel voxels have the same densities with C. According to the linked storage structure indexed by densities, the location of D is either at the start of the link or at the end of the link.

We begin with a voxel C in the inner of a certain tissue and find out the Greatest-span voxel D of C. Then travel voxels from C to D in the order of first slices (Z) , then rows (X) and last volumes (Y). At the same time, the locations of those voxels must be marked, which are belonging to the boundary voxels set B. In this way, these voxels areas among the marked boundary voxels are deleted. According to the above process, it is easy to delete the voxels that do not belong to the certain tissue T at the beginning of the pre-appointed voxel A. In succession, we find out the contiguous voxels of A and deal with these voxels by the same method in order of Z-X-Y. Otherwise, turn to the next contiguous voxel and go on until all the volume data of T have been dealt with. Obviously, there only are the operations of search and delete, and no calculations in the whole course.

2.3 Characteristics of Local Area

By Taylor expansion, Sato Y and Nakajima S expanded at $f(X)$ its one-order derivation and two-order derivation, as follows

$$f(X) = f(X_0) + (X - X_0)^T \nabla f(X_0) + \frac{1}{2}(X - X_0)^T \nabla^2 f(X_0)(X - X_0)$$

$$\nabla^2 f(X) = \begin{bmatrix} f_{xx}(X) & f_{xy}(X) & f_{xz}(X) \\ f_{yx}(X) & f_{yy}(X) & f_{yz}(X) \\ f_{zx}(X) & f_{zy}(X) & f_{zz}(X) \end{bmatrix} \tag{9}$$

$\nabla^2 f(X)$ denotes the two-order derivation of voxel's density, that is, Hessian matrix. Therefore, we describe the original densities of voxels by Hessian matrix. According to the analysis of the voxels' local character structures (linear, sheet, punctate), they draw a conclusion that if there is a special connection between the voxels' densities and its eigenvalues of Hessian matrix, like Table 1, the voxels will have the corresponding character structure, provided that the eigenvalues of the matrix separately are $\lambda 1$, $\lambda 2$ and $\lambda 3$.

Table 1. Basic conditions of local different character structures

Local character structures	Conditions of eigen-values	Conditions of decom-position	Examples
sheet structure	$\lambda_3\langle\langle\lambda_2\approx\lambda_1\approx0$	$\lambda_3\langle\langle0\&\lambda_3\langle\langle\lambda_2\approx0\&\lambda_3\langle\langle\lambda_1\approx0$	Organ, pallium
linear structure	$\lambda_3\approx\lambda_2\langle\langle\lambda_1\approx0$	$\lambda_3\langle\langle0\&\lambda_3\approx\lambda_2\&\lambda_2\langle\langle\lambda_1\approx0$	Vessel, trachea, nerve
Punctuate structure	$\lambda_3\approx\lambda_2\approx\lambda_1\langle\langle0$	$\lambda_3\langle\langle0\&\lambda_3\approx\lambda_2\&\lambda_2\approx\lambda_1$	nerve cell, node

In order to filter to the given local character structure, we use Gauss function and its two-order derivation to deal with the 3D data. The response filter of one-dimension function can be expressed R(x).

$$R(x)=-\frac{d^2G(x,\sigma)}{dx^2}*f(x)$$

The symbol " * " stands for the operation of convolution and σ stands for the standard deviation, controlling the width of the boundary. Correspondingly, the Hessian matrix changes into as following:

$$\nabla^2 R(X)=\begin{bmatrix} R_{xx}(X) & R_{xy}(X) & R_{xz}(X) \\ R_{yx}(X) & R_{yy}(X) & R_{yz}(X) \\ R_{zx}(X) & R_{zy}(X) & R_{zz}(X) \end{bmatrix} \tag{10}$$

3 Path Planning

Definition 4 Center path: It is the locus of the centers of maximally inscribed ball from one point to another point in the cavum object. It is consisted of a set of inner voxels of the object. It is named as Center path.

We note the previous center point, current center point and the next center point as C_{i-1}, C_i and C_{i+1}. O is the origin of the 3D space; S and E are the start point and end point respectively. The point $S_{i+1}(x,y,z)$ located in the direction of the vector is C_iE which is found out at first. C_{i+1} is located in the section plane including S_{i+1}, whose normal is the vector C_iE. Their positions of the 2D section plane are displayed in Fig.1.

$$\overrightarrow{OS_{i+1}} = \overrightarrow{OC_i} + \overrightarrow{C_iS_{i+1}} \qquad\qquad S_{i+1}(x)=C_i(x)+\left|\overrightarrow{C_iS_{i+1}}\right|\cos\alpha$$

$$S_{i+1}(y)=C_i(y)+\left|\overrightarrow{C_iS_{i+1}}\right|\cos\beta \qquad\qquad S_{i+1}(z)=C_i(z)+\left|\overrightarrow{C_iS_{i+1}}\right|\cos\gamma$$

The length of the vector C_iS_{i+1} is 1, that is $|C_iS_{i+1}|$ =1, cosα, cosβ, cosγ are the direction cosine of the vector CiE

$$(\overrightarrow{OP\text{-}OS_{i+1}})\bullet\overrightarrow{C_iE}=0 \tag{11}$$

The equation (11) describes the section plane including the point $S_{i+1}(x,y,z)$, whose normal is the vector C_iE.

• is the dot product of the vectors, P(x,y,z) locates in the section plane.

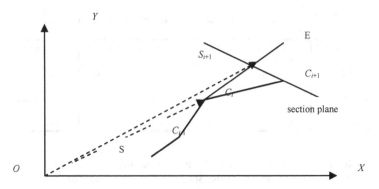

Fig. 1. Location of center points of 2D section plane

We name all the points on the section plane as the Point set, then divide Point set into *PNB*, and *PIB* and *PB* sets.

$PNB = Point \cap NOB$ $\qquad$ $PIB = Point \cap IOB$

$PB = Point \cap Boundary$ $\qquad$ $Point = PNB \cup PIB \cup PB$

dP$_m$ is the shortest distance from the point Pm belonging to the set *PIB* to all points of the set *PB*. And then, the point with the maximum dP$_m$ is the point C_{i+1}.

$$d_{Pm}=\min\{ \left|\overrightarrow{P_mP_1}\right|,\left|\overrightarrow{P_mP_2}\right|,\ldots,\left|\overrightarrow{P_mP_n}\right|,\ldots |P_1',P_2',\ldots,P_n',\ldots \in PB, P_m \in PIB\} \tag{12}$$

$$d_{Ci+1}=\max\{ d_{P1},d_{P2},\ldots,d_{Pm},\ldots |P_1,P_2,\ldots,P_m,\ldots \in PIB\} \tag{13}$$

$$Center\ path=\bigcup_{i=0}^{n} \{ C_i \} \tag{14}$$

n is the number of the set *Center path*, $C_0=S$, and $C_n=E$.

3.1 Processing Object with One Branch

A simplified procedure of calculating the distance dPm as fllows.

```
D=-1; Pnew←Point;
while Pnew≠φdo
  {
  d=d+1;
PB←extract boundary voxels from the
    set Pnew;
  Pnew←Pnew-PB;
dP_n' =d: P_n' ∈PB;
    //The distance value of each point in the set PB is evaluated.
  Remove all elements in the set PB;
  }

d_{Ci+1}=max{d_p|P∈Point};

Center path= ∪_{i=0}^{n} { C_i } ;
```

Much time can be saved to use above procedure when the section plane contains lots of points. Pick out the nearest point to the end point E as the center point, when points with the maximum distance value are more than one in the section plane.

3.2 Processing Object with Multiple Branches

Tangent plane and the object have a number of intersection in the case of multiple branching construction and each intersection has its own border voxel, internal voxel subset and center point of each branch, therefore the authors should choose the maximum value of local area instead of the maximum value of global when the authors calculate the center point. The authors have a wide range of choices when they calculate the current center point in the case of a number of center points being. If the authors calculate separately, the computation work would be amazing and time consumed would make them feel boring. Therefore, the easiest way is to make normal vector along the direction of SE to confirm the tangent plane. To make sure the unique of the center path the authors delete the branching construct Point beginning point to the ending point.

To begin with S , along the direction of **SE**, $|SE|$, 1, confirm the location of S_{i+1}, tangent plane (set *Point*) with normal vector **SE** , through point S_{i+1} , search the maximum value on the tangent plane(may be there are a number of maximum value), calculate the distance $dS_{Ci+1,m}$ from the current center point $C_{i+1,m}$ to the beginning point S, repeat this process until get the end of the ending point.

$$d_{Ci+1,m} > d_P \; : \text{(the pro points of } P \in C_{i+1}) \land (P, C_{i+1} \in PIB)$$

$$Cpt = \bigcup_{i=0}^{n} \{ C_i \} \text{ // } Cpt \text{ is temporary storage of the center points}$$

Confirm the unique center path: To delete the redundant branches on the center path, the authors will do as belows. Find the point C_j in Cpt to make $|C_i S|$ smallest (C_j and S are not necessarily connected). Then begin with point C_j, repeat the process until deal with all the points in Cpt, completion of the re-encoding to d_{SCj}. Finally reverse search the voxel brought $|CmE|$ the smallest from the ending point, if there are a number of voxel which satisfy the condition, we will choose the minimum value after re-coding, so that Cm is the point non-branch path, make C_m as the ending, and search forward for the next center point until $C_m = S$.

$$Ctemp = \bigcup_{j=0}^{n} \{ C_j \} \; : |C_j S| = \min \{|C_i S| | C_i \in Cpt \}; // Ctemp \text{ is temporary storage of}$$

the center points

$$newdS_{Cj} = newdS_{Cj} + |C_j S| : C_j \in Ctemp; \text{ // } newdS_{Cj} \text{ is the result of re-coding to } dS_{Cj}$$

$$Center \; path \leftarrow \bigcup_{m=0}^{n} \{ C_m \} \; : \; |C_m E| = \min \{|C_n E| | C_n \in Cpt\} \; : \; newdS_{Cm} = \min$$

$$\{ newdS_{Cq} | C_m E| = |C_m E| \; C_q \in Cpt\}$$

Fig. 2 is an example in 2D space. In each square there are two numbers, the above one is the original distance to the start point, the below one is the re-coded value; the squares with black color are the sole center path without the redundant branches.

0	1					7						
	1					19						
	2						9		11			
	2						17		17			
	3	4	5						11			
	3	4	5						15			
		5		7	8				12			16
		5		7	8				14			26
	5	6			10	11	12	13				
	7	6			10	11	12	13				
	6		9			12		14				18
	8		17			12		14				22
	7		10	11	12	13		15			18	
	9		16	15	14	13		15			20	
	8								17	18		
	10								17	18		
										19	20	
										19	20	
												22
												22

Fig. 2. Example of removing the redundant ranches in 2D space

4   Technology of Real-Time Processing and Scene Rendering in Two Steps

Interception the slice date in the region, divide the rendering of the current frame into two regions as close-range and far-range as shown in Fig.3 and Fig.4.

Rendering close-range based on ray casting method of voxel to choose ray casting algorithm with two-stage, and divide rendering close-range into two steps: the first step is to put the light segmentation, delaminat, and each segment has its own sampling, composition, calculated; the second step is the synthesis of the first step's results. Thus, we can obtain the current frame image after synthesis the results of rendering.

V_i is a view point, V_iE is the direction of the view line. W and h are width and height of projecting image, f is the foci, and d is the depth of close-range. The center C is projecting image.

$$C(x)=V_i(x)+f\cos\alpha \quad C(y)=V_i(y)+f\cos\beta \quad C(z)=V_i(z)+f\cos\gamma$$

$\cos\alpha$, $\cos\beta$, $\cos\gamma$ are the direction cosine of the vector V_iE. Surpose γ is the minume value, the distance among slices is1, and Volume data are coordinate translated as follows:

$$\cos\alpha' =\cos\gamma/\sqrt{\cos^2\beta+\cos^2\gamma} \qquad \cos\beta' = \sqrt{\cos^2\beta+\cos^2\gamma}$$

$$\sin\alpha' =\cos\beta/\sqrt{\cos^2\beta+\cos^2\gamma} \qquad \sin\beta' = -\cos\alpha$$

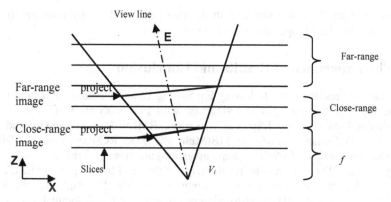

Fig. 3. Sketch map of the algorithm in 2D slice plane

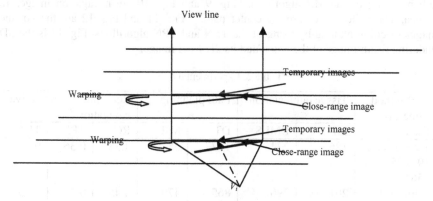

Fig. 4. Sketch map after view transformation

$$T(-V_{ix},- V_{iy},- V_{iz}) = \begin{bmatrix} 1 & 0 & 0 & 0 \\ 0 & 1 & 0 & 0 \\ 0 & 0 & 1 & 0 \\ -V_{ix} & -V_{iy} & -V_{iz} & 1 \end{bmatrix} \qquad R_x(\alpha') = \begin{bmatrix} 1 & 0 & 0 & 0 \\ 0 & \cos\alpha' & \sin\alpha' & 0 \\ 0 & -\sin\alpha' & \cos\alpha' & 0 \\ 0 & 0 & 0 & 1 \end{bmatrix}$$

$$R_y(\beta') = \begin{bmatrix} \cos\beta' & 0 & -\sin\beta' & 0 \\ 0 & 1 & 0 & 0 \\ \sin\beta' & 0 & \cos\beta' & 0 \\ 0 & 0 & 0 & 1 \end{bmatrix} \qquad S = \begin{bmatrix} 1 & 0 & 0 & 0 \\ 0 & 1 & 0 & 0 \\ \sin\alpha\sin\beta & f/(wh) & 0 & 0 \\ 0 & 0 & 0 & 1 \end{bmatrix}$$

$$M = P \cdot S \qquad P = T(-V_{ix},- V_{iy},- V_{iz}) \cdot R_x(\alpha') \cdot R_y(\beta')$$

α', β' are roted by X and Y, $V_i E$ and Z are ovelaped.

We can use the coherence of adjacent frames when dealing with the next frame and the authors can obtain the next frame image of close-range only through recalculating the smaller fraction. It can obtain most of the image of the next frame through cutting vision Image of current frame, and it can also generate the remainder of the vision image through projecting the vision image which is not rendering, then the authors combine the whole vision image with the two parts, and finally combine the next frame with the close-range image and the vision image.

5   The Experimental Results and Conclusion

We obtain the results as the following Fig.5 – Fig.12 and measure the data as table 2 by the CT data offered by Visible-Human, with PIV 3.0G Hz CPU, memory 1G. Experimental data among LS(Local structure), BMLS(Boundary model and local structure), DT(Distance transform), MB(Multi branches), RC(Ray casting), TPN(Two phase navigation) and TSN (Two step navigation) are given in Table 2.

Fig. 5 is the 3D reconstruction result image of the head by using the VHD CT head data. Fig. 6 is the segmentation result image of the Fig. 5's skull with the BMLS algorithm. Fig. 7 is the 3D reconstruction result image of the abdominal. Fig. 8 is the result image of colon's segmentation and path planning,. The red line is the center path by using of the MB algorithm. Fig. 9 and Fig. 10 are navagation images in trachea. The yellow lines are the center path.   Fig. 11 and Fig. 12 are the voyage images of colon planing by using of the TSN and TPN algorithms. Fig. 13 is the 3D rendering result image of the colon and its 2D MRI image.

Table 2. Experimental data

Methods Times(s) Data	Tissue egmentation		Path planning		Real-time interactive navigation		
	LS	BMLS	DT	MB	RC	TPN	TSN
Tracheas CT 192×256× 256	1860	272	1127	684	4.38	0.36	0.16
colons CT 256×256× 256	2019	290	865	479	4.45	0.44	0.25

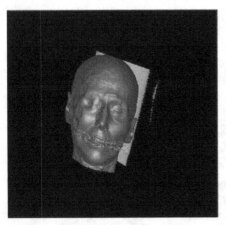

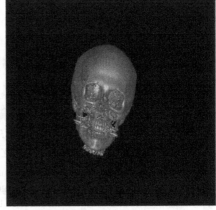

Fig. 5. The segmentation result image of the head l

Fig. 6. The segmentaion result image of the skull

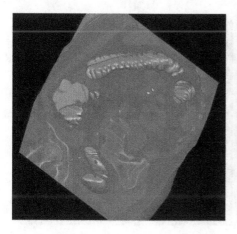

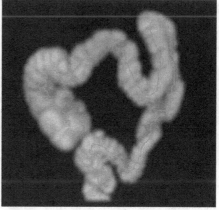

Fig. 7. The 3d reconstruction of the abdominal

Fig. 8. The result of colon's segmentation and path planning

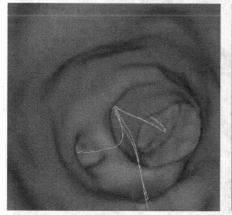

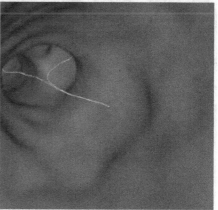

Fig. 9. Navagation image1 of path

Fig. 10. Navagation image2 of path

We can deal with the key problems of visual endoscopy quickly by using tissue segmentation, path planning, real-time processing, scene rendering argued in the paper. We also can obtain high-quality results by using visual endoscopy with the real-time speed.

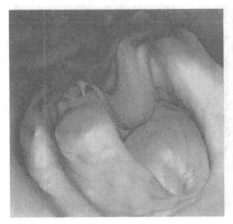 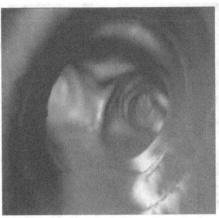

Fig. 11. The voyage image of colon planing   **Fig. 12.** The voyage image of trachea planing

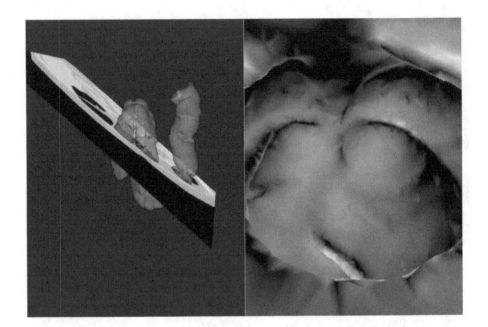

Fig. 13. The 3D rendering resukt image of the colon and its 2D MRI image

Acknowledgments. This work is supported by a grant from the National High Technology Research and Development Program of China (863 Program) (No. 2009AA062700).

References

1. Kanav, K., Mithra, V., Marshall, L.: Cognitive simulators for medical education and train-ing. Journal of Biomedical Informatics 42(4), 593–604 (2009)
2. Michael, W.L., Polly, P.A., Robert, C.H., Curry, I.G.: Accessibility and acceptance of re-sponsive virtual human technology as a survey interviewer training tool. Computers in Human Behavior 22(3), 412–426 (2006)
3. Mark, W.B., Kevin, A.S., Gilbert, M.M., Alan, V.L.: Immersive Virtual Environments for Medical Training. Seminars in Colon and Rectal Surgery 19(2), 90–97 (2008)
4. Glenn, G., Smith, H.G., Sinan, O., Yuan, Y.: Stills, not full motion, for interactive spatial training: American, Turkish and Taiwanese female pre-service teachers learn spatial visu-alization. Computers & Education 52(1), 201–209 (2009)
5. Bernhard, P., Dirk, B.: Image Analysis for Medical Visualization. Visualization in Medi-cine 34(2), 83–133 (2007)
6. Chao, Y., Huai, Z., Zhi, H.: Visualization of 3-D temperature distribution in a 300 MW twin-furnace coal-fired boiler. Journal of China University of Mining and Technol-ogy 18(1), 33–37 (2008)
7. David, D., James, M.N., Toomas, T.: Situated cognition in clinical visualization: The role of transparency in GammaKnife neurosurgery planning. Artificial Intelligence in Medi-cine 46(2), 111–118 (2009)
8. Bernhard, P., Dirk, B.: Image Analysis and Visualization for Liver Surgery Planning. Visualization in Medicine 34(3), 499–523 (2007)
9. Jinman, K., Tom, W.C., Michael, F., Stefan, E., David, D.F.: Data Visualization and Dis-play. Biomedical Information Technology 5(1), 211–227 (2008)
10. Svjetlana, M., Jianyu, Z., Weidong, X., Gary, S.R., Jerrold, L.V., Cameron, C.M.: Stereo-tactic neurosurgical planning, recording, and visualization for deep brain stimulation in non-human primates. Journal of Neuroscience Methods 162(1-2), 32–41 (2007)
11. Gordon, K., James, W.D.: Semi-automatic generation of transfer functions for direct vol-ume rendering. In: IEEE Symposium on Volume Rendering Processing, Washington, USA, pp. 79–86 (2006)
12. Sato, Y., Nakajima, S., et al.: Three-dimensional multi-scale line filter for segmentation and visualization of curvilinear structures in medical images. Medical Image Analy-sis 2(2), 43–167 (2007)
13. Sato, Y., Nakajima, S., et al.: Tissue classification based on 3D local intensity structures for volume rendering. IEEE Transaction on Visualization and Computer Graphics 6(2), 160–168 (2000)
14. Hong, L., Muraki, S., Kaufman, A., et al.: Virtual voyage: Interactive navigation in the human colon. In: SIGGRAPH 1997, pp. 27–34 (1997)
15. Zhou, Y., Toga, W.: Efficient skeletonization of volumetric objects. IEEE Transaction on Visualization and Computer Graphics 5(3), 196–209 (1999)
16. Palagyi, K., Kuba, A.: A 3-subiteration 3D thinning algorithm for extracting medical sur-face. Pattern Recognition Letters 23(6), 663–675 (2008)
17. Sramek, M., Kaufman, A.E.: Fast ray-tracing of rectilinear volume data using distance Transforms. IEEE Transaction on Visualization and Computer Graphics 6(3), 236–252 (2007)
18. Martin, L.B., Kenneth, K.J., Nguyen, H.T., et al.: Interactive volume navigation. IEEE Transaction on Visualization and Computer Graphics 4(3), 243–256 (1998)
19. Krishnan, R., William, E.H.: Interactive dynamic navigation for virtual endoscopy. Com-puters in Biology and Medicine 29(5), 303–331 (2007)

Design and Implementation of Virtual Museum Based on Web3D

JianPing Zhang[1,2] and YuHui Yang[2]

[1] Institute of educational technology, Zhejiang University,
Hangzhou, 310028, China
[2] College of teacher education, Zhejiang Normal University,
Jinhua, 321004, China
{21zjp,yyhhn2007}@163.com

Abstract. In recent years, virtual museum has become more and more wide-spread and it plays an important role for effective utilizing of collected resources and protecting historical and cultural heritage and restoration of cultural relics. Moreover, virtual museum can make museum virtual resources to be spread and shared more broadly though Internet. This article takes "We are Yi-wunese" virtual museum as an example and proposes how to develop a Web3D-based virtual museum. There are three main sections in the article: (1) Web3D technology; (2) development process of virtual museum based on Web3D; (3) functions and implementation of a practical virtual museum. The aim of the study is to provide some valuable references for development of virtual museum in the future.

Keywords: Web3D, virtual museum, virtual avatar, precise navigation.

1 Introduction

With the development and maturity of the Web3D technology, it is possible to give an omnibearing display about virtual museum and virtual cultural relics. The application of the computer network has made communication through digital information about virtual museum become more and more convenient. This article takes "We are Yi-wunese" virtual museum as an example and proposes how to develop Web3D-based virtual museum. The study mainly focuses on the crucial matters as follows: firstly, technology of Web3D; secondly, development process of Virtual Museum based on Web3D; thirdly, functions and implementation of Virtual Museum. Finally, some software will be introduced, such as virtual museum development software, virtual avatar development software, and the adaption configure software of multi-user server.

2 Web3D Technology

Web3D is a virtual reality technology which is used based on the Internet [1]. The origin of virtual world in the Internet can trace back to the 1990, with the development

Z. Pan et al. (Eds.): Transactions on Edutainment III, LNCS 5940, pp. 154–165, 2009.

of VRML (Virtual Reality Modeling Language). The first version of the standard was VRML 1.0. In 1996, VRML 2.0 was introduced at the Siggraph conference, which has been accepted as an international standard hereafter called VRML 97.

Use of this standard against other available technologies, such as Java3D, provides advantages such as rapid creation of contents for the Web. The main characteristics of VRML include: definition of 3D objects in remote locations, definition of animations, inclusion of connections to other worlds or Websites, and modification of the scene by means of events.

Even before VRML 2.0 was presented formally, a large number of working groups appeared to take new lines of design ahead. One of these groups, under the name of Living Worlds (LW), implemented the first version of a multi-user environment, in which it was possible to insert avatars in scenes defined with VRML 1.0. VRML had a new standard known as X3D in 2004. X3D is a royalty-free open standard file format and run-time architecture to represent and communicate 3D scenes and objects using XML.

Now, the LW group has disappeared. This caused numerous companies to commercialize this kind of system unremittingly and develop their own software, sometimes beyond the VRML standard. Some of them are as followings:

- Active Worlds (http://www.Active worlds.com).
- Blaxxun interactive (http://www.blaxxun.com): It is one of the most important companies that uses worlds and avatars defined in the VRML standard.
- DeepMatrix (http://www.geometrek.com): The system is split into server programs running on the web server where the VRML worlds and supporting HTML files are stored. The client is realized as a Java applet.
- WorldsServer (http: //www. worlds. com): Some of its most important characteristics are: voice-to-voice communication, audio and video streaming, multilingual text chat, etc.
- VRSpace (http://vrspace.sourceforge.net): It is free cross-platform modular 3D community software.

The common deficiency of systems listed above is the lack of visual realism. As a matter of fact, a lot of game servers currently offer new advances in real time computer graphics science. Currently, games can be also played through a computer network, including Internet. These are some reasons why they can be considered good alternatives for the systems based on VRML. The use of game servers currently available allows us to have an open modular software and multi- platform that could incorporate the new technologies developed in the fields of realtime modeling, visibility algorithms and illumination models.

3 Systematic Architecture of the Virtual Museum

Generally speaking, a virtual museum system consists of two sections: server section and client section. Server section includes ABNet server and MeChat Server. Client section includes BS Contact Client, ABNet Client and MeChat Client. ABNet is one of the multi-users Web3d Kimball Software that was developed by Rick and his colleagues. MeChat is one of the Voice and video chat software that was developed by Rhyme Computer Limited company of Guangzhou. We integrated these three kinds of software and constructed our virtual museum based on them (Figure.1).

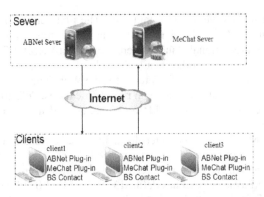

Fig. 1. Systematic architecture of the virtual museum

In the Systematic architecture of the virtual museum, ABNet sever is used for receiving information from ABNet client and BS Contact and broadcasting them to every client. Thus every user can see others' motion and interaction. ABNet client is used for collecting users' motion and interaction and sending them to ABNet sever. BS Contact is one of the browsers which is developed by Bitmanagement company. BS Contact is used for supporting 3D environment of VRML format and sending information back to ABNet client. MeChat Sever and Plug-in are used for supporting multi-user dialogs and videos. Users can do such kind of work as writing exchange through MeChat Sever and Plug-in.

4   Development Process of the Virtual Museum

Development process of the virtual museum based on Web3d generally includes five sections: (1) design of virtual museum based on Web3D; (2) development of virtual museum environment; (3) making avatars; (4) configuration of network sever and (5) synthesis of virtual museum (Figure 2).

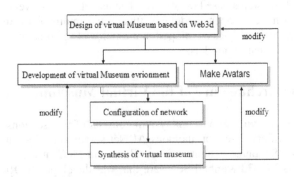

Fig. 2. Developing process of the virtual museum

4.1 Design of the Virtual Museum Based on Web3d

Design of the virtual museum based on Web3D mainly involves the rate of network, appearance of virtual museum, scale of virtual museum and content of virtual museum. In this section, we consider how to design a general structrure for topic-oriented virtual museum with integration of ABNet Sever and MeChat Sever.

"We are Yiwunese" Virtual Museum mainly includes five contents: Ancient Museum, Modern Museum, Contemporary Museum, New comers' Museum and Movie House (Figure 3). Introductions of some famous ancient Yiwunese, such as Zongze, Luo Binwang, Zhu Danxi, Yan Xiao and Zhu yiqing, would be shown in Ancient Museum. Introduction of representatives of modern Yiwunese, such as Chen Wangdao, Feng Xuefeng and Wu Han, and their hard-working styles and Yiwunese' spirit of "Chicken Feather for Sugar of" would be presented in Modern Museum. The course of development, followed by the Opening Policy, of all steps of Yiwunese and businessmen rambling all over the country would be demonstrated in Contemporary Museum. The "Yiwu Spirit" developed by newcomers and foreigners and some samples would be presented in Newcomers' Museum. And in the Movie House, we mainly broadcast Yiwu's reform and development course as well as its significant achievements achieved after the Reforming and Opening policy.

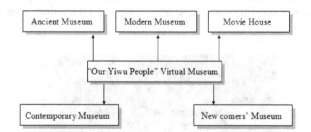

Fig. 3. Architecture of the "We are Yiwunese" virtual museum

4.2 Development of the Environment of the Virtual Museum

Sound code of the virtual museum is constructed by VRML.However, the modeling function of VRML is not very good because it don't support visual 3D model edition. Thus we ususally edit 3D model by 3DSmax or Maya software, then export it with VRML format (Figure 4).

Both 3Dsmax and Maya software are comprehensive 3D modelings with animation and they provide solutions widely used by leaders in areas of game development, television, education and so on. After 3D virtual museum is completed, some programs related to interaction and information need to be edited in VRML.

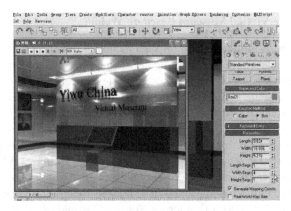

Fig. 4. Making 3D model in 3Dsmax

4.3 Making Avatars

3D virtual avatar is a computer user's representation of himself/herself or alter ego, which is in the form of a three-dimensional model used in virtual museum. It is an "object" representing the embodiment of every user. Users can make various movements through avatars. Users may choose different avatars to represent themselves in virtual museum. Avatar Studio is a specialized 3D software for making avatars. We can make different avatars by Avatar Studio, which supports designing movements, modifying faces, choosing statures, synthesizing (or integrating) user's photo and avatar (Figure 5).

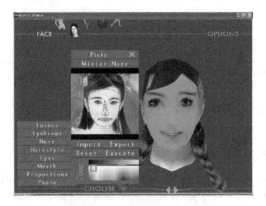

Fig. 5. Making avatar in Avatar Studio

4.4 Configuration of Network Sever and Synthesis of the Virtual Museum

Up to now, there are several multi-user network sever platforms, such as Blaxxun Commu-nication Server platform, ABNet, BS Collaborate Server, and etc.. We selected ABNet for its powerful functions and also because it is a free multi-user Web3d Kimball Software.

ABNet supports multi-user, interaction, writing exchange and some other functions. The sever needs to install ABNet Server.exe and MeChat sever before setting up path of web page. Users who want to view the virtual museum must install ABNet Client.exe, BS Contact and MeChat plug-in in their computers, then they can look over the virtual museum by the web page that integrates ABNet sever and MeChat sever.

5   Functions and Implementation of the Virtual Museum

5.1   Real-Time Walkthrough

Users can control their avatar real-time walkthrough in the virtual museum. The avatars' viewpoint replace user's eyes and through it, users could browse historical culture in the museum through avatar (Figure 6). User can automatically walk in the virtual museum with some program.

Some typical VRML code:
Program Inflation (Output)
DEF   view1 Viewpoint { position 0.0 0.0 6 }
DEF   time1 TimeSensor {cycleInterval 10 }
DEF Camera01-POS-INTERP PositionInterpolator { key [0 0.2 0.35 0.55 0.75 1]
keyValue [7 1.72 260,-7 14 167,-120 14 164,-120 14 100,-120 14 20,-50 14 20] }
Group { children [DEF botton TouchSensor { }Transform { children [Shape {appearance Appearance {material Material {diffuseColor 2.0 0.0 0.0}}geometry Box {size0.05 0 0.025}}
]}]}
ROUTE button.touchTimeTO time1.start Time
ROUTE time1.fraction_changedTO Camera01- POS-INTERP. set_ fraction
ROUTE Camera01-POS-INTERP.value_ chang TO view1. position

Fig. 6. Avatars walkthrough in virtual museum

5.2 Voice Introduction

In the museum, users can choose the function of phonetic introduction. When users click the sound switch, the history of and culture about the heritages and relics in the museum will be broadcast. The voice is similar with that in reality. Besides, the volume is lower when users are far from the sound source and higher while near the source. This function technologically depends on the AudioClip node of VRML code.

5.3 Multi-user Interaction

Users can walk in virtual museum and click the historical relics and pictures. Once one object was clicked, its information will be shown on a web page. In this way, users may obtain more information from virtual museums. We are now working to enable virtual museums present history and culture as many as possible based on limited network rate. The interaction function technologically depends on the Anchor node of VRML code.

5.4 Precise Navigation

Precise navigation is very important to users because users would lost their ways easily in a large virtual museum. The ProximitySensor node of VRML are used to locate specific position of the virtual avatar and send data back to web page. The avatar's coordinates (X, Z) are turned to One small ico's coordinates(X,Y) on the 2D map. When the avatar's coordinates alter, ico's coordinates will change accordingly (Figure 7).

Fig. 7. Precise navigation of avatar

When users click the link on the 2D map, the avatar's coordinates will become the position of the link. The related code is divided into VRML document and HTML document.

Wrl document code:

```
DEF prox ProximitySensor {
        size  1000 1000 1000
        center 0 0 0}
```

HTML document code:

```
<SCRIPT Language="JavaScript">
```

```
function start() {
   timerID1 = setTimeout("disp1()", 300); }
 function disp1(){na=document.bsContact.getNodeEventOut
('PS','position_changed');
   temp=na.split("");x=temp[0];y=temp[1];z=temp[2];
   image2.style.left=3 * x + 320;
   image2.style.top =0.95 * z + 510;
   timerID2 = setTimeout("disp1()", 200); }
</SCRIPT>
<SCRIPT Language="JavaScript">
   function SetVP( )
{bsContact.setNodeEventIn("view1","set_bind", "true")}
   function SetVP2( )
{bsContact.setNodeEventIn("view2","set_bind", "true")}
   function SetVP3( )
{bsContact.setNodeEventIn("view3","set_bind", "true")}
   function SetVP4( )
{bsContact.setNodeEventIn("view4","set_bind", "true")}
      function SetVP5( )
{bsContact.setNodeEventIn("view5","set_bind", "true")}
   function SetVP6( )
{bsContact.setNodeEventIn("view6","set_bind", "true")}
</SCRIPT>
```

5.5 Multi-user and Video Chat

In a virtual museum, every user can see each other with the function of multi-user. They can talk with each other in text, audio and video through MeChat. The functions of multi-user and video chat are realized though web server. In the virtual museum, ABNet' multi-user with video chat were integrated into one web page (Figure 8). (Note: I am not sure about the meaning of the last sentence, please check it again)

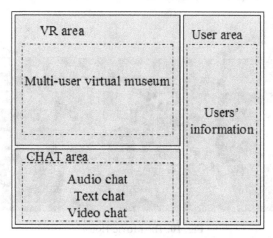

Fig. 8. A framework of the web page

Users can browse the content of virtual museum in VR area. If users want to enter a virtual museum, they need to login the system. Users' information will appear in user area, such as the number of people online and users' names. In chat area, users could send messages to others by video and audio(Figure 9).

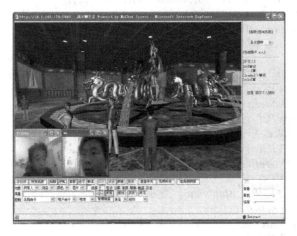

Fig. 9. Users are chatting by video and text

5.6 The Movie House

The Movie House is mainly used to broadcast the videos associated with Yiwunese achievements gained in its era of reforming and opening up, in formats of AVI, which was supported by VRML, Virtual Multimedia Stage and projectors. Virtual Multimedia Stage do a lot of work, such as stimulating functions of real Multimedia Stage in a lifelike manner, synchronizing projection and stage computer, and switching on or shutting down effect of computers and related control logic. Here we mainly adopted the Texture Replacement technique of VRML (Figure 10).

Fig. 10. The Movie House

Some typical VRML code :

```
DEF MV_01 MovieTexture {loop TRUE  url "maps/mov1.avi" stopTime 0 }
DEF MV_02 MovieTexture {loop TRUE  url "maps/mov2.avi" stopTime 0 }
DEF CtrlScript Script {
    eventIn SFTime time
    eventIn SFFloat  BB
    eventIn SFFloat  CC
    eventIn SFFloat  DD
    field SFNode MV01 USE MV_01
    field SFNode MV02 USE MV_02
    eventOut SFNodeMovieType_changed
    url      "vrmlscript:
    function CC (value)
    { if (value==1)
    { MovieType_changed=MV01;}
    }
    function DD (value)
    { if (value==1)
    { MovieType_changed=MV02;
    }} "}
ROUTE CtrlScript.MovieType_changed TO zhuping.set_texture
ROUTE CtrlScript.MovieType_changed TO lb.set_texture
ROUTE s1.touchTime TO TIME1.set_startTime
ROUTE s1.touchTime TO MV_01.set_startTime
ROUTE s1.touchTime TO MV_02.set_stopTime
ROUTE TIME1.fraction_changed TO CtrlScript.CC
ROUTE s2.touchTime TO  TIME2.set_startTime
ROUTE s2.touchTime TO MV_02.set_startTime
ROUTE s2.touchTime TO MV_01.set_stopTime
```

6 Conclusion and Future Work

Currently, the development of virtual museum is becoming more and more popular. The artistic effect of virtual museum is obvious .Thanks to Internet, for its power and diverse manners to spread all kinds of histories and cultures to as many as possible target users through free surfing. Comparing with constructing physical museum, developing virtual museum based on web3d for public could save a lot of money. At the same time, the virtual museum makes it possible for users from different areas to study history and culture together and exchange ideas by video, which makes virtual museum even more interesting. On the other hand, to make a perfect virtual museum based on web3D, it is time-consuming and also technologies of multiuser are a little complicated and challenging. If a game server could be used to design virtual museum, we could make the most use of its function because some game servers use public domain open code and they allow us to incorporate all the desired technologies. In the future, we would improve our virtual museum based on web3D by integrating some interrelated software.

Acknowledgments. It is a project supported by Chinese Computer Aided Education Committee "The construction of the adaptive learning environment based on DVR (2009CBE004,)" "The inheritance and development of Regional culture spirit in the school (SC242)" and China National Social Science Fund Education Issues "Distance learning mechanism and its application in adaptive learning support system (BCA070053)."

References

1. Stytz, M.: Distributed Virtual Environment. J. IEEE Computer Graphics and Application 16(3), 19–31 (1996)
2. Yuhui, Y., Jianping, Z.: Web3D technology and its application in the cultural relic protection. In: International Conference on Computer Science and Information Technology, Beijing, August 2009, vol. 3, pp. 10–13 (2009)
3. Jianping, Z., Bo, M., Yuhui, Y.: Design and Implementation of The 3D Virtual Learning Environment. In: 2009 World Congress on Software Engineering, Xiamen, May 2009, pp. 19–21 (2009)
4. Chittaro, L., Ranon, R.: Dynamic Generation of Personalized VRML Content: a General Approach and its Application to 3D E-Commerce. In: Proc. of the seventh international conference on 3D Web technology, pp. 145–154 (2002)
5. Celentano, A., Pittarello, F.: Observing and adapting user behavior in navigational 3D interfaces. In: Proc. of AVI 2004, pp. 275–282 (2004)
6. Lepouras, G., Charitos, D., Vassilakis, C., Charissi, A., Halatsi, L.: Building a VR-Museum in a Museum. In: Proc. of VRIC Virtual Reality International Conference (2001)
7. Patel, M., White, M., Walczak, K., Sayd, P.: Digitization to Presentation – Building Virtual Museum Exhibitions. In: Proc. of Vision Video and Graphics, pp. 1–8 (2003)
8. Pan, Z., Cheok, A.D., Yang, H., Zhu, J., Shi, J.: Virtual reality and mixed reality for virtual learning environment. Computers & Graphics 30, 20–28 (2006)
9. Ashdown, N., Forestiero, S.: A guide to VRML 2.0 and an Evaluation of VRML,Modelling Tools (1998),
   http://www.agocg.ac.uk/train/vrml2rep/cover.htm
10. Inoue, Y.: Effects of virtual reality support compared to video support in a high –school world geography class. Campus-wide information System 16, 95 (1995)
11. Ieronutti, L., Chittaro: Employing virtual humans for education and training in X3D/VRML worlds. Computers & Education 49, 93–109 (2007)
12. Chittaro, L., Ranon, R.: Wed3D technologies in learning, education and training: Motivations, issues, opportunities. Computers & Education 49, 3–18 (2007)
13. Walczak, K., Cellary, W.: Building database applications of virtual reality with X-VRML. In: Proceedings of the Web3D 2002 symposium, 7th international conference on 3D Web technology, Tempe, AZ, pp. 111–120 (2002)
14. Ibanez, J., Aylett, R., Ruiz-Rodarte, R.: Storytelling in virtual environments from a virtual guide perspective. Journal of Virtual reality 7(1), 30–42 (2003)
15. Patel, M., White, M., Walczak, K., Sayd, P.: Digitisation to presentation - building virtual museum exhibitions. In: VVG, pp. 189–196 (2003)
16. Barbieri, T., Garzotto, F., Beltrame, G., Ceresoli, L., Gritti, M., Misani, D.: From dust to stardust: A collaborative 3d virtual museum of computer science. In: ICHIM, vol. 2, pp. 341–345 (2001)

17. Hetherington, R., Farrimond, B., Presland, S.: Information rich temporal virtual models using x3d. Computers & Graphics 30(2), 287–298 (2006)
18. Sowizral, H.A., Deering, M.F.: The java 3d api and virtual reality. IEEE Computer Graphics and Applications 19(3), 12–15 (1999)
19. Lepouras, G., Charitos, D., Vassilakis, C., Charissi, A., Halatsi, L.: Building a VR-museum in a museum. In: Proceedings of the 3rd virtual reality international conference (VRIC 2001), Laval, France, May 2001, pp. 16–20 (2001)
20. Ciabatti, E., Cicnoni, P., Montani, C., Scopigno, R.: Towards a Distributed 3D Virtual Museum. In: Proc. of Working Conference on Advanced Visual Interfaces, Italy, pp. 264–266 (1998)

Large Area Interactive Browsing for High Resolution Digitized Dunhuang Murals*

Qingshu Yuan[1], Dongming Lu[1], Qi Wu[1], and Gang Liu[2]

[1] College of Computer Science and Technology, Zhejiang University,
310027 Hangzhou, Zhejiang, China
[2] The Dunhuang Academy,
736200 Dunhuang, Gansu, China
{yuanqs,ldm,wuqi1985}@cs.zju.edu.cn, liugang@gs165.com

Abstract. The Dunhuang Motao Grottoes consist of about 45000 square meters murals, which are the most important part of the Dunhuang Art. As Dunhuang murals are rich in contents, large in sizes and amounts, high resolution and high fidelity acquisition techniques are required for storage. It is significantly important to exhibit the murals vividly and tell the recondite stories to the public. How to browse these high resolution mural images effectively is an important technical issue. In the paper, a novel multi-resolution image partition method is presented, thus the system can efficiently load and splice these partitioned images with proper resolution during browsing. A natural gesture interaction approach is also brought forward for convenient browsing of the murals. Gesture detection is used to get the moving and zooming operation instructions from the user. Using gesture approaches, the user can interact with the system without wearing or operating any device, but swinging the arms. The results show that the system can effectively exhibit high resolution mural images with convenient interactions.

Keywords: the Dunhuang Mocao Grottoes, natural interaction, high resolution images, gesture detection, large display wall.

1 Introduction

The Dunhuang Mogao Grottoes [1], firstly built in 366 A.D., contain one of the largest and best preserved collections of Buddhist art treasures in the world. Located in Dunhuang, Gansu, China, they are now rich in content and large in scale after tens of dynasties. It is a huge comprehensive art palace, integrating architecture, painted sculptures and murals. There are 492 grottoes which are well restored for thousands of years, murals about 45000 square meters and painted sculptures over two thousand pieces. Therefore, the Dunhuang Mogao Grottoes was listed as UNESCO world cultural heritage in 1987.

---

* The research was partially funded by Program for Changjiang Scholars and Innovative Research Team (No. IRT0652) and China University Digital Museum Plan.

Z. Pan et al. (Eds.): Transactions on Edutainment III, LNCS 5940, pp. 166–176, 2009.
© Springer-Verlag Berlin Heidelberg 2009

Dunhuang is famous for its mural art with consummate skills. Main mural contents include Buddhist statues, narrative Buddha's stories, Sutra paintings, and so on. These murals contain rich information regarding religion, society, history and cultural values, which are helpful in museum exhibition and e-learning. However, most of the murals are recondite, and not easy to be understood. Thus interactive and large area exhibition is in urgent need.

For mural exhibitions, some problems should be addressed. Firstly, large area HCI (wall-sized display and large area interaction) should be used and implemented to simulate large sizes of murals. Therefore, users will have the immersive illusion as if he or she were in the grottoes. Secondly, in order to acquire enough details of murals, high fidelity techniques are always used, which will generate extra ultra-high resolution images. However, high resolution images are inconvenient for digital exhibitions and some caching-like techniques should be adopted, since there are not enough memories to entirely load the images. Meanwhile, we can neither put the whole image file in the disk, whose I/O delay will reduce the system display effects. Thirdly, natural interaction, especially device-free interaction techniques should be provided for the purpose of convenience, which will greatly enhance the users' experience during learning or visiting. In addition, multimedia or animation should be adopted, which can vividly tell the recondite mural stories. Lastly, for application cost considerations, the hardware should be easy to set up and not too expensive.

2 Related Work

Wall-sized displays can simulate large size murals, allowing users to stand and move freely in front of them, and interactive browsing is an important issue for such displays. In the application of museum exhibitions and e-learning, and an increasing amount of researches has been done in this field in recent years.

Touch screen usually serves as an interactive device. In [2], a kiosk system with a touch screen and a stereoscopic display was proposed. Visitors could navigate in the virtual museum, select artifacts and view more details of them interactively. Touch screen does not scale well and its restricted display space could only show a part of whole large image. Since it needs touch operation, its interaction area is constrained.

In [3], techniques for direct pen-based interaction on large high resolution displays were proposed. The system had been tested in a brainstorming tool by groups of professional product designer. A pen is used as an interactive tool to sketch and annotate directly on graphical objects or on transparent overlapping sheets. However, performing operations on wall-size displays with a pen, users may have difficulties in reaching too high, too low, or too far away spot of the display.

Several handheld devices also have been introduced into the interaction application in museum exhibition and e-learning. In [4], a gesture recognition engine using an inexpensive 6 DOF data glove was proposed and applied into immersive virtual environments. In [5], Bernardo et al. used a joystick to control a mechanical arm which takes charge of the real camera navigation, and then, the images captured by the camera are embedded in the virtual 3D environment. A system which shows both overview and detail of large images is proposed in [6]. While the user holds up a tablet tracked through ultrasonic in front of the display wall, the detail image of corresponding region is accessed on the tablet screen.

When interacting with wall-size display, users typically stand or move in front of it. Using hand-held devices [4][5][6] could be inconvenient, as it must be carried around and often requires environmental supports. The use of those handheld devices may bring device management problems, which results in inconvenience in public exhibition.

Some computer vision based approaches were also proposed. Some of them focused on marker-based interaction research. In [7], a camera tracks the LED marker placed on the user's fingertip, and then the system recognizes and processes crossing operation of the marker. In [8], in order to gain the position and orientation of the marker, IR-sensible cameras are used to recognize the pattern emitted by the marker on the input device Sceptre and the appending head tracking device. In [9], the system provides input by tracking a wand-like object using two cameras, which requires markers. The shortcoming of those marker-based approaches is similar with handheld devices. They do not accord with the users' usage pattern, and may make users inconvenient and uncomfortable. The calculation process of those approaches is usually complicated and time-consuming.

In [10], a hybrid vision and sound based system for marker-free interaction was proposed. Sixteen cameras and four microphones are used to capture the user's motion in order to detect the objects interacted with. In [11], an interactive advertisement system is described that two stereo cameras are used to recognize the users' positions. The system changes display modes obeying the recognized distance between users and display. In [12] four computers and eight cameras are mounted along the floor. Each camera image is divided into vertical slices and each slice is processed to detect 1D position, while 2D and 3D positions are determined using triangulation or inferring. Although these systems allow marker-free interaction, they need too many computers or support devices. It may cost too much for applications. In addition, users' interaction area is limited in such systems, since the intersecting camera FOV (Field of View) is limited.

3 System and Algorithm Design

3.1 System Framework

The system is composed of interaction module, image partition module and scene rendering module, the system architecture is shown in Fig. 1. The server recognizes visitor's gesture, generates instructions and sends them. The interaction client receives the instructions and passes them to the scene renderer, which maintains display parameters, such as resolution and position. Scene renderer sends these parameters to the image management module, which will return the required image set. By splicing and mapping these images as textures using OpenGL library, the system finally renders the result to the display interface.

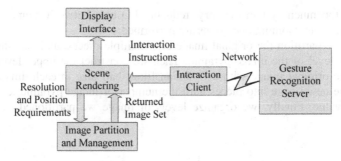

Fig. 1. System architecture

3.2 Hardware Design

The system mainly consists of projection devices, an infrared light and a camera with infrared lens. As shown in Fig. 2, a monochrome camera is used to capture visitor's motions. Since the visitor stands in front of the projection screen, the projection image alteration will be captured by the camera, which will greatly increase the difficulty of motion detection. To settle this problem, we put an infrared light near the camera and attach an infrared lens to the camera, and then, the camera will only observe the reflected infrared light.

When the infrared light is turned on, visitor's motions can be detected by subtracting frames one by one, named frame difference method. And the projection image alteration will be ignored since the projection light will not emit infrared light.

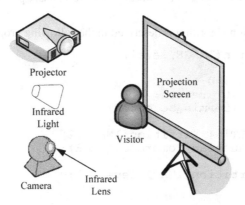

Fig. 2. Gesture detection and recognition devices

3.3 Mural Image Partition and Utilization

Since image partition is used, the system needn't load the whole image data when initializes, which avoids users waiting too long. During the process of browsing, the system only needs to render the currently viewable portion of the large image which greatly increases flexibility and browsing speed. The partition approach also avoids occupying too much system memory, reducing I/O cost between memory and disk when moving and zooming operations are performed.

Firstly, we partition the original image into multiple pieces, and take these pieces as the base level of the image pyramid. Then we construct the upper level by compressing the original image with a Gaussian filter, half size in each dimension. We partition the new image into pieces until the number of image pyramid level reaches the given value. Finally, we organize levels of image we partitioned as an image pyramid.

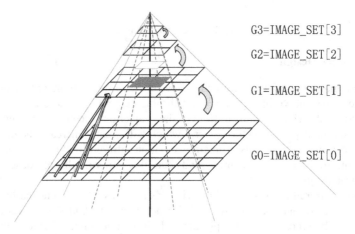

G3=IMAGE_SET[3]

G2=IMAGE_SET[2]

G1=IMAGE_SET[1]

G0=IMAGE_SET[0]

Fig. 3. Process of constructing a four-level image pyramid

The image partition algorithm is described in the following program code.

```
ImagePartition(IMAGE,level)
{
    static int i=0;
    if (level<=0) return;
    if(IMAGE.size>min_accepted)
    {
        IMAGE_SET[i]=Partition(IMAGE,2^(level-1));
        IMAGE=Gaussian_Compress(IMAGE);
        i++;
        ImagePartition(IMAGE,level-1);
    }
    else
    {
        IMAGE_SET[i]=IMAGE;
        IMAGE_SET[i];
    }
}
```

In the algorithm, the Partition function is used to partition the IMAGE into equal-sized partitions, $2^{level-1}$ pieces in each direction.

During the process of browsing, the whole image will not be observed entirely for the constraint of the projection screen resolution. According to the currently viewable region and the resolution of the display, the system chooses the nearest and lower level of resolution image in order to provide a greater visual effect. Then, the system figures out the set of image blocks needed for rendering obeying the currently viewable region. In the example of Fig.3, the viewport is projected to the level of IMAGE_SET[1]. The four image blocks covered by the blue area in the center of that level will be chosen and transferred for rendering.

In addition, we also apply a pre-fetch scheme in our system. The user views the content displayed, while the system pre-fetch the image block around the currently viewable region for moving operation the user may perform next. The adjacent resolution-images blocks back and forth of the corresponding region are also pre-fetched for the potential zooming operation. Recently referenced image blocks may be reused sooner or later due to the spatial and temporal localities. We mark each image block with a tag, in order to utilize LRU replacement policy to decide which block will be swapped out when there are too many blocks in the memory.

Let the load time of each byte be t, the color depth be bpp, the resolution of the whole image be $M \times N$ pixels, and block resolution in all pyramid level $a \times b$. If the whole image is loaded in the memory without any partition, the load time will be $(M \times N \times bpp/8) \times t$. Using our approach, when a display with resolution of $m \times n$ is used, the block number $num\_w \times num\_h$ is in the following interval

$$(num\_w \in \left[\frac{m+a-1}{a}, 1+\frac{(m-1)+(a-1)}{a}\right], num\_h \in \left[\frac{n+b-1}{b}, 1+\frac{(n-1)+(b-1)}{b}\right]),$$ then the load

time will be $(num\_w \times num\_h \times a \times b \times bpp/8) \times t$. It can clearly be seen that our approach is about $(M \times N)/(m \times n)$ times faster than the un-optimized one.

3.4 Gesture Recognition Algorithm

What should be mentioned is that the camera pose should be adjusted to the position in which it can capture the screen with no or little distortion. The rectangle area captured by the camera is named as R, which could be divided into four equal-sized sub areas. The visitor gives leftward and upward instructions with left arm, while the rightward and downward instructions with right arm. The left half of R, including the upper left sub area R_{00} and the lower left sub area R_{10}, takes charge of left arm motion detections. Similarly, the right half area R_{01} and R_{11} take charge of right arm motion detections, as shown in Fig. 4.

The gesture detection and recognition flow chart is illustrated in Fig. 5. After the camera captures the user's motion, we subtract the current image from the previous one. If all of the pixel differences are less than the threshold, it means no motion was detected, otherwise the optical flow is calculated through Lucas and Kanade's method [13]. After optical flow calculation completes, we will get the average pixel moving speed under specified sample rate in both X and Y axes. Then the operation recognition process starts.

The recognition procedure goes as follows. Supposing S is the sampled pixels set, which is equally distributed in R. Each pixel P in S will has the following properties, pixel coordinates (x,y), motion direction vector (u,v) and motion speed s, as the result of optical flow algorithm. Considering each pixel P in S, if the value $P.u$ and $P.v$

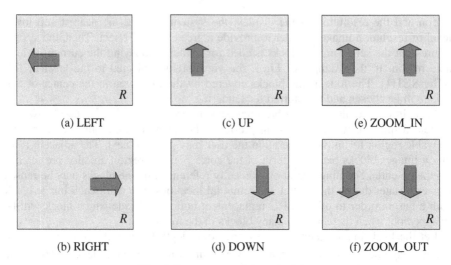

Fig. 4. Gesture recognition principles

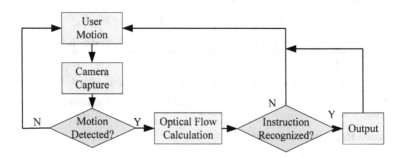

Fig. 5. Gesture detection and recognition process

equal 0, it means no motion happens in that pixel. Those pixels change insignificantly, whose u and v is less than a given threshold value, will be ignored, too. Then the operation recognition algorithm is described as:

```
Operation_Recognize (R,S)
{
   static enum INST c=NULL;
   enum INST ret=NULL;
   float count[2][2], _x=0.001, _y=0.001;
   // set to 0.001, avoid divide by zero
   set_zero(count);
   Divide R as 4 equal-sized sub-rectangles
   {
      R00 as left top one, R01 as right top one,
      R10 as left bottom one and R11 as right bottom one,
   }
   for each pixel P in S
   {
      if (P.u==0 && P.v==0) continue; //no motion in pixel
```

```
for (i=0;i<2;i++) for (j=0;j<2;j++)
{
  if (P is in R_{ij})
    count[i][j]+=1.0;
  _x+=s*P.u; _y+=s*P.v;
}
float r =   (count[0][0]+count[1][0])
          /(count[0][1]+count[1][1]);
float angle = atan(_y/_x);
if (r>5.0 && fabs(angle)<pi/8) ret=LEFT;
if (r>5.0 && fabs(angle)>3*pi/8) ret=UP;
if (r<0.2 && fabs(angle)<pi/8) ret=RIGHT;
if (r<0.2 && fabs(angle)>3*pi/8) ret=DOWN;
if (r>0.2 && r<5.0 && _y>0
    && fabs(angle)>3*pi/8) ret = ZOOM_IN;
if (r>0.2 && r<5.0 && _y<0
    && fabs(angle)>3*pi/8) ret = ZOOM_OUT;
if (c==ret) return NULL;//still previous motion
if (c==ZOOM_IN && ret==ZOOM_OUT)
  return NULL; // ignore backward motion
if (ret==NULL) return c=NULL; // no operation
}
}
```

Let $count[i][j]$ be the number of pixels in sub area R_{ij} which moves significantly, r be the ratio of $count[0][0]$ and $count[1][0]$ to $count[0][1]$ and $count[1][1]$. If r is larger than the threshold, 5.0 for example, it means that only left region has sufficient motions. Then the sum of $p.u$ in the corresponding region is compared to the sum of $p.v$, in order to determine the motion is horizontal movement or a vertical movement.

It's worth mentioning that when the visitor lifts up both arms, indicating ZOOM_IN, he will lay down them later after the gesture finishes. This downward gesture will be ignored so as not to be mistaken as ZOOM_OUT operation.

4   Results and Discussions

On the back wall of 61st grotto of Dunhuang, the mural describes the terrain from Taiyuan, Shanxi to Zhenzhou, Hebei, covering about 250 kilometers neighboring area. In the mural, there are over 100 temples, pagodas and other architectures. The mural also records beautiful sceneries, famous historical relics and ancient customs. Therefore, the mural of Wutai Mountain is the largest mural with historical relics in Dunhuang Mogao Grottoes. The mural image is shown in Fig. 6.

We have acquired the mural of Wutai Mountain with the size (with some boundary areas) of 13.45×3.42 meter, and finally got a 35000×10500 image. Since the image browsed is so large that we use the Gaussian pyramid structure [14] to organize the image blocks of different resolution levels in our system. The system only needs to load the currently viewable portion instead of the whole image, which greatly increases flexibility and avoids occupying too much system memory.

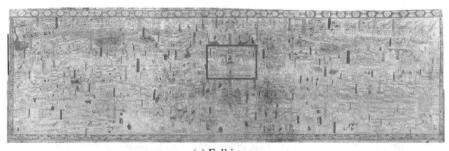

(a) Full image

(b) Sub-image of (a)   (c) Sub-image of (b)

Fig. 6. Mural of Wutai Mountain in the 61st grotto

Fig. 7 (a) is the image captured without the infrared lens, and Fig. 7 (b) is the image captured with the infrared lens, filtering the projected image which will interfere the recognition.

(a) Image without infrared lens   (b) Image with infrared lens

Fig. 7. Comparison of normal and infrared images

When system starts, it captures images frame by frame and detects motion regions by subtracting frames one by one. In Fig. 8, (a) and (b) shows two continuous frame images capture by the camera, and (c) shows the corresponding optical flow image in which the arrow length and direction means the moving speed and direction in that point. The example in Fig. 8 (c) indicates left move operation.

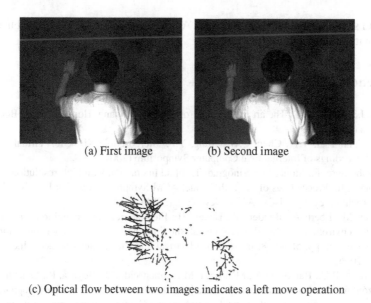

(a) First image   (b) Second image

(c) Optical flow between two images indicates a left move operation

Fig. 8. Optical flow sample

In addition, we introduce some voice explications accompanied with interpretative notes and images into the system, in order to supply more information that might interest visitors. The system also provides visitors with an automatic navigation mode, in which visitors could browse some interesting scenes with multimedia explications continuously in the mural, according to a preset VRML script.

5 Future Work

The continuous response of the same operation is ignored in the current system, which causes a stiff interaction effect. Future works can be done on dealing with the continuous operations. The more the operations are accumulated, the faster the image moves or zooms. In other words, the moving and zooming acceleration will be simulated by the system during interactions.

In the current system, visitors should stand at a fixed position when browsing because of the moving image's relative position limitations. Auto calibration should be adopted in the next version, which can greatly increase the flexibility. In addition, next version will support multi-user interaction in order to take full advantage of those digitized heritage resources and bring users more sense of participation.

A vision-based head tracking system is previously developed, which can greatly help to detect user's gaze directions. Using gaze direction information, the system can easily get user's focus spot in mural image and the spot changes as well, and then take corresponding actions. For example, a left move of focus spot can be interpreted as a right move operation.

Besides Dunhuang murals, we have collected many digitized cultural heritages, such as Dunhuang painted sculptures, unearthed artifacts excavated from Jinsha site,

Liangzhu site and Hemudu site and so on. All these models can be exhibited using the current natural interaction approaches.

References

1. Fan, J.S., Zhao, S.L.: The art of Mogao Grottoes in Dunhuang. Homa & Sekey Books, Paramus (2009)
2. Lo, W.Y., Tsai, Y.P., Chen, C.W., Hung, Y.P.: Stereoscopic Kiosk for Virtual Museum. In: Proceedings of International Computer Symposium (2004)
3. Guimbretiere, F., Stone, M., Winograd, T.: Fluid interaction with high-resolution wall-size displays. In: Proceedings of the 14th Annual ACM Symposium on User Interface Software and Technology, pp. 21–30. ACM, New York (2001)
4. Deller, M., Ebert, A., Bender, M., Hagen, H.: Flexible gesture recognition for immersive virtual environments. In: Proceedings of the International Conference on Information Visualization, pp. 563–568. Institute of Electrical and Electronics Engineers Inc., Piscataway (2006)
5. Mendoza, B.U., Ramos, G.A., Méndez, L.M., Almonacid, F.J., Boyacá, R., Santamaría, W., Pinzón, A.: Camera motion control from a java 3D environment: Virtual studio application in decorative arts museum collections. In: International Conference on Cyberworlds, pp. 58–61. Institute of Electrical and Electronics Engineers Computer Society, Piscataway (2006)
6. Sanneblad, J., Holmquist, L.E.: Ubiquitous Graphics: Combining hand-held and wall-size displays to interact with large images. In: Working Conference on Advanced Visual Interfaces, pp. 373–377. ACM, New York (2006)
7. Nakamura, T., Takahashi, S., Tanaka, J.: Double-crossing: A new interaction technique for hand gesture interfaces. In: Lee, S., Choo, H., Ha, S., Shin, I.C. (eds.) APCHI 2008. LNCS, vol. 5068, pp. 292–300. Springer, Heidelberg (2008)
8. Wienss, C., Nikitin, I., Goebbels, G., Troche, K., Göbel, M., Nikitina, L., Müller, S.: Sceptre: An infrared laser tracking system for virtual environments. In: Proceedings of the ACM Symposium on Virtual Reality Software and Technology, pp. 45–50. ACM, New York (2006)
9. Cao, X., Balakrishnan, R.: VisionWand: Interaction Techniques for Large Displays Using a Passive Wand Tracked in 3D. In: Proceedings of the 16th annual ACM Symposium on User Interface Software and Technology, pp. 173–182. ACM, New York (2003)
10. Stodle, D., Bjorndalen, J.M., Anshus, O.J.: A system for hybrid vision- and sound-based interaction with distal and proximal targets on wall-sized, high-resolution tiled displays. In: Lew, M., Sebe, N., Huang, T.S., Bakker, E.M. (eds.) HCI 2007. LNCS, vol. 4796, pp. 59–68. Springer, Heidelberg (2007)
11. Fukasawa, T., Fukuchi, K., Koike, H.: A vision-based non-contact interactive advertisement with a display wall. In: Harper, R., Rauterberg, M., Combetto, M. (eds.) ICEC 2006. LNCS, vol. 4161, pp. 394–397. Springer, Heidelberg (2006)
12. Stødle, D., Troyanskaya, O., Li, K., Anshus, O.J.: Tech-note: Device-free Interaction spaces. In: Proceedings of IEEE Symposium on 3D User Interfaces. IEEE Comp Soc., Los Alamitos (2009)
13. Lucas, B.D., Kanade, T.: Iterative image registration technique with an application to stereo vision. In: Proceeding of the 7th International Joint Conference on Artificial Intelligence, Vancouver, Canada, pp. 674–679 (1981)
14. Burt, P., Adelson, E.: The Lapacian Pyramid as a Compact Image Code. IEEE Transactions on Communications 31(4), 532–540 (1983)

Research of Autonomous Active Control for Virtual Human Based on Emotion-Driven Model

Fenhua Wang, Xiaodan Huang, and Zhiliang Wang

School of Information Engineering, University of Science and Technology Beijing, 100083
Beijing, China
hxd10243005@sina.com

Abstract. Information science has been widely used in many aspects, such as e-learning, educational games and smart home. In environment above, the study of virtual human can make human-computer interaction more natural. This paper associated emotional decision with virtual human's active control. It can make the virtual human in smart home generate some inner directed behaviors. Meanwhile, it came up with a mode called finding exit to solve the problem that there are a lot of ring-shaped obstacles. This mode improved the basic obstacle-avoiding behaviors. Then with the organic combination of emotion, memory and behavior, the autonomous active controlling system of virtual human in smart home is realized.

Keywords: virtual human; autonomous active control; emotional decision; finding exit mode; obstacle-avoiding behavior.

1 Introduction

Information science plays more and more import roles in our daily life. Technology related to it has influenced on every aspect, for instance, housekeeping, education, and entertainment.

As the concept of lifelong learning now becomes a reality and more and more people are partaking in online courses, researchers are constantly exploring innovative techniques to motivate online students and enhance the e-learning experience [1]. What is the e-learning? E-Learning is the use of telecommunication technology to deliver information for education and training. With the progress of information and communication technology development, e-Learning is emerging as the paradigm of modern education [2]. Over the past decade, the rapid developments and growth of information and communication technology (ICT) in such areas as education and training has offered new paradigms for university training and the topic of electronic learning (e-learning) has deserved careful attention [3]. As a result, the trend of using e-learning as a learning and/or teaching tool is now rapidly expanding into education [4, 5]. So, in a word, this new pedagogy does not reduce the time of training but induces much more active learning, a better comprehension of technology and the possibility for the students to progress at their own rhythm [6, 7].

Z. Pan et al. (Eds.): Transactions on Edutainment III, LNCS 5940, pp. 177–189, 2009.

Moreover, educational games are introduced to learning environments and its use is an increasingly relevant trend [8]. It is a useful tool in promoting learning within the classroom because learning through gaming is one of the natural ways for knowledge and skill acquisition [9, 10]. On this account, it can increase the students' motivation and engagement while they learn [11]. In paper [12], Children learnt fire and street safety through computer games that employed "virtual worlds" to teach recommended safety skills. And learning results suggested that this was a highly effective method.

Why could e-learning and edutainment develop rapidly? They are able to satisfy personal habitual needs better. In paper [13], researchers analyzed the factors of learners' attitudes with e-learning system. And the paper [14]'s point is that Human–computer interaction (HCI) has a key role to play in researching video games. It will be seen that human factor is important. In order to be more user-friendly, many e-learning systems have added virtual teacher. And various virtual roles with personalized feature in game have abstract players' attention. Virtual human has developed quickly in edutainment.

Information science has been widely used in smart home. For virtual human in smart environment, his action controlling will be researched in this paper. Based on an emotional transferring model led to by emotion stimulus[15], a method of driving autonomous action of virtual human by emotional decision is introduced. Furthermore, behavior-based path planning is realized with improved method of artificial potential field. Finally with the organic combination of emotion, memory and behavior, the autonomous active controlling system of virtual human in smart home is realized.

The paper is organized as follows. At first, introduce the autonomous active controlling system of virtual human. Then, describe the principles of emotion-driven mode and improved path planning algorithms based on behavior. Finally, analyze the results of simulations.

2 Autonomous Active Controlling System of Virtual Human

Emotion plays a crucial role in reasoning, learning, remembering, deciding and intelligent behavior [16]. And studies have suggested controlling style of brain is that sensory perception and emotion determine one's action jointly. Correspondingly, researchers begin to focus on the artificial emotion. It is to simulate, recognize and understand the emotion of human being, utilizing theory and technology of information science. Based on this, machines could be of subhuman emotion which brings in harmonious and natural interaction in HCI [17].

With development of the technology, robot comes close to us more and more. Not only simple and repeated service could it provides, but it also have psychological activity, such as emotion, character, will and creativity. Today, researches on endowing robot with ability of emotional interaction become a hotspot [15, 18].Robot doesn't only include physical one, but also contains software one which is named virtual robot. Research on virtual human is still a new area. In this paper, virtual robot is endowed with emotion. And then, it researches how virtual human plan path with emotion-driven model.

HMM emotional transferring model is used as emotional decision model of virtual human in smart home [15]. Emotion is brought into autonomous active controlling. System structure is shown in Figure 1.

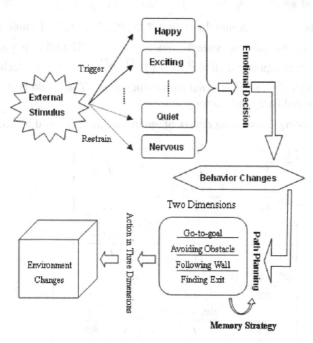

Fig. 1. Autonomous active system of virtual human is shown. When the virtual human is stimulated by external event, one type of emotions is triggered, and the other two are restrained. According to HMM, every dimension of virtual human's emotion changes. After that, utilize the changed values to decide next action of virtual human. Generally speaking, action refers to walking which has an original point and a target point. In this case, path planning is needed. In actuality, human lives in three dimensions, but his path is in two dimensions. So path planning in two dimensions using emotional decision should be got firstly. Then map the path to three dimensions to control virtual human's action.

3   Emotion-Driven Mode

This paper adopts HMM in process of emotional state stimulated transferring proposed in paper [15]. The model is set on probability space of emotional state.

According to psychological theory, with external emotional stimulating event, emotion changes with state. Moreover, there are many aspects of factors influencing on emotion. In summary, they are external stimulating event (type/ intensity), current emotional state and character which could be denoted as $\lambda = \left(N, M, \pi, \hat{A}, B\right)$, where, N is the dimension of emotion, M is the number of stimulating type, π is initial probability of emotion in HMM, $\hat{A}$ is stimulating transferring matrix of emotional state, B is the stimulating matrix.

In the stimulating transferring process of emotional state, emotional state probability is expressed as $P = [p_1, p_2, \cdots, p_N]$ which is decided by one of the probability distributions below. One is initial emotion $\pi = [\pi_1, \pi_2, \cdots, \pi_N]$ which equals to the probability of emotional state spontaneous transferring. The other is probability distribution of current emotional state $P^{(T)} = [p_1^{(T)}, p_2^{(T)}, \cdots, p_N^{(T)}]$ which is related to the type and intensity (T) of external stimulating event. That could be computed with forward vector and backward vector.

$\hat{A}$ is stimulating transferring matrix of emotional state. It could be deduced as:

$$\hat{A} = \begin{bmatrix} \dfrac{\hat{L}_1 - (N-1)}{\hat{L}_1} & \dfrac{1}{\hat{L}_1} & \cdots & \dfrac{1}{\hat{L}_1} \\ \dfrac{1}{\hat{L}_2} & \dfrac{\hat{L}_2 - (N-1)}{\hat{L}_1} & \cdots & \dfrac{1}{\hat{L}_2} \\ \vdots & \vdots & \cdots & \vdots \\ \dfrac{1}{\hat{L}_N} & \dfrac{1}{\hat{L}_1} & \cdots & \dfrac{\hat{L}_N - (N-1)}{\hat{L}_N} \end{bmatrix}$$

$$= \begin{bmatrix} \dfrac{\hat{\theta}\hat{\pi}_1^* - (N-1)}{\hat{\theta}\hat{\pi}_1^*} & \dfrac{1}{\hat{\theta}\hat{\pi}_1^*} & \cdots & \dfrac{1}{\hat{\theta}\hat{\pi}_1^*} \\ \dfrac{1}{\hat{\theta}\hat{\pi}_2^*} & \dfrac{\hat{\theta}\hat{\pi}_2^* - (N-1)}{\hat{\theta}\hat{\pi}_2^*} & \cdots & \dfrac{1}{\hat{\theta}\hat{\pi}_2^*} \\ \vdots & \vdots & \cdots & \vdots \\ \dfrac{1}{\hat{\theta}\hat{\pi}_N^*} & \dfrac{1}{\hat{\theta}\hat{\pi}_N^*} & \cdots & \dfrac{\hat{\theta}\hat{\pi}_N^* - (N-1)}{\hat{\theta}\hat{\pi}_N^*} \end{bmatrix}$$

(1)

Where, $\hat{\theta}$ is a constant and $\hat{\pi}^*$ is the emotional limited probability.

External stimulation is described with observing value, observing matrix and observing sequence. The set of observing value is as same as the set of stimulating event.

$$V = \{V_1, V_2, \ldots, V_M\} = \{1, 2, \cdots, M\},$$
$$V_m = m \quad (m = 1, 2, \cdots, M)$$

(2)

Suppose that observing matrix is stimulating one.

$$\{B(m,i)\}_{M \times N} = \begin{bmatrix} b_1(1) & b_2(1) & \cdots & b_N(1) \\ b_1(2) & b_2(2) & \cdots & b_N(2) \\ \vdots & \vdots & \cdots & \vdots \\ b_1(M) & b_2(M) & \cdots & b_N(M) \end{bmatrix}$$

(3)

Where, $B(V_m) = [b_1(m) \quad b_2(m) \quad \cdots \quad b_N(m)] \ (1 \le m \le M)$ is stimulating vector corresponding with the mth emotional state. And the type of stimulating event could be confirmed with elements of $B(V_m)$. Furthermore, equations could be satisfied.

$$\sum_{m=1}^{M} b_i(m) = 1, \quad (1 \le i \le N) \cdot \tag{4}$$

$$\sum_{i=1}^{N} b_i(m) = 1, \quad (1 \le m \le M) \cdot \tag{5}$$

According to formula below, external stimulating matrix is computed.

$$b_i(j) = \begin{cases} a, & (i = j) \\ b, & (i \ne j) \end{cases} \quad a \ge b \cdot \tag{6}$$

And stimulating matrix is:

$$\{B(m,i)\}_{M \times N} = \begin{bmatrix} a & b & \cdots & b \\ b & a & \cdots & b \\ \vdots & \vdots & \cdots & \vdots \\ b & b & \cdots & a \end{bmatrix} \cdot \tag{7}$$

Suppose stimulating impact factor is:

$$r = \frac{a}{b}, (r > 1) \cdot \tag{8}$$

According to formula (5):

$$a + (N-1)b = 1 \cdot \tag{9}$$

We could deduce that with formula (8, 9):

$$\begin{cases} a = \dfrac{r}{N-1+r}, & r > 1 \cdot \\ b = \dfrac{1}{N-1+r} \end{cases} \tag{10}$$

So, if r is determined, stimulating matrix $\{B(m,i)\}_{M \times N}$ could be got too.

According to W. Wundt's 3D emotional theory, emotion in this paper is thought as being of three dimensions. They are happy-unhappy, exciting-quiet and loose-nervous. Correspondingly, suppose that stimulating event of happy emotion is watching TV, stimulating event of exciting emotion is gaming and stimulating event of loose emotion is sleeping. So, $N = 3$, $M = 3$ is reasonable.

Other parameters used are shown as:

(1) Stimulating parameters:

$r = 1.06, T_{max} = 55, T \in [1, T_{max}]$;

(2) Stimulating transferring matrix $\hat{A}$:

Because $\hat{\pi}^* = \begin{vmatrix} 1/3 & 1/3 & 1/3 \end{vmatrix}, \hat{\theta} = 12$, matrix could be deduced as:

$$\hat{A} = \begin{bmatrix} a_{11} & a_{12} & a_{13} \\ a_{21} & a_{22} & a_{23} \\ a_{31} & a_{32} & a_{33} \end{bmatrix} = \begin{bmatrix} 0.6 & 0.2 & 0.2 \\ 0.2 & 0.6 & 0.2 \\ 0.2 & 0.2 & 0.6 \end{bmatrix};$$

(3) External stimulating matrix:

$$B = \begin{bmatrix} b_1(1) & b_2(1) & b_3(1) \\ b_1(2) & b_2(2) & b_3(2) \\ b_1(3) & b_2(3) & b_3(3) \end{bmatrix} = \begin{bmatrix} 0.5 & 0.3 & 0.2 \\ 0.2 & 0.5 & 0.3 \\ 0.3 & 0.2 & 0.5 \end{bmatrix};$$

(4) Probability distribution of initial emotional state:

$\pi = [0.35681 \quad 0.36104 \quad 0.28215]$;

Based on the model above, emotional decision can be made for the autonomous active controlling system of virtual human.

4   Improved Path Planning Algorithms Based on Behavior

4.1   Basic Path Planning Based on Obstacle-Avoiding Behavior

Robot's path planning is seemed as an important research area in robotics[19]. In terms of environment known fully or partly, path planning is thought as two parts: global or local one, which are also called static or dynamic one. Inspiration from path planning of physical robot, it is brought into the research of virtual human to realize dynamic path planning based on obstacle-avoiding behavior.

Usually speaking, path planning includes three basic actions: going to goal, avoiding obstacle and following wall. For physical robot in practice, when it has avoided obstacle and gone to goal, the mission is completed successfully. However, this paper focuses on virtual human in smart home. So going to goal is not the only task, but how to simulate human being vividly is also needed to be considered. On the scene of virtual smart home, the path planning algorithm based on behavior is improved.

There are many rooms, which are made up of three walls in smart home. That is to say obstacles exist in three directions. For this ring shape, basic path planning based on obstacle-avoiding behavior let virtual human walk along the wall with following wall strategy, when target is in front of obstacle. It is shown in Figure 2.

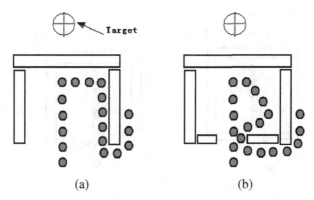

Fig. 2. It is following wall mode. In this mode, obstacles exist in three directions. And virtual human walks along the wall with following wall strategy.

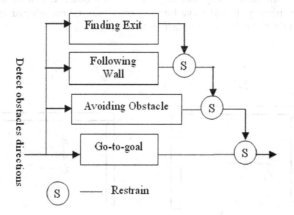

Fig. 3. Improved controlling structure of virtual human's action is shown. There are four levels in this structure with Finding Exit Mode brought in.

However, human being never walks like that in practice. After entering into room and not finding exit to target, he will go out of the room from entrance directly. Based on this view, finding exit mode is brought into the basic algorithm. Controlling structure of action with improvement is shown as Figure 3.

4.2 Finding Exit Mode

The principle of finding exit is shown in Figure 4. Under the control of going to goal and avoiding obstacle mode, the virtual human achieves the position (marked by red circle). At that time the basic obstacle-avoiding behavior will start following wall model. But the moving track does not conform to real men's movement, because people will return to the entrance after finding no way to the target point in front of ring shaped obstacle. Therefore, design a mode called finding exit.

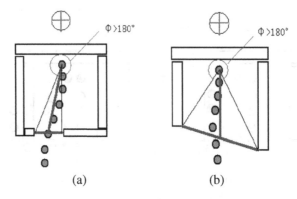

Fig. 4. Principle of finding exit mode is shown above. It connects the two ends of entrance with a line and takes the midpoint as a temporary target point. When the virtual human goes out the line, the program will temporarily store the line as a new obstacle, that is, to give the virtual human a simple memory. It will make him not enter into the ring-shaped region again. The program will not delete the line until he arrives to the target.

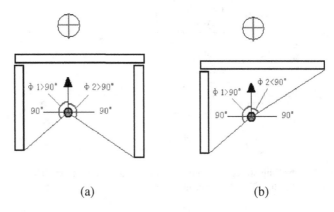

Fig. 5. The case in Figure 5(b) maybe take place, at that time, the sum of angles is greater than 180°. But its surrounding does not have three walls, and $\phi 2$ is less than 90°. So it needs to satisfy the three conditions proposed in formula (11) at the same time. Then enter the finding exit mode and restrain the following wall mode.

Considering current walking direction as front, virtual human detects obstacles towards the left and right. If requirements stated below are satisfied, finding exit mode is triggered.

$$\begin{cases} \phi 1 > 90°, \phi 2 > 90° \\ \phi 1 + \phi 2 > 180° \end{cases} \quad (11)$$

Where, $\phi 1$ is left-hand angle, $\phi 2$ is right-hand angle.

Not only the sum of angles is greater than 180°, but also both of left-hand and right-hand angles should be greater than 90°.

5 Simulation

With improved path planning algorithms based on obstacle-avoiding behavior, simulate virtual human's action driven by emotion.

5.1 Emotional Decision of Virtual Human

The three curved lines shown in Figure 6 represent three types of virtual human's emotion which are given occurrences in Section 3. They are static changing curves of emotion.

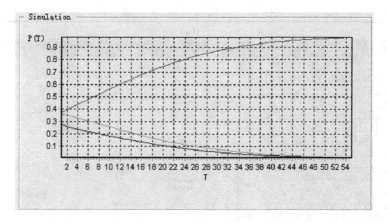

Fig. 6. Emotional simulation experiment results demonstrate that one type of emotions is triggered, while the other two are restrained using HMM in process of emotional state stimulated transferring.

For instance, when gaming action stimulates virtual human, his exciting dimension of emotion begins to increase gradually from an initial value to a high one. At the same time, happy and loose dimensions of emotion go down to a relative low level. Because emotional values in three dimensions change, virtual human's action could alter too. Maybe he would watch TV or go to sleep to turn happy or loose. Correspondingly, virtual human will move among playroom, drawing room and bedroom. We can see continuous emotional variation curve and virtual human's behavior in Figure 7. When the behavior changes, the controlling system will achieves the three-dimensional effects at last. An example was taken in Figure 8.

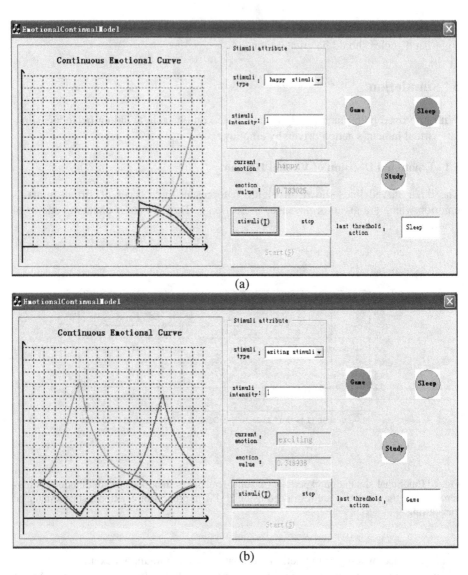

Fig. 7. In figure (a), left part of the figure are dynamic changing curves of emotion. And the right one is the performance of virtual human. The green circle shows that current action is sleep. Sleep makes him happier, which is displayed by the green increasing curve in the left part. After several seconds, curves in figure (a) change to curves in figure (b).Correspondingly, the right part in figure (b) vary too. His current emotion is exciting and his action transfer to game.

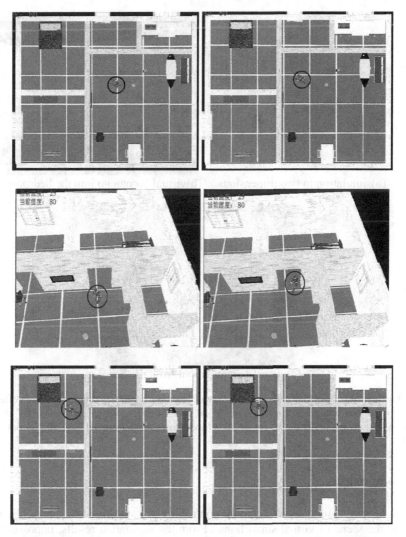

Fig. 8. This is a sequence of 3D frames that virtual human goes from drawing room to bed-room. Four of them are top views and the other two are phantom views from a certain camera angle. Because virtual human's emotion is nervous currently, emotion driven mechanism makes his active state change into sleeping. As a result, he walks into the bedroom.

5.2 Improved Path Planning

Result of improved path planning algorithms based on obstacle-avoiding behavior is shown in Figure 9. Firstly, experiments in two dimensions are done. Virtual human succeeds to going out of the room which is expectable. Then map this situation to environment in three dimensions.

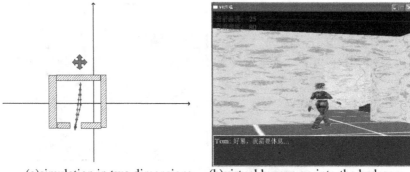

(a)simulation in two dimensions   (b)virtual human go into the bedroom

(c)virtual human go out from the bedroom

Fig. 9. Effect of path planning based on behavior is shown as above. Figure (a) shows effect in 2D with red line which demonstrates path, and with blue star which represents the goal. In addition, Figure (b) (c) is the effect in 3D which shows virtual human goes in and out separately.

6 Conclusions

Virtual human's autonomous behavior controlling system driven by emotion is realized on the scene of virtual smart home. From the simulation results, improved path planning based on obstacle-avoiding behavior makes virtual human walk out of the room in smart home with rapid and human-like behavioral habits. Simultaneously, combine emotional decision with active controlling which enhances realness of virtual human.

Human being is the subject of various society practice activities and the source of various needs. So virtual environment requires research on human being themselves for every kind of industries with virtual reality. That is to say researching on virtual human has practical significance. In recent years, virtual human becomes researching hotspot. And it has been applied in many industries, especially in area of education and game. As time goes on, it is believed that there will be more application with it, which could promote the development of educational industry especially in e-learning with humanization.

Acknowledgments. This work is supported by the High Technology Research and Development Program of China (2007AA01Z160).

References

1. Monahan, T., McArdle, G., Bertolotto, M.: Virtual Reality for Collaborative E-learning. Computers & Education 50, 1339–1353 (2008)
2. Sun, P.C., Tsai, R.J., Finger, G., et al.: What Drives a Successful E-Learning? An Empirical Investigation of the Critical Factors Influencing Learner Satisfaction. Computers & Education 50, 1183–1202 (2008)
3. Wu, J.H., Tennyson, R.D., Hsia, T.L., et al.: Analysis of E-learning Innovation and Core Capability Using a Hypercube Model. Computers in Human Behavior 24, 1851–1866 (2008)
4. Paechter, M., Maier, B., Macher, D.: Students' Expectations of and Experiences in E-learning: Their Relation to Learning Achievements and Course Satisfaction. Computers & Education (2009), doi: 10.1016/j.compedu.2009.08.005
5. Liaw, S.S., Huang, H.M., Chen, G.D.: Surveying Instructor and Learner Attitudes Toward E-learning. Computers & Education 49, 1066–1080 (2007)
6. Schaer, E., Roizard, C., Christmann, N., Lemaitre, A.: Development and Utilization of an E-learning Course on Heat Exchange at ENSIC. Education for Chemical Engineers 1(D0), 82–89 (2006)
7. Paynea, A.M., Stephenson, J.E., Morris, W.B., et al.: The Use of an E-learning Constructivist Solution in Workplace Learning. International Journal of Industrial Ergonomics 39, 548–553 (2009)
8. Pablo, M.G., Daniel, B., Iván, M.O., et al.: Educational Game Design for Online Education. Computers in Human Behavior 24, 2530–2540 (2008)
9. Ricardo, R., Miguel, N., Patricio, C., et al.: Beyond Nintendo: Design and Assessment of Educational Video Games for First and Second Grade Students. Computers & Education 40, 71–94 (2003)
10. Cai, Y.Y., Lu, B.F., Fan, Z.W., et al.: Bio-edutainment: Learning Life Science through X gaming. Computers & Graphics 30, 3–9 (2006)
11. Virvou, M., Katsionis, G.: On the Usability and Likeability of Virtual Reality Games for Education: The Case of VR-ENGAGE. Computers & Education 50, 154–178 (2008)
12. Coles, C.D., Strickland, D.C., Padgett, L., et al.: Games that "work": Using Computer Games to Teach Alcohol-affected Children about Fire and Street Safety. Research in Developmental Disabilities 28, 518–530 (2007)
13. Liaw, S.S., Huang, H.M., Chen, G.D.: An Activity-theoretical Approach to Investigate Learners' Factors Toward E-learning Systems. Computers in Human Behavior 23, 1906–1920 (2007)
14. Pippin, B., James, N., Robert, B.: Video Game Values: Human-computer Interaction and Games. Interacting with Computers 19, 180–195 (2007)
15. Teng, S.D.: Research on Artificial Psychology Model Applied in Personal Robot. Ph.D. Dissertation, University of Science and Technology Beijing (2006)
16. Picard, R.W.: Affective Computing. Cambridge, Mass, London England (1997)
17. Wang, Z.L.: Artificial Psychology–A most Accessible Science Research to Human Brain. Journal of University of Science and Technology Beijing 22(5), 478–481 (2000)
18. Zang, H.D., Liu, S.R.: Autonomous navigation control for mobile robots based on emotion and environment cognition. Control Theory & Applications 25(6), 995–1000 (2008)
19. Liu, Y.: Research of the Key Technologies in Behavior Controlling for 3D Virtual Human. Ph.D. Dissertation, Tianjin University (2003)

An XML-Based Interface Customization Model in Digital Museum

Rui Wang, Chengwei Yang, Jinyu Xu, Chenglei Yang, and Xiangxu Meng

School of Computer Science and Technology, Shandong University, Jinan, 250101, China
sharon_wr@hotmail.com, yangchengwei2006@163.com,
xunjinyu@mail.sdu.edu.cn, {chl_yang,mxx}@sdu.edu.cn

Abstract. In this paper we present a XML-based interface customization model used in the construction of digital museum. Traditional component developing methods pay more attention to the function implementation. Meanwhile the interface and function realization are generally written together. In contrast the system interface is hard to implement and bald. Indeed, users usually want to customize Web interface as they like, namely interface customization. That is they want to realize the Web interface customized and dynamically. The presented model in this paper can achieve the separation of interface and function. The system architecture is composed of three layers, which are presentation layer, operation layer and data layer. In our model we employ XML as the main technology for the system construction. And the configuration process is also depicted in the paper. At the end of the paper, we give some applications of this model: the construction of the Web interfaces of the Archaeological Digital Museum of Shandong University and the Ancient Digital Technologies Museum.

Keywords: XML, Digital Museum, Customization.

1 Introduction

With the development of reusable component technology and software customization, the difficulty of function customization is getting smaller and the interface customization is in reverse. This is because the traditional component development model only concerns about the component function reuse and neglects the reuse [1] of interface design. In the development of software component, the codes of the interface design and function realization are written together, they are closely coupled, which makes the interface configuration, customization and dynamic realization difficult to achieve.

To address this issue a variety of interface customization tools and models have been presented. And at present, the UI interface is quite mature in respect of model design [2]. With the development of web technology, the ability of design is continually to be improved in order to realize and deepen the flexible design and customization of Web applications. The research trend of the model construction is to divide interface design and system function design into two parts, such as Tadeus [3], Teallach [4], MOBI-D, FUSE, Vesuf [5], etc. However, these models are based on the

Z. Pan et al. (Eds.): Transactions on Edutainment III, LNCS 5940, pp. 190–202, 2009.

traditional desktop applications. And there are big differences between Web Graphical User Interface (WUI) which has been widely used with the traditional desktop Graphical User Interface (GUI) [6]. This is mainly caused by the difference of application environment and scope for Web system application. Specifically, on the one hand, Web systems applied in Internet/Intranet, in which there are different hardware, operating system, database, browser and network protocols. On the other hand, Web system uses C/S, B/S mode to expand the scope of the system application on the maximum extent. The user's identity is not clear and the usage is uncertain.

This paper presents a XML-based interface customization model to construct websites of digital museums. It is not only easy to set up the reusable style libraries, in order to facilitate the reuse [7] of knowledge but also can be applied to expand the Web system under a variety of platforms.

Section 2 presents the system architecture. The configuration process is presented in section 3. In section 4 we put forward the application instances of the model. The paper concludes in section 5.

2 System Architecture

The system is composed of three layers, from top to bottom are as follows: presentation layer, operation layer and data layer. Which are shown in figure 1.

2.1 Presentation Layer

The top layer is the presentation layer. This layer is the interface of the system faced to the user, and it is also the interface for the customized operation. It is designed to guide users in accordance with their actual needs or personal habits to achieve the system interface configuration via graphics, forms and command operation.

Therefore, the design of this layer which needs to be considered firstly is the system users. They determine the design requirements and characteristics of this layer. The system is designed for general system administrators and the people who charge for system maintenance. The majority of such users know a number of Web design and maintenance knowledge, but they are not professional. Most of them can not understand the meaning of the expression of structured XML documents. Therefore, the design requirement of this layer is as follows:

(1) Easy to understand: The design of this layer should make users understand the contents of the configuration items and the correspondence of the configuration items with the Web pages clearly. The human-computer interaction (mainly comprise mouse, keyboard and voice for now) is the approach of the visualized graphical configuration items. And after the completion of configuration the user can preview the changes of the configuration pages.

(2) Easy to operate: In order to make the interface configuration easy to operate, there are approaches from three aspects. One is to simplify the operation process. Second is to design humanity interaction operation, which minimize the configuration items via keyboard as possible and improve their operating by mouse. Thirdly, system makes the configuration items modularity, to put together the operations of the same type which make them user-friendly configured.

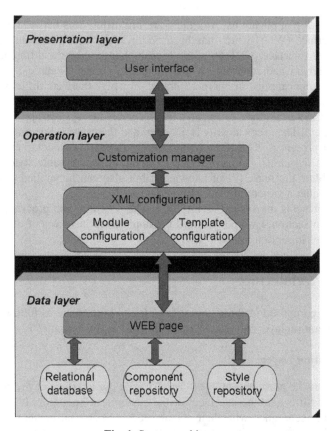

Fig. 1. System architecture

(3) Security and robustness: Web system generally provides the service for login and permission designation, it is easy to add custom users (system administrator and system maintenance staff) for interface configuration. Another thing needs to be considered is that if the custom is not satisfied with the results of the configuration operations, how to restore to a previous configuration state. We store the original configuration in the cache memory created by the SESSION variables. The SESSION memory variables preserve the information which has been initialized by the creator, and it can not be used by the other users. Thus, if the customs are not satisfied with the preview of the effect, they can restore the original configuration. In addition, we should also consider the problem of the collaborative operation on the same XML document when a number of customers access to the system simultaneously. System employs APPLICATION object to create MUTEX which operate the XML documents, and to implement mutual exclusion operation by the principle of "first-come, first operate". The APPLICATION object is different with the SESSION object, it can store the common information to all users. When MUTEX is less than zero, other users can not save the XML configuration file, and the system will prompt the pop-up window prompts to tell the users to wait for their operations. The algorithm to preserve the operation of XML configuration file can be described as follows:

```
function SaveXMLConfig()
{
Create MUTEX  MUTEX=1 (Only permit one user to do
preserve operation at a time);
While (MUTEX<=0) User should wait until the other user
complete the preserve operation of XML configuration
files;
Else modify MUTEX  MUTEX=MUTEX•1, User get the
permission to preserve XML configuration files;
Execute the operation to preserve XML configuration
files;
If  (The preservation operation is successful) modify
MUTEX  MUTEX=MUTEX+1, release resources;
}
```

2.2 Operation Layer

Operation layer is located in the middle of the system architecture which is composed of two parts: the customization manager and XML configuration file. Customs select the target which needed to be operated via WUI interface, through the DOM object to modify XML configuration files. The size of the object to compartmentalize determines the granularity of configuration. The three types of objects defined by XML documents can be manipulated by the customization manager and be described below.

2.2.1 Interface Element Object

It is the most basic unit which can be configured. It is divided into two categories: Container and Controller. Controller is the smallest independent element, it can no longer hold inside any other controller. In reverse, container can not only accommodate controllers but also be nested use or accommodate other containers. The division of the interface element objects as shown in figure 2.

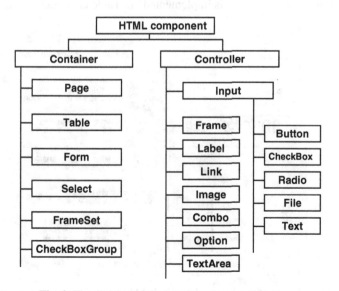

Fig. 2. The division of the interface element objects

The DTD description format of controller is as follows:

```
<!--The definition of image controller-->
<!ELEMENT IMAGE (ATTRIBUTE,INTERACTION)>
<!-- The definition of controller attributes -->
<!ATTLIST IMAGE ID CDTATA #REQUIRED>
<!ELEMENT ATTRIBUTE (WIDTH, HEIGHT•BACKGROUND ,ENABLED,
VISIABLE)>
<!ELEMENT WIDTH (#PCDATA)>
<!ELEMENT HEIGHT (#PCDATA)>
<!ELEMENT BACKGROUND (0|1)>
<!ELEMENT ENABLED (0|1)>
<!ELEMENT VISIABLE(0|1)>
<!-- The definition of controller behavior-->
<!ELEMENT INTERACTION (MOUSE_CONTRAL,KEY_CONTRAL)>
<!—Mouse event-->
<!ELEMENT MOUSE_CONTRAL (EVENT,ACTION)>
<!ELEMENT EVENT(ONMOUSEOVER|ONMOUSEDOWN|ONMOUSEOUT)>
<!ELEMENT ACTION (0|1)>
<!—Keyboard event-->
<!ELEMENT KEY_CONTRAL (EVENT,ACTION)>
<!ELEMENT EVENT(ONKEYDOWN|ONKEYUP)>
<!ELEMENT ACTION (0|1)>
```

2.2.2 Interface Module Object

One characteristic of Web system design is its prominent modularization. Figure 3 is a page of the Archaeology Digital Museum of Shandong University System. It is can be found that the entire page can be divided into eight separate parts: cultural newsletter, virtual scenes, ancient ruins, 3D cultural relics, panorama, renowned collections, as well as the famous archaeologist and archaeological classroom. The characteristics of these modules are independent to occupy a part of the page, they do not interact with each other, and the layout is implemented via Table container.

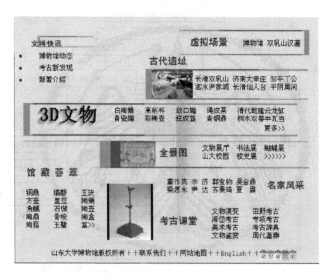

Fig. 3. A page of the Archaeology Digital Museum of Shandong University

We employ the XML + XSL approach to present the stylized module. This approach can be simply described as: firstly, we extract and define the interface elements of page modules via XML; and then define the module's performance style in using XSL; finally with transformNode() function the interface elements and the module's performance style are bind together to display on the Web page. The XML + XSL way can display the same page content as the HTML. At the same time, in order to achieve dynamic and flexible configuration module style to meet the customers' different requirements we employ XML + (n)XSL approach, that is, to define n display manners of XSL to one XML module. These XSL files are stored in the style repository, which can be retrieved repeatedly. The approach is shown in figure 4. The Web page is divided into four parts, which corresponds to the XML description of a <COMPONENT> module, each module corresponds to a set of XSL style descriptions which were stored in the XSL style repository and be unified managed.

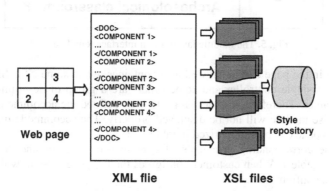

Fig. 4. Interface module configuration

2.2.3 Interface Template Object

Interface template object is the container of module objects, which determines the position of module customization in a Web page. We use figure 3 as an example, its page layout of interface template is shown in figure 5.

There are three key issues of this parts, namely the module ID, module type mapping and accommodation type.

(1) Module ID: Module ID and the XML file correspond to the module data definition block. There is no special requirement to the number manner. In this example we use the top-down and the left-to-right page order to divide the page into eight modules.

(2) Module type mapping: that is, the module is compatible with corresponding XSL style in style repository. The XML + XSL configuration approach separate the data and its presentation. XML files determine the configuration contents of the modules, and XSL files charge for the information display such as the location and size of the elements in module. According to the user's requirements, the system can directly configure interface elements in the module configuration list firstly, and then match the corresponding display style to module in the template configuration page.

(3) Accommodation type: we have classified the interface elements in the section 2.2.1, and divide the general Web elements into two types: controller and container.

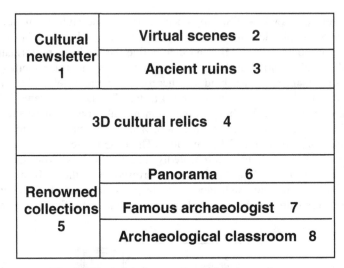

Fig. 5. The module layout of an interface template

Each module in the page can be viewed as a container, while some XSL files are the descriptions of single controller and some others are a group of descriptions in the form of container. Therefore, it is necessary to well-defined the accommodating relations, otherwise module will not be displayed properly. The accommodating relationship in a Web page can be summarized in table 1.

We get the corresponding principals of container-to-container and container-to-elements from table 1. When customer configures the template, system will check the validity of the configuration.

Table 1. Interface elements accommodating relations

Container type	Type to accommodate container	Type to accommodate controller
Page	All permit	All permit
Table	Except page	All permit
Form	Except page, Frameset	All permit
Select	All is not permitted	Only option
Frameset	Except page	Only frame
CheckBoxGroup	All is not permitted	Only checkBox

2.3 Data Layer

Data layer is designed to achieve the separation form of function and display style, the aim is to achieve reusing. Component repositories in this way can be fully concerned about the business implementation, and XML + style repositories only concern about display manner and can implement the dynamically customized services. Relational database is responsible for storing the collected data in the system. The separation form is shown in Figure 6.

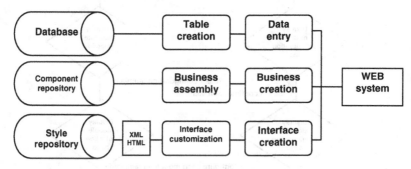

Fig. 6. The structure of data layer

The advantages of this separation are:

(1) Division of users is more explicit. Database designers, system designers, interface designers perform their respective roles. In the pre-design progress the cross interactions are reduced, and from the perspective of their own realization they can well understand the needs of users.

(2) The development efficiency has been greatly enhanced. For the well formed their own reusable repositories, developer and designer can take full advantage of past cases and codes to rapidly complete their development tasks.

(3) The Web system's flexibility has been enhanced. After assembly and customized building, it is a highly modular and structural system, which provides a more flexible approach and the latter system maintenance and evolution.

3 Interface Configuration Process

The process of interface configuration operation is to let users customize the system through the WUI interface according to their needs or habits to modify the Web system. The user's customized contents are achieved through the DOM object to modify XML files and configure different display style files. The configuration system divides user's customized operations to module configuration and template configuration. The configuration process is shown in figure 7.

There are two user customized processes in the figure 7. The configuration module is located on the left, by modifying the XML files this process customizes the display elements in the page modules. The right side of figure 7 is configuration template, the process configures the display content styles of each module in page template, and the styles are from the style repositories, while the data of the style files are from the XML files. Finally, users save their configurations and the Web interface is achieved.

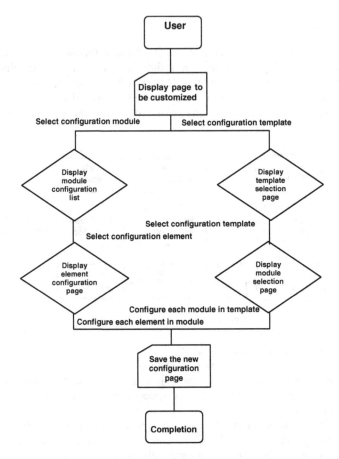

Fig. 7. Interface customized configuration process

4   Application Instances

In this section, we mainly discuss the application of this model: the construction of the Web interfaces of the Archaeological Digital Museum of Shandong University.

4.1   XML-Based Module Mapping

According to the interface customization method, each module should be defined and has been shown in Figure 3.

The XML files of the modules of Cultural newsletter and Archaeological class-room are demonstrated below. The other modules' definitions can also be added to the XML files as needed. The XSL files define the style of the corresponding XML files, which is defined by the label <SD>.

```xml
<?xml version="1.0"?>
<Map>
<!--module's id-->
    <Modules>
        <M id="WTKX"> Cultural newsletter </M>
        <M id="KGKT"> Archaeological classroom </M>
<!--Other module are defined here-->
    </Modules>
<!-- Data used by module content -->
    <XmlData>
            <Data id="data1" refm="WTKX" using="1">
                WTKX.xml
            </Data>
            <Data id="data2" refm="WTKX" using="0">
                KGKT.xml
            </Data>
            <Data id="data3" refm="KGKT" using="1">
                KGKT.xml
            </Data>
            </XmlData>
  <!-- xsl file used by showing the style-->
    <XslData>
            <SD id="sd1" refd="data1" using="0">
                WTKX.xsl
            </SD>
            <SD id="sd2" refd="data1" using="1">
                WTKX1.xsl
            </SD>
            <SD id="sd3" refd="data2" using="0">
                KGKT.xsl
            </SD>
            <SD id="sd4" refd="data2" using="1">
                KGKT1.xsl
            </SD>
            <SD id="sd5" refd="data3" using="0"> </SD>
            <SD id="sd6" refd="data3" using="1"> </SD>
    </XslData>
</Map>
```

4.2 Graphics-Based Customization

XML is one kind formalized language, and it is difficult for general users to understand and use. The graphical interface provides a convenient entry for user to manipulate theses XML files. And it also decreases the errors which happened during the process of directly modifying the XML configuration files. We have developed the graphical interface tools to satisfy the needs of digital museum. At present, these tools include three parts, which are page's display configuration, page's data configuration and page's module configuration. This three graphical configuration interfaces are shown in Figure 8, Figure 9 and Figure 10.

As shown in Figure 11 and Figure 12, we present the application of the presented model. The home pages of the archaeological museum and ancient science and technology museum have been generated as demos. We also create several other pages' templates which are used to generate content pages in the customized development process of digital museum.

Fig. 8. The graphical interface of page's display configuration

Fig. 9. The graphical interface of page's data configuration

Fig. 10. The graphical interface of page's module configuration

Fig. 11. The Web interface of Archaeological Digital Museum of Shandong University

Fig. 12. The Web interface of the Ancient Digital Technologies Museum

5 Conclusion

To fast construction websites of digital museums, we presented a XML-based interface customization model ,which is not only easy to set up the reusable style libraries to facilitate the reuse of knowledge but also can be applied to expand the Web system under a variety of platforms. We use XML technology to separate the function and interface implements. Which make the configuration, customization and dynamic realization of interface easily be implemented. Our system is complete customization which allows the user to choose the style of the interface based on the corresponding XML file. Such a model will become increasingly important as XML will be more and more widely used as a standard means of data representation and communication.

References

1. Ahmed, S., Ashraf, G.: Model-Based User Interface Engineering with Design Patterns. Journal of Systems and Software 80(8), 1408–1422 (2007)
2. Dou, R.L., Wei, X., Zheng, H.: The Architecture Design of J2EE-Based Distributed Cooperative CAD Platform. In: IEEE Symposium on Advanced Management of Information for Globalized Enterprises, pp. 1–5 (2008)
3. Stary, C.: TADEUS: Seamless Development of Task-Based and User-Oriented Interfaces. IEEE Transactions on Systems, Man and Cybernetics, Part A: Systems and Humans 30(5), 509–525 (2000)
4. Griffiths, T., Barclay, P.J., McKirdy, J., Paton, N.W., Gray, P.D., Kennedy, J., Cooper, R., Goble, C.A., West, A., Smyth, M.: Teallach: A Model-Based User Interface Development Environment for Object Databases. In: Proceedings of User Interfaces to Data Intensive Systems, Scotland, pp. 86–96 (1999)

5. Braubach, L., Pokahr, A., Moldt, D., Bartelt, A., Lamersdorf, W.: Tool-Supported Inter-preter-Based User Interface Architecture for Ubiquitous Computing. In: Forbrig, P., Lim-bourg, Q., Urban, B., Vanderdonckt, J. (eds.) DSV-IS 2002. LNCS, vol. 2545, pp. 89–103. Springer, Heidelberg (2002)
6. Schwabe, D., Esmeraldo, L., Rossi, G., Lyardet, F.: Engineering Web Applications for Re-use. IEEE Multimedia 8(1), 20–31 (2001)
7. Montero, F., Lozano, M., Gonzalez, P.: IdealXML: an Experience-Based Environment for User Interface Design and Pattern Manipulation. Technical report, DIAB-05-01-4. Univer-sity of Castilla-La Mancha, Albacete (2005)
8. Zdun, U.: Dynamically Generating Web Application Fragments from Page Templates. In: Proceedings of the 2002 ACM Symposium on Applied Computing, pp. 1113–1120. ACM Press, Madrid (2002)

Animation as an Aid for Higher Education Computing Teaching

Mark Taylor and David Pountney

School of Computing and Mathematical Sciences,
Liverpool John Moores University,
Byrom Street,
Liverpool, L3 3AF, UK
m.j.taylor@ljmu.ac.uk

Abstract. Undergraduate computing courses now cover aspects of computing ranging from the more formal computer science and software engineering, through traditional computer studies and information systems to multimedia courses and more recently specialist areas such as computer games, computer animation and computer forensics. In this paper we examine the potential use of animation for supporting teaching on the range of computing courses currently available within UK higher education. Experiments were conducted with groups of UK undergraduate computing students to compare the perceived usefulness of animated and static learning materials for teaching computing concepts such as diagrammatical design techniques, computer games development techniques and the mathematical techniques underpinning multimedia development. Overall animated learning materials appeared to be perceived as being more useful to undergraduate computing students than traditional static learning materials for learning such concepts.

Keywords: Computing, teaching, animation.

1 Introduction

Undergraduate computing courses typically contain a number of abstract concepts ranging from the mathematical modelling that underpins many computing applications to the approaches commonly used for designing computer based systems such as Data Flow Diagrams (DFDs) that are a technique for modelling the flow of data around a system. For example, Schaefer and Warren [1] commented that developing a computer game is a useful activity for educating computing students about geometric modelling and computer graphics. However, as Callan [2] commented "when you mention mathematics to many computing students their eyes glaze over, their head drops and they eagerly wait for the discussion to end". Modern computer games may often involve the use of relatively complex mathematical modelling, especially in computer games that include collisions between objects and the motion of projectiles. Such mathematical modelling is also applied to 'real world' applications such as military and aerospace systems in the software engineering field.

Z. Pan et al. (Eds.): Transactions on Edutainment III, LNCS 5940, pp. 203–218, 2009.

Two fundamental mathematical concepts that might be used in a variety of software applications that model motion are: **vectors** which are used to represent points in space such as the locations of objects, or the vertices of a triangle mesh in a computer game object; and **matrices** which are used to transform vectors by scaling, rotation or reflection [3]. However, typical traditional teaching approaches for such concepts may not make them particularly accessible to non-maths specialists. For example, a standard undergraduate mathematics text book might describe a vector as "an entity specified by magnitude and direction" and a matrix as "a rectangular array of numbers" [4], [5], and might show simple diagrams to represent them graphically. However, demonstrating their function and purpose visually by showing how a matrix can transform a vector (or a two dimensional computer game object composed of vectors) using animation makes it possible to provide students with a visual perspective of such computing concepts.

The animated learning materials (and their equivalent static versions) used in the research reported in this paper covered matrix addition, subtraction and multiplication, and rotational symmetry; the nature and application of vectors, matrices and rendering computer game development activities; and data flow diagrams [6] (as an example of commonly used commercial systems design approaches). The software development tool used to create the animations (and their equivalent static versions) described in this paper was Macromedia Flash [7], [8]. Brisbourne et al [9] commented that Flash movies are more technically efficient and easier to produce than animated GIFs and QuickTime movies for teaching purposes.

In this paper we examine whether the appropriate use of animated learning materials may potentially aid in supporting the teaching of abstract computing concepts to undergraduate computing students. In particular, the research reported in this paper aimed to examine if animated learning materials can help students to visualize what mathematical computing notation actually means; what actually happens when a computing process or procedure is followed; and how models (mathematical and more generally system design models) are actually applied in practice. In this manner, computing students will be aided in understanding the abstract computing concepts involved, and will hopefully be assisted in applying such concepts to solving problems for themselves. The outcomes of this approach should be improved teaching and learning materials. This paper is based upon an analysis and interpretation of the results reported in the following papers: [10], [11], and [12].

2 Literature Review

Tversky at al [13] and Byrne et al [14] stated that the use of pictures and visualizations as educational aids has become accepted practice. However, while static visualizations can provide a student with the essence of how something is laid out, or is constituted, animation appears better able to explain a dynamic, evolving process. Animation can be defined as the rapid display of a sequence of images in order to create an illusion of movement. Animation produces an optical illusion of motion due to the phenomenon of persistence of vision. Animation can potentially be applied to any learning activity where the subject matter to be studied can be represented in image form. Khalil et al [15] reported that in a study conducted with medical students, the participating students viewed animation as a better approach to learning when compared to static imagery. Animations may aid learners in constructing a mental model of various "processes" such as mechanical or mathematical systems. Stoffa [16] advocated the use of animation for teaching mathematical modelling, especially in topics such as probability. McGrath and Brown [17] outlined the benefits of using animation for teaching across a range of science, engineering and technology subjects including chemistry, biology, physics, mathematics, engineering and geology.

Mayer [18] and Michas and Berry [19] commented that the purpose of multimedia learning is that students can learn more deeply from well-designed multimedia messages consisting of words and pictures than from the more traditional modes of communication involving words alone. Brisbourne et al [9] stated that animations can be used to provide information that aids in understanding dynamic processes and summarizing major concepts, and can help students to construct mental models with which to organize new knowledge. In this context mental modelling is the process of constructing a framework with which to organize new knowledge and apply that knowledge to problem solving [20]. Philpot et al [21] commented that animations can be used to convey to students the broad context of mathematical processes, as well as the details of calculations.

James-Gordon and Bal [22] commented that some learners absorb information more effectively from pictures and films, whereas other learners learn best from written explanations. Mathewson [23] argued that visual-spatial thinking was an aspect of science overlooked by most educators. Visual-spatial learning in current education practice appears to be subservient to the dominant alpha-numeric encoding skills encouraged in lectures and text books. Guimaraes et al [24] commented that some students prefer to treat a given mathematical problem 'by analysis', others 'by geometry'. The first are incapable of 'seeing in space', the others are quickly tired of long calculations and become perplexed. Since the skills are complimentary to each other, there should be some effort by educators to ensure a harmonious development of their students.

It is important to determine appropriate formats for animations to be used for teaching purposes. Mayer [25] and Paivio [26] supported a dual-coding learning theory that involves verbal and visual stimuli working together cognitively to enhance understanding. They argued that multiple representations of a problem help learners understand new concepts and build connections among the representations. However, as Leishman [27] commented the issue of visualizing and developing an interesting animated on-screen display is a substantial task. Albalooshi and Alkhalifa [28] and Koschke [29] stated that some learners appear to be more "spatially oriented" (preferring pictorial and animated learning materials) whilst other learners appear to be more "verbally oriented" (preferring textual learning materials). Mayer and Moreno [30] argued that animation and corresponding narration should be displayed simultaneously rather than successively (temporal contiguity), should be present near to each other on screen (spatial contiguity) to enable effective multimedia learning. Philpot et al [20] suggested that when animations are used for teaching purposes, the animations should be of small scope. Lowe [31] suggested that the complexity of animations used for teaching purposes should be fairly basic so that students are not overwhelmed. Tversky et al [13] argued that in some situations multiple discrete diagrams may be advantageous over animations as they can allow comparison and re-inspection of the details of the actions. By contrast animations are fleeting, they disappear, and when they can be re-inspected they usually are re-inspected in motion, where it may be difficult to perceive all the minute changes simultaneously. Tall [32] provides examples of static images used for visualizing mathematical concepts before animation was practical for educational use.

Faraday and Sutcliffe [33] argued that for animation to be an effective teaching tool, it must be used to draw learners' attention to appropriate features of the presentation. Rieber [34] commented that animation should be incorporated into learning activities only when its attributes are congruent to the learning task. Tversky et al [13] stated that inappropriate animations may be distracting or even harmful to conveying important ideas. Passerini and Granger [35] argued that no extra learning effects are attributable to the use of animation, but did acknowledge that animation contributes to gathering attention. Albalooshi and Alkhalifa [27] commented that from previous research there appears to be difficulty in determining whether animation is more effective than verbal / pictorial representation or vice versa. Large et al [36] commented that ambitious educational claims are often made for multimedia learning approaches, but there is generally little empirical evidence for their justification.

Overall it appears that there is not necessarily a consensus view among educational researchers as to the benefits of animation for supporting teaching and learning activities. In particular there appears to be little if any research regarding the use of animation rather than just visualization software (such as graph plotting software packages [23] for supporting computing teaching and learning at undergraduate level). The originality of the research reported in this paper concerns the examination by means of controlled experimentation of the potential usefulness of animated learning materials compared to traditional static learning materials, for supporting the teaching of a range of computing concepts.

3   Methodology

The research method used for the research reported in this paper was experimentation. The rationale for the choice of experiments conducted and their relationship to one another was as follows: within the university computing department studied, the authors interviewed a number of teaching staff to determine those academic areas where there had been over a period of time an identified pattern of student under achievement. The areas identified by staff were then compared to the actual student performance in examinations and courseworks. The areas identified by the teaching staff did indeed show a pattern of lower than average student marks. The areas identified were mathematics, mathematics for computer games and dataflow diagrams within the computing modules delivered within the computing department studied. The rationale for the choice of experiments was therefore the academic topics where the students within the department showed the weakest performance.

In addition within the department studied, there were a significant number of students with dyslexia. These students typically achieved slightly lower grades than their non-dyslexic counterparts. The difficulties of the students with dyslexia were known to the special educational needs co-coordinator within the department studied. Analysis of the marks for the students with dyslexia showed that of the three areas already identified as generally displaying weaker performance by students within the department, the dataflow diagram marks were lower for the dyslexic group.

Three groups of 32, 30 and 26 undergraduate computing students were chosen from the student population within a UK computing department. The first group viewed animated and static learning materials relating to the mathematics underpinning multimedia development, the second group viewed similar materials relating to computer games development techniques, and the third group viewed similar materials relating to diagrammatical design techniques (data flow diagrams).

The rationale for the design of the experiments was as follows: animation had not been used for teaching purposes in the department studied previously. The classes where mathematics, mathematics for computer games and dataflow diagrams were taught were not particularly large. For these reasons it was felt by the authors that it would be more appropriate to conduct experiments that that measured the students' perception of the usefulness of the animations (in order to determine if animations would be useful and appropriate for supporting teaching in those areas in the future) rather than attempt to assess students' performance pre and post experiment, or have two groups being taught differently given the small class sizes. It would have been difficult to analyze in a meaningful statistical manner the results of student performance given the small group numbers.

Half of each group of students viewed the animated version of the learning material for a given topic to be taught, then the static version, and so on through the set of topics. The other half of each group viewed the static version of a given topic and then the animated version, and so on through the set of topics. This approach aimed to remove any bias due to viewing either the animated or static material for a given topic first.

Tversky et al [13] stated that lack of comparability of static and animated diagrams can cloud any conclusions concerning the benefit of animation for learning and teaching purposes. In order to investigate if animation itself assists learning, animated graphics must be compared to informationally equivalent static graphics. Only in this manner can the contributions of animation be separated from the contributions of graphics alone without confounding with content. In order to assess the usefulness of animation for supporting undergraduate computing teaching and learning activities, the animated version of the material for a given topic was presented along with an informationally equivalent static version of the material. By informationally equivalent was meant that all the 'information' in terms of text, numbers, symbols, lines and shapes that was displayed during the animation was present in the static version. Both the animated and static versions of the given topics were displayed to the student participants in the experiments for the same length of time. The animated and static versions of the topics presented were displayed to the student participants using the Blackboard [37] system in use at the university where the experiments were conducted. The animated learning materials presented to the student participants allowed no user interaction other than starting the animation. The reason for this approach was to assess the usefulness of animation for supporting computing teaching and learning, rather than having any results clouded by competing aspects of animation and interaction [13]. The animations developed included no audio component, and were informationally equivalent to the static versions of the material for each topic. This meant that all the information present in the animation was present in the static version and vice versa. The only difference was that the animations showed the material appearing over a period of time, or moving over a period of time, compared to the static versions that showed all the information at once.

When designing the animations, the authors consulted the staff who taught the areas identified for the experiments (mathematics, mathematics for computer games, and dataflow diagrams) and undertook a literature review of the design of animations for teaching purposes. The staff teaching the areas identified stated that the students typically found difficulty in matching the visual elements with the textual elements in these areas. For example, in the mathematics for computer games area, some students could fairly easily manipulate matrices on paper, but found difficulty visualizing what the result of a matrix manipulation was in terms of computer games objects. Some students found the visual aspects of rotation and enlargement straightforward, but found the written notation for matrices and vectors confusing. Similarly with regard to dataflow diagrams, some students could fairly easily understand how to textually identify the elements of a dataflow diagram, but drew such diagrams poorly. Other students could understand the visual layout of the diagrams, but found difficulty in analyzing text in order to generate the elements of the diagrams.

Based upon the above analysis the authors identified that a dual coding approach, that is one that displays both the textual and visual aspects simultaneously, would be an appropriate basis for the design of the animations. This approach was also advocated by researchers from the literature review [25], [26].

The aim of the first set of animated and static learning materials was ultimately to examine if animated learning materials could be useful for supporting the teaching of mathematical concepts and processes used in computing applications, and in particular if they could benefit the teaching of mathematical concepts and processes involving the use of visio-spatial abilities. The first set of animated and static learning materials attempted to examine the students' perceptions regarding the usefulness of the animations in assisting the visualization of such mathematical concepts and processes. Matrix addition and multiplication and rotational symmetry were the topics chosen for the animated and static learning materials because they are all mathematical topics that require a degree of visio-spatial ability. Rotational symmetry can potentially appear confusing because it requires the ability to mentally picture a given shape in different positions. Matrix addition and multiplication require the ability to mentally join certain elements of one matrix with the relevant elements in another matrix.

The topics for the second set of animated and static learning materials presented to the student participants were vectors, rendering and matrices. The vectors and rendering topics were chosen because these are fundamental to the manner in which computer game objects are defined in terms of computer game programming [38]. The topic of matrices, and in particular matrix manipulation of computer game objects defined by vectors, was chosen since this is necessary to understand how computer game objects can be manipulated (for example, rotated or enlarged) in mathematically based programming. In addition, animations concerning these topics can also potentially allow students to visualize how computer game objects are generated and manipulated, and how these activities relate to mathematically based computer programming concepts.

The aim of the third set of animated and static learning materials was to ascertain if by animating the text and the construction of Data Flow Diagrams it might assist textual analysis and diagrammatical construction activities by undergraduate computing students. Data Flow Diagrams are a diagrammatical technique used for systems analysis and design and are commonly taught to undergraduate computing students in the UK. This topic was chosen since Data Flow Diagrams are typically constructed from an analysis of a written scenario or case study. In essence, a passage of written text is analyzed and then represented in a standardised diagrammatical format using rectangles, ellipses and arrows along with text labels.

The aim of the experiments reported in this paper was to undertake an investigation of the perceived usefulness of animation as a teaching and learning aid rather than attempting to measure in some manner the actual effect of the animation in terms of increased knowledge or abilities of the student participants.

The experiments reported in this paper were conducted in controlled conditions. In particular, the same room with the same lighting was used for the experiments, the experiments were conducted with minimal background noise, and uniform display of materials was used (similar computer screens with the same resolution, window sizes, and brightness).

The three groups of undergraduate computing student participants were presented with a questionnaire after they had viewed both the animated and static versions of the learning materials. For the group that viewed the materials relating to the mathematics underpinning multimedia development, the questions presented had a ten-point Likert scale answer that went from Static version more useful (1) to Animated version more useful (10).

The questions presented to this group of undergraduate student participants were as follows [10]:

How did the static and animated versions compare with regard to:

- the overall concepts being presented (e.g. order of rotational symmetry)?
- the elements of the concepts presented (e.g. what is a matrix?, what is matrix multiplication?)
- how the elements of the concepts are interrelated (e.g. why some matrices can be multiplied together and some cannot)?
- the mathematical symbols used (e.g. the symbol for a matrix)?
- how useful was the material on rotational symmetry?
- how useful was the material on matrix addition?
- how useful was the material on matrix multiplication ?
- your speed of understanding the concepts?

The group of student participants who viewed the learning materials relating to computer games development techniques were presented with a similar questionnaire. The questions on the questionnaire were as follows [12]:

How did the static and animated versions compare with regard to:

- the overall concepts presented (e.g. how a rotation matrix is applied to the vectors constituting a two-dimensional computer game object)?
- how the concepts presented are applied in actual computer game development (e.g. rotating a two-dimensional game object)?
- your understanding of vectors?

- your understanding of matrices?
- your understanding of rendering?
- how the elements of the concepts presented are interrelated (e.g. how a computer game object defined by vectors is transformed by a matrix)?
- the mathematical symbols used (e.g. the mathematical symbols for a matrix and a vector)?
- the overall speed of understanding?

The participating undergraduate students who viewed the materials relating to diagrammatical design techniques (data flow diagrams) were given a similar questionnaire containing the following questions [11]:

How well compared to each other did the static and animated versions assist your understanding of the following?

- The overall concept presented (Data Flow Diagrams).
- The concept of a process within a Data Flow Diagram.
- The concept of a data flow within a Data Flow Diagram.
- The concept of a data store within a Data Flow Diagram.
- The concept of levelling of Data Flow Diagrams.
- How the elements of the overall concept interact, for example data flows move between external entities, processes and data stores.
- How the concept is applied in actual practice, for example creating a Data Flow Diagram for a transaction.
- The different symbols used and the diagrams produced using the symbols, for example arrows for data flows.
- How well compared to each other did the static and animated versions assist your speed of understanding the concepts.

4   Animation Design

Examples of the actual animations used to assess the usefulness of animation for supporting the teaching of computing concepts are depicted in Figures 1 to 6, which show the informationally equivalent static versions of the learning materials presented to the undergraduate student participants.

Figure 1, [10], depicts the animation used to present the concept of matrix addition for two 2 X 2 matrices. In animation 1, the number values of the corresponding elements of the two matrices are superimposed on the appropriate elements in order (that is first row and first column in each matrix and so on). The two numbers then move across the screen to be positioned in the appropriate position of an answer matrix. An addition sign then appears between the two numbers, and the final answer value then appears in the relevant position in a final answer matrix. This process is repeated for each of the corresponding elements in the two matrices. This was done in order to assist students in visualizing the process of matrix addition, and to encourage them to perform matrix addition in an organized and systematic manner (that is first, row first column, then first row, second column etc) as a means of avoiding simple arithmetic errors in the process.

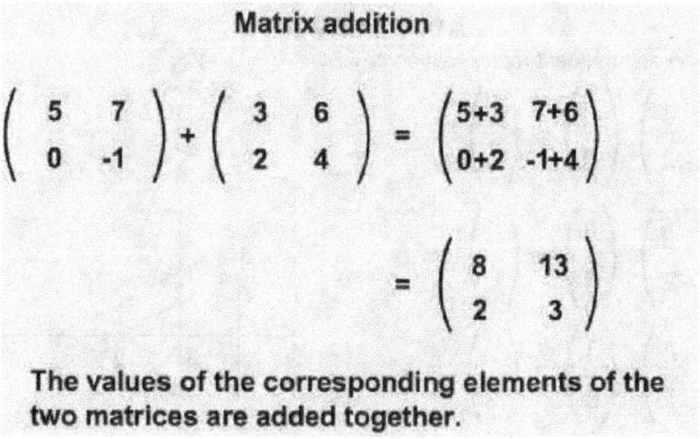

Matrix addition

$$\begin{pmatrix} 5 & 7 \\ 0 & -1 \end{pmatrix} + \begin{pmatrix} 3 & 6 \\ 2 & 4 \end{pmatrix} = \begin{pmatrix} 5+3 & 7+6 \\ 0+2 & -1+4 \end{pmatrix}$$

$$= \begin{pmatrix} 8 & 13 \\ 2 & 3 \end{pmatrix}$$

The values of the corresponding elements of the two matrices are added together.

Fig. 1. Animation for the addition of two 2X2 matrices [10]

Figure 2, [10], depicts the animation used to present the concept of matrix multiplication for a 2 X 2 matrix with a 2 X 2 matrix.

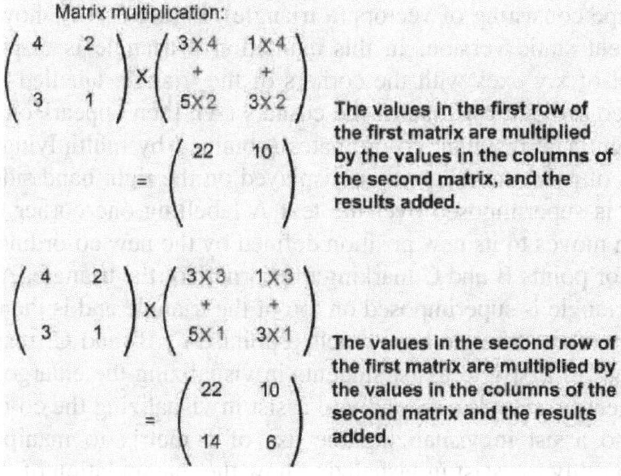

Matrix multiplication:

$$\begin{pmatrix} 4 & 2 \\ 3 & 1 \end{pmatrix} \times \begin{pmatrix} 3\times4 & 1\times4 \\ + & + \\ 5\times2 & 3\times2 \end{pmatrix}$$

$$= \begin{pmatrix} 22 & 10 \\ & \end{pmatrix}$$

The values in the first row of the first matrix are multiplied by the values in the columns of the second matrix, and the results added.

$$\begin{pmatrix} 4 & 2 \\ 3 & 1 \end{pmatrix} \times \begin{pmatrix} 3\times3 & 1\times3 \\ + & + \\ 5\times1 & 3\times1 \end{pmatrix}$$

$$= \begin{pmatrix} 22 & 10 \\ 14 & 6 \end{pmatrix}$$

The values in the second row of the first matrix are multiplied by the values in the columns of the second matrix and the results added.

Fig. 2. Animation for the multiplication of two 2X2 matrices [10]

During animation 2, the number values in the rows of the first matrix are superimposed on the appropriate elements of the matrix, and then move to position themselves alongside the appropriate number values in the columns of the second matrix. This is done in order, that is the first row moves to the first column, then the first row moves to the second column and so forth. When the values of the rows of the first matrix are positioned by the values of the columns in the second matrix a multiplication sign appears between each of the two relevant values, and an addition sign appears between each of these calculations. An answer value then appears in the appropriate position within an answer matrix. This was done in order to assist students in visualizing the process of matrix manipulation, and to encourage students to develop visio-spatial abilities to enable them to approach matrix multiplication in an organized and systematic manner.

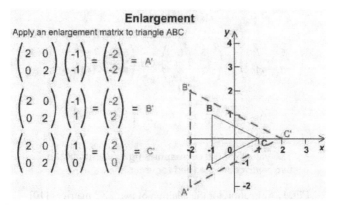

Fig. 3. Animation for illustrating how a matrix can be used to enlarge a simple 2D shape consisting of vectors [12]

The third animation depicted how a matrix can be used to enlarge a simple two-dimensional shape consisting of vectors (a triangle). Figure 3 [12] shows the informationally equivalent static version. In this animation a triangle is displayed superimposed over a set of x,y axes with the corners of the triangle labelled A, B and C. A matrix and the co-ordinates of one of the corners (A), then appears on the right hand side of the screen. The resultant co-ordinates (obtained by multiplying the matrix by the co-ordinates of point A) A' are then displayed on the right hand side of the screen and the text A' is superimposed over the text A labelling one corner of the triangle. The text A' then moves to its new position defined by the new co-ordinates. This process is repeated for points B and C marking the corners of the triangle. A dotted outline of the original triangle is superimposed on top of the triangle and is then enlarged until the three corners of the triangle have reached points A', B' and C' respectively. This was done in order to firstly to assist students in visualizing the enlargement of a two-dimensional object (a triangle), secondly to assist in visualizing the co-ordinates of the object, thirdly to assist in visualizing the use of a matrix to manipulate such co-ordinates and fourthly to assist in visualizing how the manipulation of the co-ordinates results in the transformation of the object (in this case enlargement).

The fourth animation shows how a matrix can be used to rotate a simple two-dimensional shape consisting of vectors (a triangle). Figure 4 [12] shows the informationally equivalent static version. In animation 4, the process is similar to animation 3, except that this time the matrix effects the rotation of a triangle 90 degrees anti-clockwise about the origin.

Animation 5 presented an overview of the symbols and terminology used in Data Flow Diagrams. Figure 5 [11] shows the informationally equivalent static version of the animation. During animation 5 a textual description of an external entity, a dataflow, a process, a further dataflow and a data store appear in turn down the left hand side of the screen. As each of these appear a corresponding image of the symbol for an external entity etc. appears on the right hand side of the screen. This was done in order for students to mentally associate the word representing each of the elements of a Data Flow Diagram with its pictorial representation, and also to encourage students to visualize how the textual and pictorial aspects of a dataflow diagram fit together.

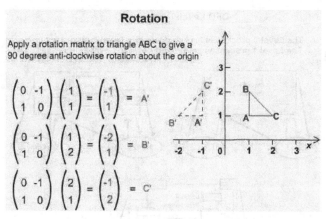

Fig. 4. Animation for illustrating how a matrix can be used to rotate a simple 2D shape consisting of vectors [12]

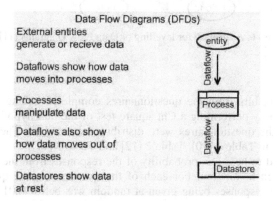

Fig. 5. Animation for the overview of the symbols and terminology used in Data Flow Diagrams [11]

For example, to visualize that a dataflow moves between an external entity and a process (or vice versa) or between a process and a data store.

Animation 6 presented the concept of levelling in Data Flow Diagrams. Levelling shows how a process is broken down into 'levels' of sub-processes. Figure 6, [11], shows the informationally equivalent static version containing three separate images of the same Data Flow Diagram at different levels of detail. In animation 6, the large rectangle that represents the level 0 process fades out to be replaced by a dotted outline, within which a number of smaller rectangles appear representing the level 1 processes. Then these smaller rectangles fade out to be replaced by dotted outlines within which a number of even smaller rectangles appear representing the level 2 processes that comprise each level 1 process. This was done in order to assist students in visualizing how the overall level 0 process is broken down into a number of more detailed level 1 processes and how each of these may be broken down into yet more detailed level 2 processes.

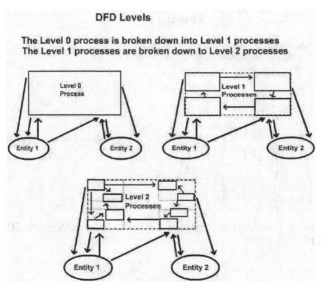

Fig. 6. Animation for levelling of Data Flow Diagrams [11]

5 Results

Analysis of the results from the questionnaires completed by the participants was firstly undertaken by performing a Chi square test of the null hypothesis that the answers given on the questionnaires were distributed at random. The Chi square test results are shown in Table 1 [10], Table 2 [12] and Table 3 [11].

There appeared to be a low probability of the responses from the students participating being given at random. For each of the questions in the questionnaire, the probability of the responses being given at random was below 0.01 in nearly all the cases. Given that the responses provided by the students participating appeared not to be random, analysis of the responses could then meaningfully be undertaken in order to attempt to discover any consensus views of the participating students.

Table 1. Chi square test for the mathematics animations [10]

Questions	Mean	Chi square	P
Comparison with regard to:			
Overall concepts	8.44	81.75	<0.001
Elements of concepts	8.53	56.13	<0.001
Interrelation of elements of concepts	7.81	40.45	<0.001
Mathematical symbols	6.97	29.25	<0.001
Rotational symmetry	8.53	71.13	<0.001
Matrix addition	8.59	45.16	<0.001
Matrix multiplication	8.72	49.25	<0.001
Speed of understanding concepts	8.66	59.63	<0.001

Table 2. Chi square test for the computer games development animations [12]

Questions	Mean	Chi-square	P
Overall concepts presented	6.73	24	<0.01
How concepts presented are applied in computer game development	6.97	24	<0.01
Understanding of vectors	6.77	22	<0.01
Understanding of matrices	7.00	27.33	<0.01
Understanding of rendering	6.97	22.66	<0.01
Interrelation of elements of concepts presented	6.97	39.28	<0.001
Mathematical symbols used	6.23	10.66	0.30
Overall speed of understanding	6.60	18	<0.05

Overall the mean responses provided by the participating students appeared to indicate that they viewed the animated versions of the different learning materials as being more useful than the equivalent static versions. The mean responses ranged from 6.15 to 8.72 on a scale of 1 = static version more useful to 10 = animated version more useful.

The participating students appeared to consider the animated learning materials capable of speeding up their understanding of the computing concepts presented compared to the static counterparts. This was rated by the student participants as one of the more positive aspects of the animated learning materials with mean scores of 8.66, 6.60, and 7.23 for the three sets of learning materials, with 10 being animations more useful and 1 being static versions more useful.

Table 3. Chi square test for the data flow diagram animations [11]

Questions	Mean Score Dyslexic students	Mean Score Non-dyslexic students	Chi square	P
Understanding the overall concept (DFDs)	7.23	8.23	38.61	<0.001
Understanding the concept of a process within a DFD	6.69	7.92	21.69	<0.01
Understanding the concept of a data flow within a DFD	7.00	8.46	31.69	<0.001
Understanding the concept of a data store within a DFD	6.92	8.00	23.23	<0.01
Understanding the concept of levelling of DFDs	6.77	7.69	23.23	<0.01
Understanding the interactions between the elements of a DFD	7.46	8.08	20.15	<0.05
Understanding how DFDs are applied in actual practice	7.62	8.08	29.38	<0.001
Understanding the symbols used in a DFD	6.15	8.31	34.00	<0.001
Speed of understanding a concept	7.23	8.38	26.31	<0.01

The responses were on a scale of 1 = Static version more useful to 10 = Animated version more useful.

The animations covering the different topics within each group of learning materials appeared to be roughly equal in terms of their perceived usefulness compared to the static equivalents. Animation controls were not used in order to assess the usefulness of the animation alone, rather than the combined effect of animation and interaction.

The weakest aspect of the perceived usefulness of the animated versions of the learning materials over the static versions was in terms of mathematical symbols and dataflow diagram symbols. These were given mean scores of 6.97, 6.23 and 6.15 in the experiments.

The third set of animated and static learning materials that were viewed by two sub-groups of dyslexic and non-dyslexic computing students appeared to indicate that animated learning materials can be useful for students with dyslexia, however the students with dyslexia still appeared to find such materials less useful than their non-dyslexic counterparts. On average, the perceived usefulness of the animations for the non-dyslexic students was 16% higher than for the students with dyslexia. The difference in perceived usefulness between the two groups varied from 6% (with regard to how DFDs are applied in practice) to 35% (with regard to understanding the symbols used in a DFD).

Overall, the animated learning materials appeared to be more useful for teaching mathematical concepts (average score 8.28) than computer systems design concepts (average score 7.57) than computer games development concepts (average score 6.78).

6 Conclusions

The results of the experiments reported in this paper appeared to indicate that animated learning materials may be more useful to undergraduate computing students than equivalent static learning materials for the teaching of a range of computing topics. Animated learning materials for mathematical modelling techniques such as matrix addition and multiplication that involve the use of visio-spatial abilities were perceived as being on average 33% more useful than equivalent static materials. Animated learning materials for vectors, matrices and rendering in computer games development appeared on average to be 18% more useful than equivalent static materials, and animated learning materials for systems design techniques such as dataflow diagrams on average 26% more useful.

It would appear from the results reported previously that animation can potentially be a useful teaching aid for undergraduate computing teaching from the student perception of such. In particular, for teaching more abstract concepts with which some computing students may struggle. However, there is a need to ensure that the animations provide something useful with regard to the learning task. As indicated in the results with regard to the understanding of mathematical and diagrammatical symbols, animated learning materials may have little to offer, if a simple diagram can be equally effective in teaching terms. Overall, the animated learning materials appeared to be more useful for presenting a "visual demonstration" of a computing procedure or process.

The perceived added value of the animations based upon analysis of the results was that they can show how a process or sequence of actions develops, for example the high scores of 8.59 and 8.72 for the processes of matrix addition and matrix multiplication. Animations can more clearly show the process involved and the sequence of actions in developing a dataflow diagram (high scores of 7.62 and 8.08 in the dataflow diagram animations), and they can also more clearly show the process and sequence of mathematical operations in applying a matrix to a vector (high score of 7.00 in computer games development learning materials).

References

1. Schaefer, S., Warren, J.: Teaching computer game design and construction. Computer Aided Design 36(14), 1501–1510 (2004)
2. Callan, R.: Mathematics for computing. Letts Educational, London (1998)
3. Lengyel, E.: Mathematics for 3D game programming and computer graphics. Charles River Media, Hingham (2002)
4. Mustoe, L., Barry, M.: Mathematics in Engineering and Science. John Wiley and Sons, Chichester (1998)
5. Davies, G., Hicks, G.: Mathematics for scientific and technical students. Longman, Harlow (1998)
6. CCTA: SSADM 4+ Reference Manual, CCTA. NCC Blackwell, Oxford (1995)
7. Flash: Flash animation tool, Adobe Systems Incorporated (2008),
   http://www.adobe.com/products/flash
8. Mohler, J.: Flash MX: graphics, animation and interactivity. Delmar Learning, Clifton Park (2002)
9. Brisbourne, M., Chin, S., Melnyk, E., Begg, D.: Using web-based animations to teach histology. The Anatomical Record 269, 11–19 (2002)
10. Taylor, M.J., Pountney, D., Malabar, I.: Animation as an aid for the teaching of mathematical concepts. Journal of Further and Higher Education 31(3), 249–261 (2007)
11. Taylor, M.J., Duffy, S., Hughes, G.: The use of animation in higher education to support students with dyslexia. Education and Training 49(1), 25–35 (2007)
12. Taylor, M.J., Pountney, D., Baskett, M.: Using animation to support the teaching of computer game development techniques. Computers and Education 50(4), 1258–1268 (2008)
13. Tversky, B., Morrison, J., Betrancourt, M.: Animation: Can it facilitate? International Journal of Human-Computer Studies 57, 247–262 (2002)
14. Byrne, M., Catrambone, R., Stasko, T.: Evaluating animations as student aids in learning computer algorithms. Computers and Education 33, 253–278 (1999)
15. Khalil, M., Johnson, T., Lamar, C.: Comparison of computer based and paper based imagery strategies in learning anatomy. Clinical Anatomy 18, 457–464 (2005)
16. Stoffa, V.: Modelling and simulation as a recognizing method in education. Educational Media International 41(1), 51–58 (2004)
17. McGrath, M., Brown, J.: Visual learning for science and engineering. IEEE Computer Graphics and Applications 25(5), 56–63 (2005)
18. Mayer, R.: The promise of multimedia learning: using the same instructional design methods across different media. Learning and Instruction 13(2), 125–139 (2003)
19. Michas, I., Berry, D.: Learning a procedural task: effectiveness of multimedia presentations. Applied Cognitive Psychology 14, 555–575 (2000)

20. Park, O., Gittelman, S.: Dynamic characteristics of mental models and dynamic visual displays. Instructional Science 23, 303–320 (1995)
21. Philpot, T., Hall, R., Hubing, N., Flori, R., Oglesby, D., Vikas, Y.: Animated instructional media for stress transformations in a mechanics of materials course. Computer Applications in Engineering 11(1), 40–52 (2003)
22. James-Gordon, Y., Bal, J.: Learning style preferences of engineers in automotive design. Journal of Workplace Learning 13(6), 239–245 (2001)
23. Mathewson, J.: Visual-Spatial thinking: An aspect of science overlooked by educators. Science Education 83(1), 33–54 (1999)
24. Guimaraes, L., Barbastefano, R., Belfort, E.: Tools for teaching mathematics: A case for Java and VRML. Computer Applications in Engineering Education 8(3), 157–161 (2000)
25. Mayer, R.: Multimedia learning: are we asking the right questions? Educational Psychologist 32(1), 1–19 (1997)
26. Paivio, A.: Mental representations: a dual coding approach. Oxford University Press, New York (1990)
27. Leishman, D.: Visual literacy and learning: finding some online territories for the slow learner. On the Horizon 12(1), 26–30 (2004)
28. Albalooshi, F., Alkhalifa, E.: Multimedia as a cognitive tool. Educational Technology and Society 5(4), 49–55 (2002)
29. Koschke, R.: Software visualization in software maintenance, reverse engineering, and re-engineering: a research survey. Journal of Software Maintenance and Evolution: Research and Practice 15, 87–109 (2003)
30. Mayer, R., Moreno, R.: Animation as an aid to multimedia learning. Educational Psychology Review 14(1), 87–99 (2002)
31. Lowe, R.: Extracting information from an animation during complex visual learning. European Journal of Psychology in Education 14, 225–244 (1999)
32. Tall, D.: Intuition and rigour: the role of visualization in mathematics In: Zimmerman, W., Cunningham, S. (eds.) Mathematical Association of America Notes, vol. 19, pp. 105–119 (1991)
33. Faraday, P., Sutcliffe, A.: Designing effective multimedia presentations. In: Proceedings of the ACM SIGCHI 1997 Conference on Human Factors in Computing Systems, pp. 272–278 (1997)
34. Rieber, L.: Animation in computer-based instruction. Educational technology research and development 38, 77–87 (1990)
35. Passerini, K., Granger, M.: Integration of instructional approaches through media combination in an undergraduate information systems course. Campus-Wide Information Systems 16(5), 162–170 (1999)
36. Large, A., Beheshti, J., Breuleux, A., Renaud, A.: Multimedia and comprehension: The relationship among text, animation and captions. Journal of the American Society for Information 46(5), 340–347 (1995)
37. Blackboard: Blackboard Academic Suite, Blackboard Inc., Washington, DC, USA (2008), http://www.blackboard.com
38. LaMothe, A.: Tricks of the Windows game programming gurus. Sams Publishing, Indianapolis (2002)

Bringing Integrated Multimedia Content into Virtual Reality Environments

Paulo N.M. Sampaio and Laura M. Rodríguez Peralta

Laboratory for Usage-centered Software Engineering (LabUse), Centro de Ciências Matemáticas (CCM), University of Madeira (UMa), Campus da Penteada, 9000-390 Funchal, Madeira, Portugal
{psampaio,lmrodrig}@uma.pt

Abstract. Most of the tools and languages for modeling Virtual Reality environments, such as VRML, X3D, Java3D, etc. do not allow the description of synchronized presentation of multimedia content inside these environments. Multimedia capabilities motivate users capturing their attention, which is actually an asset when we want to provide them with a higher degree of immersion inside Virtual Reality applications. This paper presents a robust and generic solution for the integrated presentation of different kinds of media objects inside virtual environments based on the Graphical Engine OGRE.

Keywords: Virtual Reality, Interactive Multimedia Documents, OGRE, OGRE-Multimedia.

1 Introduction

Multimedia has been applied in different applications as a helpful tool for providing insight about a subject being presented. At the same time, it has been proved that human is more receptive to new information and construct easier cognitive models if this information is presented in different modalities [1]. The integration of multimedia content inside Virtual Environments (VEs) is a promising and interesting trend in the development of Virtual Reality (VR) applications. Multimedia captivates users´ attention inside the VE enhancing interaction, promoting user´s interest, facilitating learning and improving user´s immersion.

Some important issues must be considered for the integration of multimedia content inside a VE such as the specification of the temporal and logical synchronization of different media objects (with at least one audio or video) to be rendered inside the 3D environment, and determining which events (e.g., user interactions) will be applied for the communication between the 2D/3D worlds. Unfortunately, most of the existing languages for describing 3D environments (such as VRML [2], X3D [3] or Java3D [4]) are mono media and non-interactive since they support only the presentation of isolated media objects without any synchronization relations among them. One exception to this is MPEG-4 which by means of BIFS allows the creation of rich 2D/3D graphical scenarios with synchronized multimedia [5]. Nevertheless, the authoring of the MPEG-4 BIFS is still too complex and intuitive tools and approaches are still lacking.

Z. Pan et al. (Eds.): Transactions on Edutainment III, LNCS 5940, pp. 219–230, 2009.
© Springer-Verlag Berlin Heidelberg 2009

Many VR systems have been proposed in the literature addressing different application domains: e-learning [6], [7], [8], [9], collaboration among workgroups [10], augmented collaborative spaces [11], multimodal VR applications [12], cultural computing [13], 3D reconstruction [14], special needs assistance [15], among others. The rapid prototyping, modeling and authoring of VEs has been a major concern to many authors, as presented in [16], [17], and [18]. Although, most of the systems propose the development of VEs, few of them explore the presentation of integrated multimedia content inside VEs [19].

This paper presents a solution to provide the integration of multimedia content inside a VE based on the Graphical Engine OGRE [20]. The API implemented is called OGRE-Multimedia, and can be applied to any VR application to allow their customization with multimedia content. OGRE (Object-Oriented Graphics Rendering Engine) is a scene-oriented, flexible 3D engine written in C++ designed to make it easier and more intuitive for developers to produce applications using hardware-accelerated 3D graphics. When comparing OGRE with other existing languages and approaches for describing virtual worlds, we decided to adopt this platform based on its design quality, flexibility and clear documentation.

This paper is organized as follows: Section 2 presents a solution to customize a VE with multimedia presentations; Section 3 presents the main architecture of the API developed; Section 4 illustrates a Multimedia and Virtual Reality application; Section 5 introduces some current and future perspectives to this work, and; Finally, Section 6 presents some conclusions.

2 Customizing Multimedia Presentations with XML

The main goal of our work was to propose and develop a solution for providing the presentation of multimedia content within an OGRE´s virtual environment (VE). This multimedia content is related to: the output of any embedded multimedia player (such as RealPlayer [21], GRiNs [22], etc.); a Flash executable content [23], or; a web-browser content.

The definition of Interactive Multimedia Documents (IMDs) is related to the synchronized presentation of different types of media objects where at least one of these media objects is continuous (such as audio or video). The main idea behind our proposal is to apply the paradigm of IMDs to a virtual environment. In other words, the virtual environment is considered as an IMD itself, where all the multimedia objects can be rendered as textures over any 3D object being synchronized inside this virtual environment.

When proposing the integration of multimedia content inside a VE, we had to come up with a customized solution to meet the need for specifying synchronization relations among the media objects, supporting user interactions with these objects, ensuring interoperability of multimedia players, and mapping 2D objects into the 3D world. Unfortunately, the existing languages and models for describing multimedia presentation such as SMIL [24] do not support the description of three-dimensional channels, that is, the specification of the x, y and z coordinates for the presentation of the multimedia content inside the 3D environment. For this reason, the solution relied on the proposal of a simpler XML-based meta-language for describing synchronized multimedia content to be presented inside virtual environments, or as we called the *meta-multimedia document.*

The *meta-multimedia document* was strongly inspired on the syntax of SMIL and can be applied as a multimedia authoring language where users can customize the virtual environment and describe what is going to be presented, where and when they will be presented. Briefly, it describes all the components of the multimedia presentation and their temporal and logical synchronization. The particularity about this presentation is that all the media objects (multimedia documents, flash, web-browsers, and primitive media objects such as video, image, text, audio, etc.) are synchronized and rendered anywhere inside the virtual environment. The interpretation and coordination of this document presentation inside the VE is done by the API developed for OGRE, the *OGRE-Multimedia.*

As presented in Figure 1, the structure of the *meta-multimedia document* is composed of four main elements: *panel, trigger, eventHandler* and *event.*

Each *panel* element describes a presentation panel for media objects inside the virtual environment. The container called *panels* is a set of the panel objects that must be rendered inside a VE.

```
<multimediaControl>
  <panels>
    <panel name='MainUMa' width='1024' height='768' scale='0.2' position='-745, -150, 0' verRotation='90°' />
    <panel name='LeftUMa' width='640' height='480' scale='0.3' position='-745, -150, 225' verRotation='90°' />
    <panel name='TopLeftUMa' width='640' height='480' scale='0.3' position='-700, 25, 225' verRotation='90°' horRotation='45°' />
    <panel name='TopUMa' width='640' height='480' scale='0.3' position='-700, 25, 0' verRotation='90°' horRotation='45°' />
    <panel name='TopRightUMa' width='640' height='480' scale='0.3' position='-700, 25, -225' verRotation='90°' horRotation='45°' />
    <panel name='RightUMa' width='640' height='480' scale='0.3' position='-745, -150, -225' verRotation='90°' />
  </panels>
  <triggers>
    <trigger name='TriggerUMa' position='-535, -174, 0' scale='2.5' verRotation='45°' />
  </triggers>
  <eventHandlers>
    <eventHandler triggerName='TriggerUMa' action='click' loopEvents='true'>
      <event source='Moby.ogg' volume='25' />
      <event panelName='MainUMa' source='http://www.uma.pt/' />
      <event panelName='LeftUMa' source='Cantina2.swf' start='3s' stop='14s' fadeOut='3s' />
      <event panelName='TopLeftUMa' source='FachadaInf.swf' start='3s' stop='14s' fadeOut='3s' />
      <event panelName='TopUMa' source='Biblioteca1.jpg' start='3s' fadeIn='4s' stop='14s' fadeOut='3s' />
      <event panelName='TopRightUMa' source='ESC.swf' start='3s' stop='14s' fadeOut='3s' />
      <event panelName='RightUMa' source='Biblioteca2.jpg' start='3s' fadeIn='4s' stop='14s' fadeOut='3s' />
      <event panelName='RightUMa' source='Anfiteatro1.swf' start='18s' fadeIn='4s' stop='30s' />
    </eventHandler>
  </eventHandlers>
</multimediaControl>
```

Fig. 1. Example of a meta-multimedia document

Each element *trigger* characterizes an object inside the VE which controls the activation and deactivation of a multimedia presentation. The container called *triggers* is a set of all the trigger objects that will be used to control the multimedia presentations inside a VE.

Each element *EventHandler* characterizes how the presentation of the media objects associated with a given *trigger* will be controlled (e.g., start their presentation when the user clicks on the trigger or when he approximates it). The container called *eventHandlers* is a set of all multimedia presentation described by all the elements *eventHandler*.

Each element *event* characterizes how and when the presentation of each media object of a given *eventHandler* will be carried out.

The structure of the meta-multimedia document was defined to make the process of authoring the multimedia document easier and intuitive. The *meta-multimedia document* is the key-solution for the integration of multimedia content inside VEs. With this document, the author of the application is able to customize his virtual environment with new multimedia content without changing a single line of his code.

3 OGRE-Multimedia: Integrating Multimedia within Virtual Environments

Most of the libraries available for creating Virtual Reality applications do not have appropriate APIs for the integration of multimedia content inside a VE. Some languages and platforms such as VRML, X3D, Java3D and OGRE, provide only APIs for the presentation of single media objects (such as video or audio) without integrating or synchronizing these objects. The solution proposed with OGRE-Multimedia is to provide an API to integrate the presentation of different multimedia objects (rendered by different plug-ins or APIs) around the definition of the *meta-multimedia document*. Therefore, the meta-multimedia document describes all the synchronization relations among all the components (media objects, Flash presentation, web-browsers, etc.) of the document. Taking advantage of the OGRE´s component-based architecture, this API can be easily instantiated and integrated with the remaining available library. This section presents the main architecture of OGRE-Multimedia

The architecture of OGRE-Multimedia describes the integration of the *meta-multimedia document* with the Virtual Environment, which are supported by the implemented software modules and some existing APIs. This architecture is depicted in Figure 2.

The architecture of *OGRE-Multimedia* is composed of four main components:

(1) *External modules*, which are represented by those APIs developed by other projects, or which were already provided by the OGRE´s library, such as (i) TinyXML [25] (XML syntactic analyzer parser), (ii) OIS [26] (Interactions management), (3) OgreAL [27] (Presentation of audio objects), (4) DevIL [28] (Presentation of images inside VEs), (5) Navi [29] (Presentation and interaction of a web browser inside the VE), and (6) OGRE graphic engine which is the main module of the system being responsible for creating, managing and updating the tri-dimensional model;

(2) *Elementary module*, which describes the non-functional components of the architecture used as a support for the application (*Meta-multimedia document* and *Virtual Environment*);

(3) *System startup*, which is in charge to set up the presentation of multimedia content inside VEs, and;

(4) *System Update*, which is in charge to control and update the multimedia presentation inside the VE according to possible user interactions.

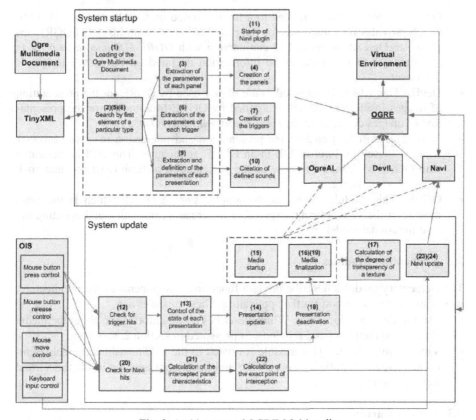

Fig. 2. Architecture of OGRE-Multimedia

The architecture of *OGRE-Multimedia* is composed of four main components: (1) *External modules* (TinyXML, OIS, OgreAL, DevIL, Navi and OGRE), (2) *Elementary modules* (*Meta-multimedia document* and Virtual Environment), (3) *System startup*, and (4) *System Update*. These components are presented on the following sections.

3.1 External Modules

The external modules are represented by those APIs developed by other projects, or which were already provided by the OGRE´s library. These modules were helpful for the implementation of OGRE-Multimedia, and demonstrate how this API can be integrated straightforward with other plug-ins to enable the presentation of multimedia content inside VEs. These modules are:

- TinyXML: This API [25] provides an XML syntactic analyzer (parser) developed in C++. TinyXML is applied for reading information described on the *meta-multimedia document*;
- OIS: This module [26] describes a simple solution for managing the interaction through the input devices (such as mouse, joystick, keyboard, etc.) and feedback devices (vibrating commands, etc.);

- OgreAL: This module is related to a library, based on the library OpenAL [27], which provides functionalities for the presentation of audio inside an OGRE application. OgreAL is applied in conjunction with *OGRE-Multimedia* to provide the presentation of all the audio information declared on the *meta-multimedia document*.
- DevIL: This API [28] is related to the library used by OGRE for the presentation of images inside VEs. DevIL is applied by OGRE-Multimedia for the presentation of images declared on the *meta-multimedia document*;
- Navi: This API [29] enables the presentation and interaction of a web browser window (based on Firefox 2.0) in an OGRE application. This API is integrated with OGRE-Multimedia to provide the presentation of flash (.swf) content such as video or animations;
- OGRE: This module represents the graphic engine OGRE which is the main module of the system being responsible for creating, managing and updating the tri-dimensional model.

3.2 Elementary Modules

The elementary modules describe the non-functional components of the architecture, which are used as a support for the application. These modules are:
- Meta-multimedia document: Which describes all the information about the media objects and their temporal relations, as presented in section 2, and;
- Virtual Environment: This module is related to the tri-dimensional models (*panels* and *triggers*) applied to support the multimedia presentation inside the Virtual Reality application.

3.3 System Startup

This component is in charge to set up the presentation of multimedia content in VEs. Therefore, the modules of this component are executed only once when the application is launched. These modules are numbered following the sequence they are executed:

1) *Loading the meta-multimedia document*: This modules reads and loads into memory the multimedia document (XML), building a DOM [30] out of this file. The API TinyXML is used for this purpose;

2) **5) and 8)** *Search by the first element of a particular type*: This module analyses DOM and search for the first element of a given type. This step is executed three times, each one searching for the first occurrence, respectively, of a *panel*, a *trigger* and an *eventHandler*;

3) **6) and 9)** *Extraction and definition of the parameters for each presentation*: These modules extracts and loads all the parameters necessary for the creation of each *panel*, *trigger* and *eventHandler* (and *events*);

4) **7) and 10)** *Creation and rendering each panel, trigger and defined audio*: These modules create the respective *panel*, *trigger* and prepare the presentation of the audio, based on the parameters defined on the *meta-multimedia document*, and;

11) *Startup of the Navi plug-in*: This module prepares the system for the utilization of texture-based videos, animations and web pages, using the functionalities of *Navi*.

3.4 System Update

This component is in charge to control and update the multimedia presentation inside the VE according to possible user interactions. Therefore, the modules of this component are executed several times, once the modules of the component *startup* are executed. Similar to the modules of *startup*, the modules of this component are also numbered following the sequence of execution inside the architecture:

12) *Checking for user interaction on triggers*: This module verifies if a user interacted with a trigger by clicking over it. This module uses the functionalities of OIS and OGRE;

13) *Controlling of the state of each presentation*: which updates the control parameters related to the state of each presentation (active or inactive), according to their triggering type (selection or proximity) and user interaction;

14) *Updating the presentation*: This module is responsible for timing each multimedia presentation and controlling each media object being presented. This module also monitors and activates a *trigger* object based on the proximity of the user;

15) *Media startup*: This module launches the presentation of a media object. For this purpose, the appropriate plug-in is applied for the presentation (by the creation of a multimedia texture for visible objects), such as *DevIL* for images, *Navi* for video, animation and web pages, and *OgreAL* for audio;

16) and **19)** *Media finalization*: This module interrupts the presentation of a media object, eliminating the respective texture for visible media objects. This interruption is done based on the presentation duration for this object declared on the *meta-multimedia document*;

17) *Calculation of the degree of transparency of a texture*: This module calculates the degree of transparency of a given texture, in case there is a appearing/fading effect associated with it;

18) *Deactivation of presentation*: This module is responsible for interrupting a given presentation by invoking the module *media finalization* to interrupt the presentation of the media objects currently being presented;

20) *Checking for user interaction on Navi*: This module verifies if there was a user interaction with a panel whose texture is a Navi web browser. This module is useful to determine, in the future, the exact interaction point with the web browser;

21) *Calculation of the intercepted panel characteristics*: This module determines the characteristics of the 3D object target of the user interaction. These characteristics include the number of polygons, position of polygons, etc. This information is useful to determine which polygon the user interacted with;

22) *Calculation of the exact point of interception*: This module determines the exact point of a user interaction with the Navi web site presentation. This is helpful to follows hyper-links defined in a web site, and;

23) and **24)** *Navi update*: which is in charge of updating a Navi web browser texture. The texture is updated as a result of a web page navigation, introduction of text in the web site, etc.

Some implementation details and issues are further discussed on the next section.

4 The Prototype Implemented

This section illustrates the prototype implemented by the presentation of an OGRE-Multimedia application. This application applied a virtual world (also called map) which describes a three-store building where the capabilities (distribution, communication, physics, Artificial Intelligence, enhanced textures, emission of particles, etc.) of OGRE and its related APIs were exploited. Figure 3 illustrates a global view of this application.

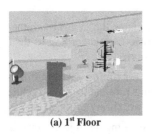 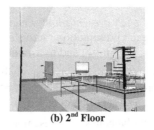 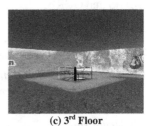

         (a) 1ˢᵗ Floor   (b) 2ⁿᵈ Floor   (c) 3ʳᵈ Floor

Fig. 3. Global view of the virtual three-store building

OGRE-Multimedia was easily integrated to this OGRE application, where the methods of OGRE-Multimedia were invoked to enable the presentation of multimedia content previously defined on the *meta-multimedia document*, called "MMDocument.mmc".

In the case of this VR application, the first floor of the building is reserved for the presentation of multimedia content as an exposition area. This floor is an open-wide area, where in front of each wall there is a sensitive column which can be activated by the user's click or proximity (depending on its previous configuration on the *meta-multimedia document*) in order to trigger the multimedia presentation on the wall (Figures 3a and 4a). Figure 4(b) illustrates the interactive column in the virtual environment. In particular, this column (which is represented by a *trigger* element on the *meta-multimedia document*) is able to launch a presentation by a user´s click.

The multimedia presentation is launched after the user interacts (by clicking) with the sensitive column (Figures 4c). When the media objects start to be presented, their level of transparency is gradually changed producing the effect of fading-in. As we can see in Figure 4(d), a web-browser is also presented as one of the multimedia textures. This browser is rendered by the API Navi which allows the user to navigate on the Web. Figures 4(d), 4(e) and 4(f) present an example of this navigation.

All the media objects presented inside the VE are synchronized and managed by OGRE-Multimedia which keeps pace of each presentation starting and interrupting all the media objects according to their previous configuration on the *meta-multimedia document*. OGRE-Multimedia enables the multimedia presentation inside the VE making of it a more realistic environment and, above all, keeping the user´s focus.

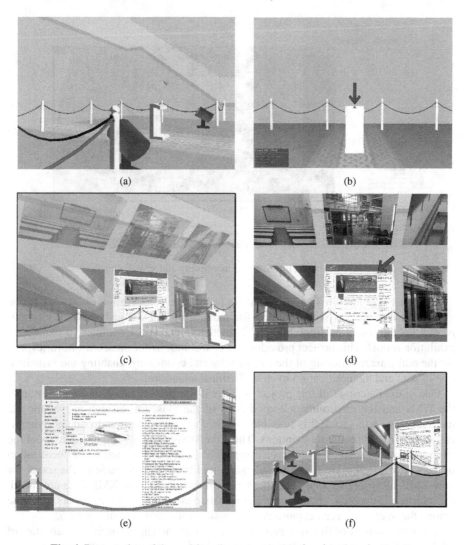

Fig. 4. Presentation of the multimedia content inside the virtual environment

5 Customizing Virtual Environments with XML

Based on the previous experiences with the development of OGRE-Multimedia, some extensions to this work have been made in order to provide a full customization of virtual environments by the utilization of XML and the dynamic rendering of the 3D environment using OGRE. These extensions include a 3D visualization tool for monitoring the environment conditions of a museum using a Wireless Sensor Network (WSN) [31].

Fig. 5. OGRE-based Interface for monitoring and visualizing WSNs

Monitoring a museum´s environment for preventive conservation of artwork is one major concern. The WSN is applied for monitoring continuously several environmental conditions (e.g., humidity, CO2, light, pollutants, etc.) either in storage or exhibition rooms. This project provides low cost solutions for museums, libraries, etc. for the real-time monitoring of their environmental conditions, enabling the visualization of data and the notification in case of critical situations.

One of the outcomes of this project is the real-time visualization and monitoring of the WSN and the environmental conditions of the museum through a dynamic 3D interface. Using this tool, it is possible to customize the virtual environment dynamically applying XML file descriptions. Thus, the WSN captures information about the environment and sends it to a server using an XML format (related to the localization of the sensors, status, etc.). The visualization tool browses continuously the server for new XML files in order to update the 3D environment. As new XML files are found, the interface is updated, and the user can visualize the state of all the sensors, navigate among them, etc. A screen capture of this application is depicted in Figure 5.

The development of this tool provided us with an insight on further capabilities of OGRE and how to provide dynamic customization of virtual environments using XML. Further developments include the integration of our previous results in order to provide an authoring tool for the dynamic customization and rendering of distributed multimedia virtual environments which can be applied in several domains.

6   Conclusions

This paper presented the development of an API for the presentation of integrated multimedia content inside Virtual Environments based on the Graphical Engine OGRE, called OGRE-Multimedia. The integrated presentation of multimedia content inside VEs relied on the proposal of an XML-based representation to describe all the media objects to be presented and their synchronization relations, the *meta-multimedia document*. OGRE-Multimedia can be applied straightforward in different OGRE Virtual Reality applications since it is the result of an open-architecture where different APIs were applied in conjunction to provide the presentation of different kinds of media objects including the traditional images, audio, video, animations, etc., and also multimedia documents such as FLASH, and web-browsers as well. Indeed, the combination of Multimedia and Virtual Reality can be successfully applied to the design of robust applications where users feel more comfortable and have their focus inside the VE, definitely improving their feeling of immersion.

Acknowledgments. We would like to thank Roberto Ivo C. de Freitas, Gonçalo Nuno P. Cardoso and Marco Paulo Domingos Louro who have been actively involved in this project.

References

1. Sorden, S.D.: A cognitive approach to instructional design for multimedia learning. Informing Science Journal 8(1), 263–279 (2005)
2. VRML: Virtual Reality Modeling Language, http://www.w3.org/MarkUp/VRML/
3. ISO/IEC 19775:2004 — Extensible 3D (X3D),
   http://www.web3d.org/x3d/specifications/
   ISO-IEC-19775-X3DAbstractSpecification/
4. Java3D API, http://java.sun.com/products/java-media/3D/
5. ISO/IEC JTC 1/SC 29/WG 11N7608 — MPEG-4 BIFS white paper,
   http://www.chiariglione.org/MPEG/technologies/
   mp04-bifs/index.htm
6. Chee, Y.S.: Network Virtual Environments for Collaborative Learning. Invited talk. In: Proceedings of ICCE/SchoolNet 2001—Ninth International Conference on Computers in Education, Seoul, S. Korea, pp. 3–11. ICCE/SchoolNet (2001)
7. McArdle, G., Monahan, T., Bertolotto, M., Mangina, E.: A Web-Based Multimedia Virtual Reality Environment for E-Learning. In: Proceedings Eurographics 2004, Grenoble, France (July 2004)
8. Halvorsrud, R., Hagen, S.: Designing a Collaborative Virtual Environment for Introducing Pupils to Complex Subject Matter. In: NordiCHI 2004: Proceedings of the third Nordic conference on Human-computer interaction. Tampere, Finland, pp. 121–130 (2004) ISBN: 1581138571
9. Hamada, M.: An Example of Virtual Environment and Web-based Application in Learning. The International Journal of Virtual Reality 7(3), 1–8 (2008)
10. Bochenek, G.M., Ragusa, J.M.: Virtual (3D) collaborative environments: an improved environment for integrated product team interaction? In: Proceedings of the 36th Annual Hawaii International Conference on System Sciences, 2003, p. 10 (2003)
11. Pingali, G., Sukaviriya, N.: Augmented Collaborative Spaces. In: proceedings of the 2003 ACM SIGMM workshop on Experiential telepresence, International Multimedia Conference, Berkeley, California (2003)
12. Carrozino, M., Tecchia, F., Bacinelli, S., Cappelletti, C., Bergamasco, M.: Lowering the development time of multimodal interactive application: The real-life experience of the XVR Project. In: ACM SIGCHI International Conference on Advances in Computer Entertainment Technology (2005)

13. Bartneck, C., Hu, J., Salem, B., Cristescu, R., Rauterberg, M.: Applying Virtual and Augmented Reality in Cultural Computing. The International Journal of Virtual Reality 7(2), 11–18 (2008)
14. Zhu, T., Tian, F., Zhou, Y., Soon Seah, H., Yan, X.: Plant Modeling Based on 3D Reconstruction and Its Application in Digital Museum. The International Journal of Virtual Reality 7(1), 81–88 (2008)
15. Sik Lányi, C., Geiszt, Z., Károlyi, P., Tilinger, Á., Magyar, V.: Virtual Reality in special needs early education. The International Journal of Virtual Reality 5(4), 55–68 (2006), http://www.ijvr.org/issues/issue4/7.pdf
16. Rodrigues, S.G., Oliveira, J.C.: ADVICe - um Ambiente para o Desenvolvimento de ambientes VIrtuais Colaborativos. In: XI Simpósio Brasileiro de Sistemas Mutimídia e Web - WebMedia2005, Poços de Caldas, MB, Brasil (2005)
17. Osawa, N., Asai, K., Saito, F.: An interactive toolkit library for 3D applications: it3d. In: Proceedings of the workshop on Virtual environments 2002, ACM International Conference Proceeding Series, Barcelona, Spain, vol. 23, pp. 149–157 (2002)
18. Garcia, P., Montalà, O., Pairot, C., Skarmeta, A.G.: MOVE: Component Groupware Foundations for Collaborative Virtual Environments. In: Proceedings of the 4th international conference on Collaborative virtual environments, Bonn, Germany, pp. 55–62 (2002)
19. Walczak, K., Chmielewski, J., Stawniak, M., Strykowski, S.: Extensible Metadata Framework for Describing Virtual Reality and Multimedia Contents. In: Proceedings of the 7th IASTED International Conference on Databases and Applications DBA 2006, Innsbruck, Austria, pp. 168–175 (2006)
20. OGRE 3D: Open source graphics engine, http://www.ogre3d.org/
21. RealPlayer - Real Networks (2004), http://www.real.com/player/
22. GRiNS – SMIL 2.0 Player Home Page, http://www.oratrix.com/GRiNS/SMIL2.0/
23. Adobe – Flash Player, http://www.macromedia.com/software/flash/about/
24. SMIL 2.0 - Synchronized Multimedia Integrated Language, http://www.w3.org/AudioVideo/
25. TinyXML – XML Parser, http://www.grinninglizard.com/tinyxml/
26. OIS – Object Oriented Input System, http://sourceforge.net/projects/wgois/
27. OpenAL – Cross-Platform 3D Audio, http://www.openal.org/
28. DevIL Development Team. DevIL – A full featured cross-platform Image Library, http://openil.sourceforge.net/
29. Simmons, A.: Main Page – NaviWiki, http://navi.agelessanime.com/wiki/index.php/Main_Page
30. DOM – Document Object Model, http://www.w3.org/DOM/
31. de Brito, L.M.P.L., Peralta, L.M.R., Santos, F.E.S., Fernandes, R.P.R.: Environmental Monitoring of Museums Based on Wireless Sensor Networks. In: Lina, M. (ed.) Proceedings of the Fourth International Conference on Wireless and Mobile Communications - ICWMC 2008, Athens, Greece, July 27 - August 1, 2008, pp. 364–369. IEEE Computer Society Press, Los Alamitos (2008)

Virtual Reality House for Rehabilitation of Aphasic Clients

Milán Horváth[1], Csaba Dániel[1], Jacqueline Stark[2], and Cecília Sik Lanyi[1]

[1] Department of Electrical Engineering and Information Systems, University of Pannonia, Veszprém, Hungary
[2] Austrian Academy of Sciences, Department of Linguistics and Communication Research, Vienna, Austria
horvim86@gmail.com, daniel.csaba@freemail.hu,
lanyi@almos.vein.hu, jacqueline.stark@oeaw.ac.at

Abstract. In this paper, the rationale for the development and the process of creating the Virtual ELA® (Everyday Life Activities)-House are described. The Virtual ELA®-House is an innovative therapy program designed for use with clients with language and speech disorders and/or with other cognitive neuropsychological disorders, which result from brain damage, e.g. aphasia, apraxia of speech, neglect, etc. The Virtual Reality setting is chosen as a modern and relevant therapy setting which imitates real everyday life scenarios. Computer supported cognitive and language therapy allows for repetitive application in the clinical and home setting which is necessary for learning to take place. The advantages of employing a software program based on a Virtual Environment, in particular the Virtual ELA® -House, are discussed.

1 Introduction

In modern educational technology the unity of form and content and their relationship is one of the most prominent issues. This special unity is seen in the promising features of the present day virtual environments [1]. Virtual Reality (VR) or Virtual Environment (VE) offers a wide range of applications in the field of cognitive neuropsychology, both in diagnosing cognitive deficits and in treating them.

Standen and Brown published a paper on general issues of Virtual Reality in the Rehabilitation of People with Intellectual Disabilities [2]. Takacs gave a detailed summary on "Special Education & Rehabilitation" and described their new virtual environment and emotional avatar [3]. This paper presents a unique human-computer interface, which uses reactive, animated human models. Such agents help to create a personal relationship and make the application more effective due to the emotional modulation method. The human models are endowed with perceptive abilities: a deep-layer communicative intelligence and a surface artificial vision. The goal was to imitate the exchange of human information by the amalgamation of surface computer animation, perception and deep-layer artificial intelligence [4]. Heldal showed that the usability of shared VEs can be enhanced not only by improving the systems and features of the environment, but also by improving the awareness of the users regarding the activities of their partners in the different settings [5].

Z. Pan et al. (Eds.): Transactions on Edutainment III, LNCS 5940, pp. 231–239, 2009.

Virtual Reality is also a useful tool for skill-building and training by creating a virtual setting, which imitates the real environment including the attributes to be trained. The virtual world is a computer-based, simulated environment intended for its users to inhabit and interact via avatars. This habitation is usually represented in the form of two-or three-dimensional graphical representations of humanoids (or other graphical or text-based avatars) [6].

A Virtual ELA®-House was created to provide an alternative means of language and cognitive rehabilitation for use with clients suffering from various disorders of higher cortical functioning resulting from brain damage [7]. The decision to create a Virtual ELA®-House was based on the impressive language therapy results from single case studies of aphasia based on the analogue version of the ELA- Photo Series [8, 9].

One possible reason for the significant improvement in language skills following provision of ELA®-based therapy protocols is that the picture stimuli are realistic and relevant for everyday life. Thus, an important goal in this project was to attain a high degree of correspondence with the analogue ELA®-picture stimuli, which is also required for an authentic virtual world. In a virtual world the designer of a task attempts to capture all aspects which a particular task requires, but it is very crucial for it to be true to nature. If the virtual world established reaches this level, the user will feel that he/she is part of the Virtual Environment. The term Virtual Environment can refer to a room, a place, a house, etc.

During the design process of a Virtual World, the designer should be aware of the available possibilities. To design or model a virtual world, a personal computer is needed with 3D modeling software and a programming environment.

2 First Steps of the Development – Design, Modeling and Converting

2.1 Design and Modeling

Before modeling the Virtual World, the entire project must be designed. Figure 1 depicts the layout of the house, which consists of various rooms located on two floors and a basement.

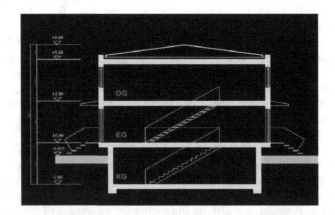

Fig. 1. The floor layout for the ELA®-Virtual House

After completion of the room layout for ELA®-Virtual House, modeling the components for the ELA®-Virtual House was initiated. For this operation, of the several available programs, we chose the Autodesk Maya[10] program for the ELA®-Virtual House.

Criteria for selecting the Autodesk Maya

3D modeling is the process of creating three-dimensional surfaces using a computer for the purpose of rendering them into a picture or a sequence of pictures [11]. Maya is a manifold 3D modeling program, which encompasses textures, thus allowing for animating software. This program is very versatile due to its wide range of applications. The Maya software has a scene where the house is modeled and built by means of a wide range of tools. To model a building - such as the ELA®-Virtual House – the first step was to create a polygon cube. This cube can be transformed, rotated or scaled to achieve the desired position and size. The cube must then be divided for the next modeling steps. Every polygon object has faces, vertices and edges. In the case of a cube there are 8 vertices, 6 faces and 12 edges. It is possible to transform, rotate or scale these vertices, faces and edges. The subdividing process generates more vertices, faces and edges, which allows the building of more exact and realistic objects. Figure 2 shows the basic form of the cube after its creation. In Figure 3 the result of the subdividing process is shown, namely, that there are more vertices, faces and edges which are necessary to model the task.

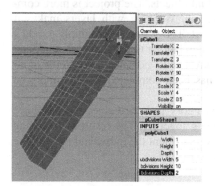
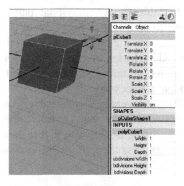

Fig. 2. A cube with rotation, translation and scale   **Fig.3.** A simple cube

In Maya software there are eight fundamental polygon objects: sphere, cube, cylinder, cone, plane, torus, pyramid and pipe. With Maya software it is possible to build any objects from these polygons with the aforementioned transformations, rotation and scales. An object can consist of one polygon object, or several polygon objects. In the second case, objects which belong together can be combined by using the Combine polygons tool.

2.2 Providing Realistic Textures and Materials

In the modeling process, after the object has been completed, the next step is to give it texture. For this operation texture mapping was used. Texture mapping is a method for adding detail, surface texture, or color to a computer-generated graphic or 3D model [12]. A virtual house has many textures, mostly in JPEG format. Maya can work easily with this format as well as with almost all of the other picture formats. The ELA®-project requires the use of precise and realistic images, therefore the analogue photos from the original ELA®-Photo Series were scanned and additional digital photos were made of components of the real rooms. These images provide the basis for the modeling of the entire house and the individual rooms. The important parts of the pictures were copied and used to texture the objects in Maya. There are several methods for texturing an object, but the simplest way is to assign a material to an object. First of all, the type of material is chosen. In this project, lambert material was used for the wall material. This is a material (shader) that represents lusterless or dull, mat surfaces (such as chalk, sheenless paint, unpolished surfaces) without mirroring qualities. For metal-like materials, blinn material is used. It is a material (shader), that is particularly effective at simulating metallic surfaces (for example, brass or aluminum), which typically give soft specular, i.e., mirroring, highlighting. It must be stressed that Maya software supports many types of materials. With Maya software it is even possible to design one's own material by adding special colors, transparency, ambient color or incandescence. Maya software saves the configurations and these can be used for other models.

In the process of modeling and texturing, numerous objects were created, including walls, windows, floors, doors, etc. It is very useful to use layers in Maya software, especially if the project consists of many individual objects. The project is more comprehensible, if the individual parts are categorized. Working with layers makes it easier to maintain an overview of the whole project. The procedure is simply to add a new layer to the project, and select the objects which belong to the same category, and then add selected objects to the layer. First, the layer must be named. When the modeling and texturing part of the layer's objects has been completed, it can simply be hidden, if necessary.

Proper layers represent categories. In each category there are objects which have their own texture map or color, and which belong together. The result of modeling and texturing is shown in Figure 4, where the layers present the individual parts of the house, such as the roof, the inside walls, the furniture, etc.

Fig. 4. The ELA®-House in Maya

2.3 Converting: An Advantage of Software Independence

This project was developed in the programming environment Eclipse [13], where the programming language is C++. Use of the engine Irrlicht [14] enables the user to walk around in the Virtual House, click on several objects and respond interactively. Irrlicht is a free open source 3D engine. However, one problem involved in using Irrlicht is that it does not support the Maya binary files. It was a challenge to find a way to export the model to a file type supported by Irrlicht. Maya software can export its models to object format, but this format contains only geometry, and textures cannot be saved in this format. The solution to this problem was the program Right Hemisphere's Deep Exploration[15].

The advantages of using Deep Exploration
Deep Exploration supports almost all 3D or 2D file types, including Maya's scenes. When the program runs, a scene, a file browser, and a little viewer appears. It is possible to open a saved Maya file in the scene field of Deep Exploration. Deep Exploration is not merely a file converter. When the file is loaded, the user is able to turn or fly around the object, zoom in or zoom out, but it is not possible to modify the object. Deep Exploration can assign textures or colors to the objects, but this operation and the possibilities are very far from those which one is able to accomplish with Maya.

Once the scene is loaded, the software is ready to export the result to all file types that Deep Exploration supports. A very popular format is the DirectX file format. The DirectX file format is an architecture- and context-free file format. It is template-driven and is free of any user-knowledge or experience. The file format may be used by any client application and currently is used by Direct3D Retained Mode to describe geometry data, frame hierarchies, and animations [16]. If the exporting process is done correctly, the resulting file is an .x file consisting of the whole geometry and inside the file the paths of the texture files are also included. As of this point the resulting .x file is ready to be imported into the Irrlicht.

3 The Second Step of the Development: Making the Model Interactive by Using Irrlicht

The Irrlicht Engine is an open source, high performance, real time 3D engine written and usable in C++ and also available for .NET languages. It is completely cross-platform, using D3D, OpenGL and its own software renderer, and it integrates all the state-of-the-art features for visual representation such as dynamic shadows, particle systems, character animation, indoor and outdoor technology, and collision detection, which can be found in commercial 3D engines. It is a powerful, high level API for creating complete 3D and 2D applications required in games or scientific visualizations. It comes with an excellent documentation, which is very useful in the development of software.

This engine is being used in many projects. There are enhancements for Irrlicht all over the web, including alternative terrain renderers, portal renderers, exporters, world layers, tutorials, editors, language bindings for java, perl, ruby, basic, python, lua, and so on.

Irrlicht has its own graphical file manager, named irrEdit [17], to load, rebuild and test our C++ project every time. In irrEdit it is possible to load many .x files, position, rotate or scale the object, but it cannot be modified. After the house model was loaded, some furniture models were added, so it became possible to furnish the whole house according to the layout. The irrEdit loader can save the objects, transformations, rotations and scales in its own file format, which at the moment is best for Irrlicht. These saved scenes, which can be modified for the specific exercises, are loaded into the program.

4   The Main Features of the Software

The Virtual ELA®-House program can be executed on Windows following installation. The project supports two languages for the clients: German and English. Before beginning the program, the user can choose between a male and a female voice. After that the user selects an exercise from the various types of exercises. The picture stimuli used for all of the language therapy tasks are taken from the ELA®- Photo Series. A constant blue-red figure shows the user where he/she is looking at the moment, when he/she is walking in the house.

4.1   Types of Exercises for the Virtual House

4.1.1   Discovery Task
In this task, the avatar wanders through the house on his/her own to learn the vocabulary of the objects and activities in each room of the house. Two different symbols are used for showing the active object. A blue cube is for an object, as shown in Figure 5 and a yellow sphere is for an activity.

Fig. 5. A virtual table with chairs

When the client clicks on an object by means of the right mouse button, a window appears. In the window an image of an object or an activity and four buttons are shown. With three of these buttons the user can read or hear separately, or see and hear the description of the image simultaneously. With the fourth button he/she can close the window, and continue discovering the components of the house.

4.1.2 Structured Discovery Task

A variation of the first task is that the avatar is standing outside the house. The avatar receives either an auditory command or one in written language to which it must respond. The following questions are included in this task:

- 'Where does activity 'x' usually take place?' or, 'Where is activity 'x' usually performed in the house?' A sentence is heard or is written on the screen requesting the avatar to move to that location in the house, where he/she thinks the activity could be performed. For one level of difficulty, when he/she clicks on the correct room, a certain symbol blinks. At a more difficult level, the avatar has to be more specific and click on the exact location, where the activity takes place. For example, if it is a picture of a boy brushing his teeth, for the first level the avatar would move into the bathroom, to be more specific, the avatar must click on or near the sink in the bathroom. If the avatar makes a mistake in the selection of the room, some response is heard or seen, signaling to him/her to continue the search. If the avatar is in the right room and makes a mistake pertaining to the exact position, then he/she also hears/sees a response: 'You are getting closer, keep trying/looking'.
- 'Where does 'x' object belong in the house?' The avatar clicks on an icon on the screen and an object appears. He/She should then look for the location where that object should be placed in the house. The same types of responses are used as in the previous exercise.

4.1.3 Memory Task

Several items (i.e. objects) are shown on the screen and the program then puts these pictures in different places in the house, one at a time. (Range of difficulty: the number can be set to include 3 to 5 objects). The avatar's task is to find the hidden items in the house in the same order as they were shown. The items can be hidden in different places. These are a few of the exercises included in the present version of the Virtual ELA®-House.

5   Conclusion

The software development and the designing and modeling of a Virtual ELA®-House is a very complex task. The project has two significant parts, which can be completely separated from each other. The first part is the software development, and the second is the modeling and texturing. During the modeling, the most difficult task was to produce a house which gives the users a feeling that the house exists, and that they are actually walking in the house. For this task digital photographs were used from a real house. Difficulties arose during the texturing part of the project. New images were created based on the actual photos, with different resolutions and compilation. In this project, the programming task was completed after being tested only once in a simple building. This was necessary because the software development and the modeling tasks were performed at the same time. After the second task was completed, the two tasks were integrated into the software environment, where the finished project was built and tested. In the future, other exercise types will be added to the program which will be based on feedback from the clients and an analysis of the data collected while clients are using the ELA®-virtual house program. An author system will also be developed for the therapists working with individual clients to adapt the program according to the individual needs of each client.

6 Future Vision

Augmenting the multimedia and virtual reality programs with devices such as data gloves is still expensive, but with the evolution of the VR game industry more and more new equipment will be on the market and will hopefully become cheaper. In this case the "old" but usable PC-s and game hardware could be used at home or in the clinic for rehabilitation of disabled people. VR researchers are investigating the possibility of delivering VE over the Internet. Eventually it will be possible to offer VR services to patients under the supervision of special teachers, doctors or therapists in their homes. In this case the patient and the therapist could go into the same VE at the same time, or hopefully in the near future more patients could work collaboratively with their therapist in the same VE at the same time [18]. Some contributions have been developed in order to provide customizable multimedia and collaborative virtual environments, where a patient would be able to interact with his therapist or with other patients by means of communication tools inside the VE, and also being able to explore and acquire information, improving his treatment with the help of the multimedia content [19]. Benkő presented a model of faces which show various emotions [20]. This model is based on a deterministic finite automaton. It will be improved upon by applying methods and tools based on EFSM (extended finite state machine) in order to personalize the possible interactions among the participants and to enable collaborative work with therapists. For this it is necessary to incorporate the common middleware services provided by domain-specific servers applying the SDL Macro-patterns method from [21], that offer EFSM-based methods for the analysis steps that focus on reuse and refactoring with design patterns from generic implementation frameworks, and on testability before the code generation. In the context of a patterns-integrated architecture, the identification and mapping of roles in the therapists' domain becomes easier, and the concept space of patterns aid in translating and integrating them into the Virtual House and Virtual Therapy Room implementation framework. In summary, future developments and applications of the Virtual House are promising.

Acknowledgements. The authors would like thank the Austrian Science and Research Liaison Office (project number: 2007.ASO-N/4/5) for their support in the development of the ELA®-Virtual therapy room.

References

1. Sik Lányi, C., Geiszt, Z., Károlyi, P., Tilinger, Á., Magyar, V.: Virtual Reality in special needs early education. International Journal of Virtual Reality 5(4), 55–68 (2006), http://www.ijvr.org/issues/issue4/7.pdf
2. Standen, P.J., Brown, D.J.: Virtual Reality in the Rehabilitation of People with Intellectual Disabilities. Review, CyberPsychology & Behavior 8(3), 272–282 (2005)
3. Takacs, B.: Special Education & Rehabilitation: Teaching and Healing with Interactive Graphics. Special Issue on Computer Graphics in Education IEEE Computer Graphics and Applications 25(5), 40–48 (2005)
4. Takacs, B.: Cognitive mental and Physical Rehabilitation Using a Configurable Virtual Reality System. International Journal of Virtual Reality 5(4), 1–12 (2006), http://www.ijvr.org/issues/issue4/1.pdf
5. Heldal, I.: The Impact of Social Interaction on Usability for Distributed Virtual Environments. International Journal of Virtual Reality 6(3), 45–54 (2007), http://www.ijvr.org/issues/issue3-2007/7.pdf
6. Stark, J.A.: Analysing the language therapy process: The implicit role of learning and memory. Aphasiology 10/11, 1074–1089 (2005)
7. The National Aphasia Association, http://www.aphasia.org/
8. Stark, J.A.: Everyday Life Activities Photo Series, Manuals to Set 1 to Set 3. Bösmüller/Jentzsch, Vienna (1992-1998)
9. Stark, J.A.: Everyday Life Activities Object Photo Series Set 1, Jentzsch, Vienna (2003)
10. Maya, A.: http://usa.autodesk.com/adsk/servlet/index?siteID=123112&id=7635018#
11. Mastering MAYA Complete 2, Perry Harovas, John Kundert-Gibbs and Peter Lee, SYBEX, Inc.
12. Texture mapping, http://en.wikipedia.org/wiki/Texture_%28computer_graphics%29
13. Eclipse – an open development platform, http://www.eclipse.org
14. Irrlicht Engine, http://irrlicht.sourceforge.net/
15. Deep Exploration, http://www.righthemisphere.com/products/dexp/
16. DirectX file form, http://local.wasp.uwa.edu.au/~pbourke/dataformats/directx/
17. Ambierra: irrEdit, http://www.ambiera.com/irredit/
18. Sik Lányi, C.: Virtual Reality in Healthcare. In: Ichalkaranje, A., et al. (eds.) Intelligent paradigms for assistive and preventive healthcare, pp. 92–121. Springer, Berlin (2006)
19. Sampaio, P.N.M., de Freitas, R.I.C., Cardoso, G.N.P.: OGRE-Multimedia: An API for the Design of Multimedia and Virtual Reality Applications. In: Lovrek, I., Howlett, R.J., Jain, L.C. (eds.) KES 2008, Part III. LNCS (LNAI), vol. 5179, pp. 465–472. Springer, Heidelberg (2008)
20. Benkő, A., Sik Lányi, C., Stark, J.: Interacting via a Virtual Language Therapy Room. In: Computer-Based Intervention and Diagnostic Procedures - Applications for Language-Impaired Persons Workshop, Vienna, Austria, July 7-8, pp. 19–22 (2008)
21. Medve, A., Ober, I.: From Models to Components: Filling the Gap with SDL Macropatterns. In: Int. Conf. Innovation on Software Engineering CIMCA/ISE 2008, Vienna, Austria (2008)

Investigating the Effects of Educational Game with Wii Remote on Outcomes of Learning

Jeng Hong Ho, Steven ZhiYing Zhou, Dong Wei, and Alfred Low

Interactive Multimedia Lab (IML), National University of Singapore
elezzy@nus.edu.sg
http://www.iml.org.sg

Abstract. In this study, a Health Education based game using the Nintendo Wii remote was developed and then tested on groups of students. To validate our claim that the use of Tangible User Interfaces (TUIs) in educational games, in particular the Nintendo Wii remotes leads to favorable outcomes of learning, a four-part construct have been explored: memoability with regards to learning, fun, enjoyment, and interest and motivation in learning. First it is hypothesized that the use of TUI in the game enhances memoability and improves subject proficiency. Second, it is hypothesized that the use of TUI in the game enhances fun and enjoyment, interest and motivation in learning, which in turn leads to improved quality of learning. Results of the study yielded positive outcomes for both subjects. Given these positive results, we conclude that the uses of TUIs in educational computer games can lead to favorable outcomes of learning.

1 Introduction

In the past decade, computer game has become an integral part of people's lives, especially for the young generation. Statistics have shown that majority of people in developed countries have access to computer games and have engaged themselves in these games [1]. It is apparent that computer games are reaching out to more people than ever and the trend is growing. This changing paradigm has led to the notion of synergizing computer games with education to produce better learning results. In recent years, the military, medical, industrial and academic fields have been forging ahead in the development of increasingly complex educational games and simulations [3] with positive results achieved.

To achieve better outcomes of learning, research has shown that instructional strategies shall be embedded within computer *games-play schemata* [2], which refers to the structure of a digital game that can be reflected in the schemata structure of the player's cognitive system. This is the cognitive structure and algorithm determining the attentiveness and other cognitive, perceptual and motor resources required to realize the task involved in game-play. In addition, there is a common consensus of the inert knowledge problem whereby students routinely fail to apply the information in school contexts to their lives. Computer games have the potential to induce students to apply knowledge that they learn

Z. Pan et al. (Eds.): Transactions on Edutainment III, LNCS 5940, pp. 240–252, 2009.

in school to their lives without the risk of getting hurt, suffer shame or running into financial troubles of one kind or the other.

In this paper, a PC game developed for children's Health Education using Nintendo Wii remote as an input device is implemented. A user study involving two groups of Primary Grade-2 students was conducted to study the effectiveness of the game. To validate our hypothesis that use of TUIs, which is Nintendo Wii reomote here, in educational games, would lead to better learning outcomes, a user study was conducted to explore these four important aspects involved in learning: memorability of learning activity, enjoyment level during learning process, interesting level of learning process and motivation effect after learning.

1.1 Computer Games in Education

Research has shown that there are learning principles embedded within computer games which can be harnessed for education purposes. Crucial elements in computer games such as interactivity, goals, outcomes, feedback, problem solving, social interaction, etc, can be applied to education to improve learning activity. Also, computer games may inspire players to explore more across a range of related fields. They influence players to make valid comparisons and observations with the real world and reinforce hypotheses formed while playing computer games [4].

In the report 'What Teachers Need to Know about the Video Game Generation' [5], Simpson analyzed why games appeal to people, which gives us an idea why students are more interested in games than learning in classrooms. Several reasons she cited are that games are empowering, motivating, individualized differentiated learning environments with set rules which value the efforts of the individual child. In addition, roles are clearly defined in games; every action has an attached outcome and is linked to an objective. Our discussions with school teachers and students also echo these findings. Therefore, our game design finally utilized Wii remote as input device to create individualized learning experience. The game design also has been developed according to the curriculum to show the clear objective and the outcome of the right and wrong behaviors acted by the students, e.g., brushing the teeth in a wrong way can cause damage to the adamantine layer.

1.2 Using Wii Remote as a Tangible User Interfaces in Learning

Studies have shown that children can often solve problems when given concrete materials to work with before they can solve them symbolically, for example, pouring water back and forth between wide and narrow containers eventually helps young children discover that volume is conserved. In addition, it had been proven that locomotion supports children in categorization and recall in tasks of perspective taking and spatial imagery, even when they typically fail to perform in symbolic versions of such tasks. Also, research has shown that touching objects helps young children in learning to count, not just in order to keep track of what they are counting, but in developing one-to-one correspondences between numbers words and item tags [6]. There are several reasons why TUIs could benefit students' learning:

First, TUIs require little time to learn how to use the interface therefore the user can focus more on the task itself rather than learning how to use the interface.

Second, TUIs offer users an alternative way of interaction and control of the computing environment. The fact that the use of TUIs is interactive underlines the big benefit in integrating it into education, because interactivity in tasks grasps students' imagination and transforms the learning process into a natural extension of the students' daily activities.

Third, TUIs induce the element of fun in performing the task and fun is a very important factor in students' learning experience and will also result in them not losing their interest easily [8]. Psychological study [17] also shows that tangible and physical interaction is essential of the human enjoyment of life. Wii remote has been widely used in consumer games and has been well received by millions of users to be a fun gaming experience. Using Wii as TUI in our educational game can bring the fun and enjoyment element into the content to be learnt. The fact that the use of TUIs promotes fun through kinesthetic also underlines the main benefit in integrating it into education for young children. It is differentiated feature to enhances the process of knowledge acquisition and may be the key to successful learning. TUIs when combined with graphics offer users with the freedom to visualize and imagine how manipulation of the TUIs itself can translate into task operation. This access to visual imagery facilitates knowledge retention [7].

Fourth, In Kenneth P. Fishkin's analysis of TUIs [9], he mentioned that TUIs can be characterized by various levels of metaphors they represent, namely none, noun, verb, noun and verb, full. It is these metaphors that enable users to identify and bridge the gap between the physical and virtual world, which facilitates effective learning . Wii remote is able to represent most of these metaphors, which makes it an effective TUI. For example, Wii remote can signify 'a noun and verb' metaphor in games like The Legend of Zelda where the players use Wii remote as a sword and swing it to replicate a slashing motion. Also, Wii remote can signify a 'verb' metaphor when players swing Wii remote to roll a bowling ball in Wii Sports. Thus we chose Wii remote as a good candidate of TUI to be implemented in our educational game.

2   Related Works

Video games have been used in serious education and have demonstrated positive outcomes. 'Replaying History' [10] is an example of educational game, whose doctorial dissertation involved a case study research in using Civilization III within a classroom setting, an after-school setting and a day camp, had made a breakthrough in the area of edutainment. The project used the popular video game series to help students learn about geopolitical struggles, global economic clout, geographic details contributing to regional power and many other socio-historical concepts with much success. Another example is the Quest Atlantic Project [11], which is a learning and teaching project that employs a multiuser, virtual environment to immerse children, ages 9 - 12, in educational tasks . Quest Atlantis has over 4500 users and has been adopted by more than four dozen teachers in various locations around the globe. Studies have shown that elementary students who used Quest Atlantis demonstrated statistically significant learning over time in the areas of science, social studies and sense of academic efficacy. Both of these two games employed crucial elements in games to develop edutainment effects successfully. In our Health Education curriculum context, unlike the topics covered in the games mentioned above, we will need to educate the students the kinetics behavior, which will be impossible to be achieved by using traditional interface like mouse and keyboard. We explored the use of Wii Remote as a TUI to enhance the kinetics learning outcomes as well as to inject the fun elements into the learning process.

Although there has been a variety of applications using Wii remote are published, most of the applications only used it as wireless sensor for location and orientation detection. Very few applications have been reported to use Wii as a tangible educational tool, especially for young children application. Soga [12] et al has used Wii remote to develope an interactive learning environment for astronomy. However, Wii remote was only used like a button on a mouse or a keyboard, e.g, user presses Wii remote button to denote the target star. We would like to fully explore the affordance of Wii remote as a TUI, especially its capability of detecting kinetics movements which are generally difficult to convey in normal education media.

3   Game Description

3.1   Game Content and Interaction Scenarios

We followed the design rules proposed by John W. Rice [13] to develop our game. In particular, the context of the games should be aligned to the curriculum. We have discussed with teachers from local primary schools in Singapore to identify the topics that can be enhanced by using Wii remote as a TUI. Finally the Singapore's Ministry of Education (MOE) curriculum of Health Education [14] was chosen as the subject because there are quite a few topics involving the physical actions (e.g., the correct way of brushing the teeth) that are traditionally difficult to be taught. These topics can make good use of the affordance of Wii remote. For example, part of the Health Education curriculum teaches students about dental care like brushing the teeth correctly. This can be simulated physically with Wii remote, inducing the element of fun and interactivity into the curriculum. The game consists of six different scenarios relating specific curriculum and activities extracted from the Primary School Health Education syllabus (Primary 2 - 4). The scenarios are: food nutrition and balance, personal hygiene and cleanliness, dental care, road safety, environmental cleanliness, and mosquitoes breeding prevention (as shown in Fig. 1).

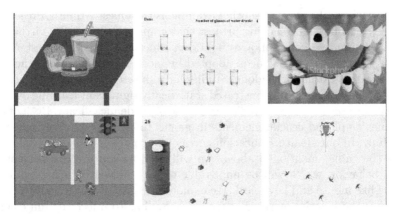

Fig. 1. The six game scenarios in our game. First row (from left to right): food nutrition and balance, personal hygiene and cleanliness, dental care scenarios; Second row (from left to right): road safety, environmental cleanliness, and mosquitoes breeding prevention scenarios.

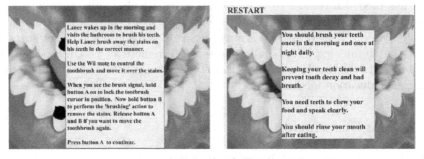

Fig. 2. The instructions and curriculum contents embedded in the game. Left: simple instruction is displayed on how to play when each scenario starts; Right: Once the task is finished, reading stuff about the topic just played is displayed in text.

Fig. 3. A screen shot captured from the 'dental care' scenario. By 'brushing' the teeth in the correct way, the number of the blobs on the teeth reduces from six (image on the left) to three (image on the right).

Each game scenario relates to a topic in the Health Education syllabus, starts with a set of instructions (see Fig. 2 left) to inform students how to play and ends with a set of syllabus (see Fig. 2 right) from the topic being played by students for reading purpose when they have successfully completed the scenario. During each scenario students should follow the instruction to play the educational game; for instance during the dental care scenario, they should use Wii remote to clean the small blobs on teeth. As shown in Fig. 3.

3.2 Game Development

In order to make use of Wii remote on any desktop or laptop, we have created a bar which contains two infrared LEDs. Each LED is fixed at one end of the bar. We used Wii Software Development Kit (SDK) which manipulates signals received from Wii remote via Bluetooth to track the LED lights. The tracking results are then translated into user action descriptions. For example, detecting the Wii mote's movements of up and down may possibly mean that the user is brushing the teeth in a correct manner. The Wii SDK used to develop our game is Wii Flash, which uses Macromedia Flash as the editor for scripts to emulate keyboard and mouse commands and the game is being build on Adobe Flash CS3 Professional [15], because Flash only requires little resource from PC. As a result, our game can easily run at 30 frame per second on any mainstream PC or laptops available nowadays in the schools.

4 Study Design

In order to determine whether students improved subject proficiency as well as improved outcomes of learning, four important aspects involved in learning activity were being identified and conceptualized into concrete observable and measurable parameters [16] in the user study. These four aspects are: memorability of learning activity, enjoyment level during learning process, interesting level of learning process and motivation effect after learning. These four aspects are evaluated upon our educational game.

The user study was conducted with two groups of users (10 primary grade-2 students for each group), i.e., the experimental group and the control group to make comparisons. The experimental group participated in the user study by using the Wii remote to complete the game scenarios. On the contrary, the control group participated in the user study by watching pre-recorded on-screen demos of the same game scenarios. Both groups need to complete all game scenarios. The main difference between these two groups is: users in experimental group experience active participation in learning activity with the use of Wii remote while users in control group only experiences passive participation in learning activity. Setup of the user study is shown in Fig. 4.

Memorability with regard to learning refers to how much of information a student can remember after it is shown to him. This is essential because learning is considered effective if students are able to remember the knowledge being

Fig. 4. A student is 'brushing' her teeth with Wii remote during dental care scenario in the user study

imparted to them. Hence, memorability with regard to learning can be used as a criterion of learning performance. In order to measure memorability of students, a set of test questions were designed for students to answer. These questions are directly related to the information that they have been exposed to through the Nintendo Wii scenarios; full mark for these questions is 10. We denote this set of questions by 'Memorability Test'.

Fun and enjoyment derived from any learning experience can also lead to more effective learning activity [8]. The game scenarios designed enable students to learn the syllabus through practical work which can lead to fun and enjoyment. Therefore, it is necessary and useful to measure the enjoyment level experienced by the students through the course of learning process in the game scenarios. A self-report approach was used to measure this with a set of two interview questions for students to answer. Besides, increase in interest and motivation levels also result in better learning activity as it induces interests in students and spurs them to desire more knowledge about a particular topic. This is an outcome that is desired from being engaged in the Nintendo Wii Health Education game scenarios. Another set of two interview questions was designed for students to answer in order to measure these two factors. Refer to Appendix for interview questions.

5   Results

Students from both groups were asked to answer ten questions. Every correct answer will give the student one score. Score distribution of 'Memorability Test' for both groups is shown in Table 1. The mean score for the experimental group is 8 while the mean score for the control group is 7.1.

For interview question 1, 5 students from the experimental group gave a score of 3 out of 5, 3 students gave a score of 4 out of 5 and 2 students gave a score of 5

Table 1. Score distribution for 'Memorability Test'

Score	5	6	7	8	9	10
Experimental group	0	1	2	4	2	1
Control group	2	2	1	3	2	0

out of 5 for the fun factor of playing the game. For the control group, 4 students gave a score of 2 out of 5, 4 students gave a score of 3 out of 5 and 2 students gave a score of 2 out of 5 for the fun factor of viewing the onscreen demos of the game scenarios. As for the enjoyment level (which is measured using question 2) of the experimental group, 3 students gave a score of 2 out of 3 and 7 students gave a score of 3 out of 3 as they rated on how much more enjoyable it is to learn Health Education by playing the game than to learn by reading the textbook. For the control group, 1 student gave a score of 1 out of 3, 7 students gave a score of 2 out of 3 and 2 students gave a score of 3 out of 3 as they rated on how much more enjoyable it is to learn Health Education by viewing the onscreen demos of the game scenarios than to learn by reading the textbook.

For interview question 3, the experimental group had 3 students giving a score of 2 out of 3 and 7 students giving a score of 3 out of 3 as they rated on how much more interested they are in the subject of Health Education after playing the game. As for the control group, 2 students gave a score of 1 out of 3, 5 students gave a score of 2 out of 3 and 3 students gave a score of 3 out of 3 as they rated on how much more interested they are in the subject of Health Education after viewing the onscreen demos of the game scenarios.

For interview question 4, the experimental group had 7 students rating 2 out of 3 and 3 students rating 3 out of 3 of their motivation level in learning more detailed information on the topics of Health Education to which they had been exposed after playing the game. As for the control group, 2 students rated 1 out of 3, 6 students rated 2 out of 3 and 2 students rated 3 out of 3 of their motivation level in learning more detailed information on the topics of Health Education to which they had been exposed after viewing the demos of the game on screen .

6   Analysis and Discussion

6.1   Result Analysis

For the results of 'Memorability Test', we use the One–Way Analysis of Variance (ANOVA) method to test whether there is any significant difference between the 2 means. The user study results are tested at 5% confidence level, where the hypothesis is that using TUIs in educational games would lead to better memorability, and it will be accepted if $p \leq 0.05$ and rejected otherwise. The p value computed is $p = 0.154$ (see Table 2), which is greater than $p = 0.05$. This means that there wasn't any significant difference in the test results between

Table 2. One–way ANOVA for 'Memorability Test'

ANOVA

Source of variation	SS	df	MS	F	P-value	F crit
Between groups	4.05	1	4.05	2.216	0.154	4.414
Within groups	32.9	18	1.83			
Total	36.95	19				

Table 3. One–way ANOVA for fun factor

ANOVA

Source of variation	SS	df	MS	F	P-value	F crit
Between groups	4.05	1	4.05	6.231	0.023	4.414
Within groups	11.7	18	0.65			
Total	15.75	19				

the 2 groups which also implies that there wasn't notable difference between the memorability of the students from both groups after being engaged in their respective activities.

For interview question 1, students from both groups were asked to rate how fun the activity was respectively. Again, using the One–Way Anova, the results are tested at 5% confidence level. The p value computed from the results is p = 0.0225 (see Table 3) which is less than p = 0.05. This proves that there was a significant difference in the fun factor experienced by the students between the experimental group and control group, which supports the hypothesis that using TUIs in educational games, would provide more fun to students and hence lead to better learning activity.

For interview question 2, students from both groups were asked to rate how enjoyable the activity was respectively as compared to learning Health Education by reading the textbook. Using the One–Way ANOVA method, under the confidence level at 5%, the p value computed is p = 0.0203 (see Table 4) which is less than p = 0.05. This once again implies that the experimental group felt that learning Health Education by playing the game was more enjoyable than learning by reading the textbook as compared to the control group, which reaffirms the hypothesis that using TUIs in educational software would provide more enjoyment to students and hence lead to better learning activity.

For interview question 3, students were asked to rate their interest level in the subject of Health Education after being engaged in their respective activities of

Table 4. One–way ANOVA for enjoyment level

ANOVA

Source of variation	SS	df	MS	F	P-value	F crit
Between groups	1.8	1	1.8	6.48	0.020	4.414
Within groups	5	18	0.278			
Total	6.8	19				

Table 5. One–way ANOVA of score ratings for interest level

ANOVA Source of variation	SS	df	MS	F	P-value	F crit
Between groups	1.8	1	1.8	4.629	0.045	4.414
Within groups	7	18	0.389			
Total	8.8	19				

Table 6. One–way ANOVA of score ratings for motivation level

ANOVA Source of variation	SS	df	MS	F	P-value	F crit
Between groups	0.45	1	0.45	1.328	0.264	4.414
Within groups	6.1	18	0.339			
Total	6.55	19				

the experimental and control group. Using the One–Way ANOVA, the results are tested at 5% confidence level and the p value computed is p = 0.0453 (see Table 5) which is less than p = 0.05. This means that students from the experimental group had a significantly higher interest level than students from the control group on the subject of Health Education after being engaged in their respective activity.

For interview question 4, students were asked to rate their motivation level of wanting to learn more detailed information with regard to the Health Education topics that they were exposed to through the Nintedo Wii game scenarios. Again, using the One–Way ANOVA and testing at 5% confidence level, the p value computed is p = 0.264 (see Table 6) which is more than p = 0.05. This implies that there was no significant difference in the motivation level of the students from both groups.

6.2 Discussion

Through the analysis we find that, on half of the four chosen important aspects with regard to learning activity, the user study gave out positive results, that is, enjoyment level and interests level. This means the use of TUIs in educational games can bring more fun to young children who learn through usage of Wii remote in educational games compared to through reading textbook, as well as can improve the attractive level of the content to be learned itself because the increase in interest level is validated by results from the user study. However, on the second half, the results didn't give us affirmative answers that we had desired. For the memorability aspect, though the experiment group gained obvious higher scores in 'Memorability Test' after experienced active participation of Nintendo Wii game scenarios than the control group who only experienced passive participation by viewing Nintendo Wii game scenarios did, but due to the relatively small size of samples and the negative feedback from one–way ANOVA, we cannot make the inference that it is the use of TUIs that leads to higher scores in experimental group. As for the motivation aspect, it's quite understandable that there is no significant difference observed between experimental group and control group. It's always hard to induce young children to learn spontaneously.

In general, this study truly validated the positive and promising aspects of using TUIs in educational games to improve learning activity performed by young children, which is quite encouraging for further studies on this topic as well as more educational applications using TUIs. However, to disambiguate the conflict between mean and negative conclusion from p-value that happened in the memorability case, further study that is designed more carefully and with more users is needed to find out the actual reason for higher scores in experimental group, that is, whether the manifestation comes from the use of TUIs or not. Furthermore, more factors known or unknown needs to be explored to enhance the motivation effect of TUIs in educational games.

7   Conclusion

In this study, the use of Nintendo Wii remote is utilized as a TUI in an educational game for the Health Education subject for young children, and its effect was tested in a user study involving 20 Primary Grade-2 students. Our hypothesis is that use of Tangible User Interfaces (TUIs) in educational games, which is Nintendo Wii reomote in this study, would lead to better learning activity. Thus, we explore these four important aspects involved in learning: memorability of learning activity, enjoyment level during learning process, interesting level of learning process and motivation effect after learning.

On one hand, this study indicates that the use of TUIs in educational games can bring more fun to young children who learn through use of TUIs in educational games compared to through reading textbook, as well as can improve the attractive level of the content to be learned itself. This can be categorized as subjective factors in learning activity. Given these positive results, we can conclude that the use of TUIs in educational computer games leads to favorable outcomes of learning. On the other hand, the user study doesn't give out an affirmative inference on one of the objective factors in learning activity, which is the improvement on memorable effect during learning process. In addition, motivation effect of TUIs in educational games needs to be further explored because it revealed not that ideal in our study.

It is important to note that any results obtained from these samples are not strongly representative for the general population but only applicable to the sample population itself due to the small sample size. In the future work, we intend to do a larger scale studies, i.e., class-size study.

In general, we would still conclude that benefits of using TUIs in educational games for children are apparent, and this technique is quite promising, has great potential to be used prevailing. Although, further studies designed more carefully are needed to explore deeper and broader on this topic.

References

1. LaPointe, D.: Will Games and Emerging Technologies Influence the Learning Landscape? In: Learners in a Changing Learning Landscape, vol. 12, pp. 227–249. Springer, Heidelberg (2008)
2. Lindley, C., Sennerstien, C.: Game Play Schemas: From Player Analysis to Adaptive Game Mechanics (2007), DigiPlay Initiative at http://hindawi.com/GetPDF.aspx?doi=10.1155/2008/216784 (Retrieved on April 10, 2009)
3. Rice, J.W.: Computer games in the classroom: A History and Brief Review of the Research. University of North Texas (2008)
4. Jenkins, H., Squire, K.: Harnessing the Power of Games in Education. Insight 3(1), 5–33 (2003)
5. Simpson, E.S.: Evolution in the Classroom: What Teachers Need to Know about the Video Game Generation. In: TechTrends: Linking Research and Practice to Improve Learning, vol. 49(5), pp. 17–22. Springer, Boston (2005)
6. O'Malley, C., Stanton Fraser, D.: Literature Review in Learning with Tangible Technologies. Technical Report 12, NESTA Futurelab (2004)
7. Ibrahim, M., Al-Shara, O.: Impact of Interactive Learning on Knowledge Retention. In: Smith, M.J., Salvendy, G. (eds.) HCII 2007. LNCS, vol. 4558, pp. 347–355. Springer, Heidelberg (2007)
8. Xu, D.: Tangible User Interface for Children – An Overview. Department of Computing, University of Central Lancashire, Preston, UK (2005)
9. Fishkin, K.P.: A Taxonomy for and Analysis of Tangible Interfaces. Personal and Ubiquitous Computing 8(5), 347–358 (2004)
10. Squire, K.D.: Replaying History: Learning World History Through Playing Civilization III. Indiana University, Indianapolis, IN, USA (2004)
11. Barab, S., Thomas, M., Dodge, T., Carteaux, R., Tuzun, H.: Making Learning Fun - Quest Atlantis, A Game without Guns. Educational Technology Research and Development 53(1), 86–107 (2005)
12. Soga, M., Matsui, K., Takaseki, K., Tokoi, K.: Interactive Learning Environment for Astronomy with Finger Pointing and Augmented Reality. In: IEEE International Conference on Advanced Learning Technologies (ICALT 2008), Santander, Cantabria, Spain, July 1-5. IEEE, Los Alamitos (2008)
13. Rice, J.W.:, Evaluating the Sustainability of Video Games for K-12 Instruction. University of North Texas (2005)
14. Ministry of Education, Singapore, Subject Syllabuses (2008), http://www.moe.edu.sg/education/syllabuses/
15. WiiFlash.org (2008), http://wiiflash.org/
16. Price, I.: Research Methods and Statistics, Lecture and Commentary Notes, University of New England, http://www.une.edu.au/WebStat/unit_materials/index.htm (2000)
17. Bowlby, J.: Attachment and Loss: Attachment, vol. i. Basic Book, New York (1983)

Appendix: Questionnaire for User Study

Interview Questions for the Experimental Group

1. On a scale of 1 to 5, how fun was it to learn about Health Education by playing the Nintendo Wii game? 1 - Very boring 2 - Boring 3 - Average 4 - Fun 5 - Very fun
2. On a scale of 1 to 3, how enjoyable is learning Health Education by playing the Nintendo Wii game as compared to learning from the Health Education textbook? 1 - Less enjoyable 2 - Same 3 - More enjoyable
3. On a scale of 1 to 3, rate how much more interested you are in Health Education after playing the Nintendo Wii health education game? 1 - Less interested 2 - Same 3 - More Interested
4. On a scale of 1 to 3, rate how much you are motivated to find out more detailed information on the topics of Health Education that you just learned about? 1 - Less motivated 2 - Same 3 - More motivated.

Interview Questions for the Control Group

1. On a scale of 1 to 5, how fun was it to learn Health Education by viewing the video recordings of the Nintendo Wii game? 1 - Very boring 2 - Boring 3 - Average 4 - Fun 5 - Very fun
2. On a scale of 1 to 3, how enjoyable is learning Health Education by viewing the onscreen demos of the Nintendo Wii game as compared to learning from the Health Education textbook? 1 -Less enjoyable 2 -Same 3 -More enjoyable
3. On a scale of 1 to 3, rate how much more interested you are in Health Education after viewing the onscreen demos of the Nintendo Wii game? 1 - Less interested 2 - Same 3 - More Interested
4. On a scale of 1 to 3, rate how much you are motivated to find out more detailed information on the topics of health education that you just learned about? 1 - Less motivated 2 - Same 3 - More motivated.

Using Computer Games for Youth Development

Ruwei Yun, Yanyan Jiang, and Yi Li

Edu-game Research Center, School of Education and Science,
Nanjing Normal University, 210097, Nanjing, China
yunruwei@njnu.edu.cn

Abstract. Correlation studies have shown that games can influence self-development of youth, resolve conflict and discord in their development, and develop their skills, etc. Referring to R.M.Gagne's theory of learning outcomes, the paper demonstrates the impacts of games on youth development from the perspective of the object, specifically including four aspects: games and the learning of verbal information, games and the development of intellectual skill, games and the development of psychomotor skill, and games and the formation of attitude.

Keywords: Games, Youth development, Verbal information, Intellectual skill, Psychomotor skill, Attitude.

1 Introduction

As people change forms of entertainment, more and more young people choose online games. Made by Game publications working committee of Chinese Publishers Association and IDC (International Data Corporation) together, "2008 China Game Industry Report Summary" shows the actual income of China's online game market was 18.38 billion yuan in 2008 and grew 76.6% compared to the same period in 2007, and it is expected that the actual s income of China's online game market will reach 39.76 billion yuan in 2013[1].

However, as related to the healthy growth of broad masses of young people, the family, schools, and the harmonious and orderly society, the evaluation of online games should not only refer to economic index, but also be more concerned with the healthy development of young people. The problem of youth development and games is the main problem that troubles scholars both at home and abroad currently. Around the issue, many scholars have done active researches and carried out lots of domestic and international academic seminars in recent years. International conferences include: "International Conference on E-learning and Games" (Edutainment), "Digital Game and Intelligent Toy Enhanced Learning" (DIGITEL), "International Conference on Web-based Learning" (ICWL), "International Games and Learning Forum" that is supported by HEWLETT Fund and held by the Massachusetts Institute of Technology and Peking University in Shanghai.

From the present research results, we can draw the conclusion that games can be effectively used in education. For example, Natale's study suggested that games can be used to enhance learners' ability of learning and memory [2]. Klawe's study

Z. Pan et al. (Eds.): Transactions on Edutainment III, LNCS 5940, pp. 253–273, 2009.

concluded that computer games can be used to encourage learners who are lack of interest and self-confident [3]. Ritchie and Dodge et al. concluded computer games have a positive effect on the learners who are lack of self-esteem in a study [4]. Li Yi et al. suggested that games are conducive to the space intelligence of students [5].

However, there are also significant risks while games are applied in education. For example, Clark concluded that when learning goals and game objectives aren't matched well game players will concentrate on the completion of tasks, scoring and winning, which will cause learning distraction and faith vacillation, so it is difficult for learners to maintain learning in the game environment [6]. Becta proposed worse disadvantages: games might be too easy or too difficult, which will lead to decline in motivation; games are addictive, which causes harm to learners; many games with a gender identity or violent tendencies, etc [7].

Correlation studies have shown that games can influence self-development of youth, resolve conflict and discord in their development, and develop their skills, etc. Referring to R.M.Gagne's theory of learning outcomes, learning is divided into five types: verbal information, intellectual skill, cognitive strategy, psychomotor skill and attitude [8]. The paper demonstrates the impacts of games on youth development from the perspective of the object, specifically including four aspects: games and the learning of verbal information, games and the development of intellectual skill, games and the development of psychomotor skill, and games and the formation of attitude.

2   Games and the Learning of Verbal Information

Around the problem that whether games are in favor of verbal information learning, main studies include four aspects: learning environment, learning method, learning content and the keeping of information, which support verbal information learning. Games can provide young people with learning environment, including: simulation environment, situational context, background knowledge, learning opportunities, etc.; games can provide young people with different learning styles of conditions, including trial and error learning, cooperative learning, discovery learning, etc.; games are available for young people to learn knowledge in various disciplines, including geography, agriculture, environment, economy, government, society, science and other disciplines of knowledge; games can cause young people's attention, which will help young people short-term memory and long-term memory.

2.1   Verbal Information

Verbal information is also known as "verbal knowledge" or "declarative knowledge" , which is saved in the proposition network form in line with rules of the language, and it is factual information of something with regard to tag, time, spot, definition and character[9]. Verbal information is defined as conscious clues extraction for individuals, factual knowledge or event information that could be stated directly by Gagne. The answers to the following questions such as which year the People's Republic of China was founded, how much land area of China and the number of China's population are good examples for the definition. Verbal information defined by Gagne includes two parts: knowledge and ability. Knowledge is mainly used to answer the question of what the world is, such as the division of the continents of the Erath in geography. Ability mainly refers to people's memory capacity, such as the number of Pi one can recite from memory and so on.

Gagne subdivided verbal information into four major parts: fact, tag, principle and generalization, such as "the earth is round" is fact, "keyboard" named as computer devices used to input characters is tag, "after using other people's things we must return them" is principle, and "his temper is better" is generalization of other people's character. The generalization in Gagne's definition is extracting the main characteristics of complex things, and forming the meaning. For example, the fruit is the meaning extracted form a series of things with common ground such as apple, pear and banana, etc. Learning verbal information is a process and it is full of a person's life. The sustained and abundant acquisition of verbal information is the basal guarantee of a person's development on intellectual skills and cognitive strategies, and also it can be extended to affective domain and motor skills domain.

2.2 Games and the Learning of Verbal Information

The learning of verbal information is mainly manifested as perception of knowledge and understanding. Learners can get the meaning by linking new information and prior knowledge through the two kinds of process, and then they can bring the meaning into their cognitive structure [10]. As Trcicher's experimental result have shown that the information accessed by human 83% comes from vision, 11% comes from hearing, and both together accounted for 94%. Human's original learning always come from sense, while vision and hearing are two main sense manners. Computer games show a master hand in revelation and amalgamation image and sound, which can simulate complicated three-dimensional space, color and voice in the real world. Then youth can acquire knowledge in games by intuitive knowledge manners (mainly consist of intuitive models and intuitive verbal). According to actual demand, focus and metal factors of virtual models can be highlight in game space, which can help students form general appearance of things. At the base of general appearance, students can acquire generic and rational understanding about related things from virtual object in games by some processes of rational thinking such as analysis, synthesis, comparison, abstraction, and summarization. Games can provide speech communication, image or other clues, and it can facilitate learners to combine huge and organized knowledge networks to new fact, which is propitious to search and extract information from memory for students.

From the perspective of games, games have the ability of carrying verbal information, which has been verified successfully in some games. Take "Snapshot Adventures" (as shown in Fig. 1) for example, the game was developed by a computer game company called Large Animal in American, and it provided knowledge of various birds, further more it also provided bird building tools for players to let them build birds according to their own cognition. The "Uncharted Waters" described and classified knowledge of many sails in details. The "Civilization" introduced knowledge that affects city health by terrain, fresh water, resources, urban population, buildings, as well as the implementation of the internal affairs of the Act in the game. The knowledge of birds and sails can be acquired directly in games, while the acquisition of the knowledge of city health need multi-try and rational thinking such as analysis, synthesis and generalization at the basement of perception for players.

Fig. 1. Snapshot Adventures: Secret of Bird Island

Around the problem that whether games are in favor of verbal information learning, main studies include four aspects: learning environment, learning method, learning content and the keeping of information, which support verbal information learning.

Games Can Create an Effective Learning Environment. Kirriemuir's study suggested that games can create a context-sensitive learning environment. He thinks the key to the attractiveness of games was to provide students with learning opportunities in relative and attractive context-sensitive environment, which not only can promote students' learning but also can make players combine the interactive nature of games with learning goals in a familiar but still new environment, and in practice, it is proved to be very effective [11]. Through the study of the simulation games, Leutner confirmed that they can provide students with background knowledge which learning needs and suggestions on initial system operation, and that it is the most effective in encouraging the use of discovery learning [12].

Simulation games are mainly to make some learning activities that are expensive, dangerous, difficult or impractical [13], or can not be achieved through other means [14], are possible in the classroom.

Flexible Learning Methods Can be Used in Games. Through the study on the simulation games, Sedighian and Kirriemuir et al., found that such games have the characteristics of the flexibility and complexity. In a simulation game, students can use appropriate learning methods according to their needs and the surrounding environment [15, 11]. They promote cooperative learning and meaningfully game-related discussions. Leutner considered that games are to encourage students in the location of decision-makers, so that they directly face more difficult challenges, which will enable them to learn in repeated experiments and errors by doing. Another study confirmed the simulation games are the most effective in encouraging discovery learning [12]. In the VISOLE (Virtual Interactive Student-Oriented Learning Environment) research project, Shang Junjie and Zhuang Shao-Yong et al. launched a game called "Farm Rhapsody", where they enable students to learn academic knowledge through collaborative learning [16].

The Combination of Games and Discipline-specific Knowledge. In the combination of games and discipline-specific knowledge, some scholars and enterprises have also made a useful attempt. Jayakanthan's study suggested that strategy games (such as Simcity) can be used in schools to encourage students to study specific subjects (such as geography) [17] . In the game "Farm Rhapsody", each student or group could create a farm. Through operation and management on the farm, students could learn many kinds of academic knowledge together, including geography, agriculture, environment, economy, government, society and so on [16]. Will Wright, the author of "Simcity", ever developped a game "SimAnt". He put a mini-encyclopedia on the ants in an on-line database, and many elements might be involved in game operation. He hoped that through the game, people could read this encyclopedia, so that people could learn a lot the knowledge about ants while they were playing [16].

Table 1. The relationship between games and the learning of verbal information

First-grade	Second-grade	Description
Verbal Information	Learning Environment	Games provide young people with simulation environment, situational context, background knowledge, and learning opportunities.
	Learning Styles	Games provide young people with different learning styles of conditions, including trial and error learning, cooperative learning, discovery learning, etc.
	Learning Content	Games are available for young people to learn knowledge in various disciplines, including geography, agriculture, environment, economy, government, society, science and other disciplines of knowledge.
	Learning Memory	Games can cause young people's attention, which will help young people short-term memory and long-term memory.

Games and the Keeping of Verbal Information. Verbal information, such as the English words, historical names, geographical knowledge, etc., is a bit dull to young people in the learning process. They often have a single learning form, so young people learn them uninterestedly, and it's hard to attract their attention. Relevant information is also difficult to contribute to the instantaneous memory into the short-term memory, too. The entertainment of computer games just makes up the tedious memory processes of some knowledge, because the fine, fantastic, and bizarre images and the beautiful music in the game can attract audiences' attention strongly. The challenge, inherent in the game, allows players become involved with the spirit of a high concentration. In the course of enjoying the game, players will master knowledge unconsciously. VanDeventer and White concluded that in the game students need participation of perception and thinking, such as self-control, pattern recognition, problem recognition, high-level problem solving, principled decision-making, qualitative thinking and so on, which is conducive to students in the short and the long-term memory [18]. Randel et al. concluded that simulation games require students to actively participate through the operation, which allows the game to provide the learning materials have the opportunity to be integrated into the learner's cognitive structure, thus contributing to the relevant information into long-term memory and to maintain [19]. Gaming experience, including: interactive narrative, cooperate to solve complex problems, foster digital lifestyle, virtual communities, explore the fine simulation of the world and use authoring tool with features [20].

The relationship between games and the learning of verbal information can be shown in Table1.

3   Games and the Development of Intellectual Skill

Intellectual skill includes four parts, which are identification, concepts, rules and advanced rules (problem solving) from bottom to top in sequence. From the perspective of identification, games can train young people's ability to distinguish images, and develop their spatial ability and cognitive skills; from the perspective of concept, it is conducive to the development of concept capacity by ebbing concept, difficult to be directly percept, in a particular type of game to promote young people's concept formation through the thinking process; from the perspective of regulation, with the combination of games and discipline-specific knowledge, a number of specific problems or skills needs young people to resolve by the application of relevant rules, which will benefit the development of their concept ability; from the perspective of high-grade regulation, complex games are able to train the innovative spirit of young people, develop their creativity, enhance their problem-solving ability, promote the development of their critical thinking.

3.1   Intellectual Skill

Intellectual skill, defined by Gagne, is an ability to act by using the symbols, and its role is mainly to answer the question how to do things. According to the definition, students have to own two kinds of abilities: one is the ability to understand and apply the concepts and rules; the other is logical reasoning ability.

Gagne divided the intellectual skill into four parts, and adjacent parts are of the composition dependence of the hierarchy according to the order of development. That is to say the mastery of the upper wisdom skills must be based on the mastery of the lower skills. The four parts are: identification, concepts, rules and advanced rules (problem solving).

3.2 Games and the Learning of Intellectual Skill

Nowadays, the considerable progress of computer games not only reflect in more colorful images, sweet sound and high degree of simulation of the real world, but also in the more complicated rules and process. Particularly, the rules of games, which implicit in the images and sounds and embodied in the process that the players interact with computer games, is similar to the complex issues inherent in the provisions of the real life , because of its high degree of complexity and intelligence. In real life, people always master intellectual skill by solving problems they encountered in the acquisition, but the games also offer young peoples possibilities to develop their intellectual skill by means of imitating the reality. Here are some progressive exercise approaches to improve intellectual skill:

(1) Seeing from the explicit images and sounds—intuitive feeling is the beginning of learning

People's learning always begins with the intuitive feelings like vision, hearing and so on. The so-called progressive exercise approach means that one has to practice from the most basic skills, and then increases the difficulties step by step, ultimately achieves the required level of technology. As for a specific "intellectual skills", students may have different levels of development before starting learning, so the most suitable development of the "basic skills" are different. Therefore, when determining the basic skills there comes a problem that "fits-all".

From the above-mentioned hierarchical classification of intellectual skill by Gagne, we can know that the development of "distinguish skill" is the beginning of the learning of intellectual skill. Distinguish skill can be described as "the ability to find out differences between objects or symbols", and this kind of ability is conducted on the basis of the most intuitive feelings such as visual, auditory and other sensory. Similarly, "specific concept learning", which is formed after mastering "distinguish skill" is no doubt conducted on the basis of the most intuitive feelings (such as visual, auditory and other sensory), and we can know this easily from the specific definition of "specific concept". The so-called specific concept, refers to "essential feature of the common things can be known by direct observation", just like cups, fans, computers and so on. The learning process of specific concept has to undergo four stages which are "perceptual identification", "hypothesis", "testing hypothesis" and "summary". And among the four stages, the first and the third stage is under the way of direct perception. When playing the computer games, players can see images and hear sounds at all times from the beginning to the end, and they identify, understand, and respond to them to get feedback. Using images and sound to convey information makes computer games meet almost everyone's requirements of practice.

(2) Seeing from the implicit rules and targets—from easy to difficult is the basic requirement of the games

In many computer games, players can choose the level of difficulty or the game itself will partition automatically according to the player's grades before the start of games. According to the different levels of difficulty, the pre-set rules and goals of the game process are different, and thus the difficulty of games will be different too. An action role-playing game "Diablo" produced by Blizzard Entertainment is a good example. The conduct of the game is divided into three difficulty levels: normal level, nightmare level and Hell level, and the beginning of the game by default for normal level.

Compared to this kind of choice, there are some games allow more flexible choices, for example, players can change the difficulty level when they are in games. Such as the famous CS (Counter-Strike), in the most classic version 1.5, the difficulty of games is mainly reflected in the robot's "IQ" setting, and there are 5 level of difficulty in all: Rookie class, fields and then class, master-level, expert-level and God-level. When they are playing games, the players can "kicking" the existing robots at any time, and then "add" a new robot of a new IQ Level.

Corresponding to the requirement of effective learning that "Students must have appropriate basic skills and be able to learn the skills with the forthcoming link", computer games offer game practice mode, allowing players to choose a degree of difficulty at the beginning and change difficulty level when they are in games, allowing them to play games from easy to difficulty, and providing them with a good help from the beginning to the end. By doing so, players can obtain the "target skills" pre-designed in the game step by step.

Face to the question that whether games help to develop intellectual skill, some people have already given affirmative answers. By studying simulation games, Pillay(1999), Kirriemuir(2002), Ko(2002), Green and Bavelier (2003) suggested that games play a great role in many aspects, such as Mental Models, Strategic Thinking and Insight, Better Psychomotor Skills, analytical and spatial skills, Visual Selective Attention, Computer Skills and so on [21, 11, 22, 23]. Here we are going to summarize the roles that games play in the development of teen-age intellectual skill from the four aspects: identification, concept, regulation and high-grade regulation (problem solving), as follows:

Games are Conducive to the Learning of the Identification Ability. Greenfield, et al, through the research on militant and adventuresome computer games, suggested that imagination is more important than words in games. The change from words to chart for performance enables the player visually identifies the pictures from different angles on the screen (as shown in Fig. 2). By this way, players can develop their capabilities of spatial skills and understanding. This is very important for many computer applications, so long-term playing games can help players adapt to the computer-oriented society [24]. Shang Junjie, Zhuang Shao-Yong, etc. and Capital Normal University have jointly conducted a "4D" research project, which is an online game providing an opportunity for students to learn the concept of multidimensional space. In this game, students can play the role of Sun Wukong, explore Monkey Park, temple and other activities to experience the one-dimensional, two-dimensional or even multidimensional space. Through these activities, students' abilities of identifying will be trained [16].

Games are Conducive to the Learning of the Concept Ability. Now many games have done very well in the integration of concepts and games. They no longer simply tell players by word of specific concepts, but hide concepts in the relevant elements of games so that players need percept and think to process derived concepts. Take the "Civilization" for example: there are religious, legal, diplomatic and other concepts, which are conducive to the development of players' conceptual ability. Natale suggests that even quite simple games can also be designed for us to learn specific

Fig. 2. To Find Differences

knowledge [2], such as exploratory and interactive games which can be embedded in math or science that is difficult for direct perception in reality. The aim is to help students develop the concept [25]. There are indications that the meaning construction in games is an important process of migration, which has nothing to do with the process mainly through induction or deduction [24].

Games are Conducive to the Learning of the Regulation Ability. Pillay's study showed that playing entertainment computer games may affect children's computer-based education tasks on the results. The extent of this impact depends on games' types students play during their study period. The linear, causal and responsible games tend to promote the formation of the analysis strategy while the adventure games can promote Inferential and Proactive Thinking [26]. Griffiths suggested that when the computer games are "designed to solve a particular problem or to teach a specific skill" [27], are very effective. For example, in the teaching courses such as mathematics, physics and language arts, specific objects have been provided [19], and there are options arrangement with the learning ability and learning goals of the content [11] . Henry M. Halff did the study of adventure games applied in Natural Science Teaching [28]. In the study, he pointed out that the main features of the natural sciences are: complex structure, difficult abstract reasoning and quantitative problem-solving leading to challenges, which were the features that such games are designed to follow. In his paper, he mentioned an example that physical balance in the capacitor with two capacitors known, seeking a third. The problem can be achieved through a dial in the game. In this way, it can eliminate the negative factors induced by boring and enable students to actively participate in "games".

Henry M. Halff did the study of adventure games applied in Natural Science Teaching [28]. In the study, he pointed out that the main features of the natural sciences are: complex structure, difficult abstract reasoning and quantitative problem-solving leading to challenges, which were the features that such games are designed

Table 2. The relationship between games and the development of intellectual skill

First-grade	Second-grade	Description
Intellectual skill	Identification Skill	Games can train young people's ability to distinguish the image, and develop their spatial ability and cognitive skills.
	Concept Skill	Games are conducive to the development of concept capacity by ebbing concept which is difficult to be directly percept in the particular type of game to promote young people's concept formation through the thinking process.
	Regulation Skill	With the combination of games and discipline-specific knowledge, a number of specific problems or skills needs young people to resolve by the application of relevant rules, which will benefit the development of the their concept ability.
	High-grade Regulation	Complex games are able to train the innovative spirit of young people, develop their creativity, enhance their problem-solving ability, and promote the development of their critical thinking.

to follow. In his paper, he mentioned an example that physical balance in the capacitor with two capacitors known, seeking a third. The problem can be achieved through a dial in the game. In this way, it can eliminate the negative factors induced by boring and enable students to actively participate in "games".

Games are Conducive to the Learning of the High-grade Regulation Ability. Lazarsfeld and Merton, American scholars, have pointed out: The mass media is a kind of tool that does not only good service but also evil. As the most sensitive level of the whole society members, youth are suffering from more and more study pressure and society pressure. They need to find a way to show their rapid response capability, strong desire and active exploration for new knowledge and things. The virtual space created by online games precisely meets this demand [29]. Gee and other researchers confirmed that students can participate in the story through games, which can change the relationship between students and the plot. Students complete games by seeing, experiencing matters, and discovering new methods, which is conducive to their creativity formation [30]. In the experiment of "Rhapsody Farm", after the in-depth qualitative and quantitative analysis of the game logs and summary reports submitted by students, and their operation behaviors in the game, Shang Junjie, Zhuang Shao-Yong, Lee Fong-lok, etc., found that students' capabilities of solving problems, planning, response and financial management had had improved to varying degrees [16].

Complex games are benefit to acquire encouraging change in the attitude, support the development of critical thinking, and develop the capacity of solving problem and making decision [31, 20]. Doolittle successfully applied games of puzzles and exploration to enhancing the creativity and some critical thinking cultivation of university students [25].

The relationship between games and development of intellectual skills can be shown in Table 2.

4 Games and the Development of Psychomotor Skill

Psychomotor skill consists of two components: one is the rule that describes how to act, namely action procedures, and the other is real muscle movement that becomes accurate and consistent due to gradually practice and feedback. In this paper, people's internal movements including the ability of hand-eye coordination, accurate actions, visual attention, spatial perception and strong gross psychomotor skill, are called the quality of psychomotor skill. From the perspective of the quality of psychomotor skill, games can be used to help young people develop hand-eye coordination, spatial perception, and visual attention; from the perspective of the practice of psychomotor skill, games can provide young people with practice environment, related knowledge and a specific training opportunity of psychomotor skill, where practice can be repeated.

4.1 Psychomotor Skill

Psychomotor skill is an ability that can be learned, and behaviors based on it are reflected in the body movement speed, accuracy, strength and continuity [8]. Structurally, psychomotor skill includes three basic components: feeling part, main center part and action part. When People are supposed to complete a special action task, their sense organs, under the particular stimulus from internal and external environment, will quickly input the information into the human brain for information processing, and then make regulating command and activities of effect controlling the effect organs. So that a variety of movement acts coordinately and their muscle activity adapts to changing environmental conditions and result in some kind of movement rhythm. Psychomotor skill consists of two components: one is the rule that describes how to act, namely action procedures; the other is real muscle movement that becomes accurate and consistent due to gradually practice and feedback.

4.2 Games and the Learning of Psychomotor Skill

Although Computer games have no direct training function on the psychomotor skill, many computer games (especially the high degree of simulation computer games) need to respect scientific rules and keep basically the same with the laws of the real operation when operating the object, which is conducive to the cognition and training of psychomotor skill. The learning of psychomotor skill in cognitive stages mainly depends on speech or action demonstration to explain. Its aim is to have a general understanding of movement and action to form images in the brain. And computer games do quite well in the present of verbal information and the formation of detailed, truthful and easy manipulated visual images. So the use of computer games for the learning of psychomotor skill in cognitive stages is very beneficial. Training of psychomotor skill is a learning activity aiming for the formation of certain skills and a repeated operation process aiming for mastering certain action. Training includes repetition and feedback. Computer games can provide a virtual operation and feedback. And it also contributes to mastery of psychomotor skill.

The implementation of psychomotor skill reflects intellectual skill that constitutes the movement order of muscle activity, and the activity needs to meet the standards of speed, accuracy, strength, fluency and so on[8]. From the perspective of speed, students need have a higher ability of hand-eye coordination; from the perspective of accuracy, students need accurate actions, visual attention and spatial perception ability; from the perspective of power, students need have strong gross psychomotor skill; from the perspective of fluency of implementation, students need practice repeatedly. In this paper, people's internal movements including the ability of hand-eye coordination, accurate actions, visual attention, spatial perception and strong gross psychomotor skill, are called the quality of psychomotor skill. Therefore, we will sum up the roles of games in the development of young people from two aspects: the quality of psychomotor skill and the practice of psychomotor skill:

Games are Conducive to Improving the Quality of Psychomotor Skill. The games playability is manifested in the extent and characteristics of interactivity in games, and it describes the way how the players play the game and how the game world reacts to the players [32]. Many computer games require players to respond quickly and the operational requirements of the players are also very high, such as The King of Fighters series of fighting games, Counter-Strike and Doom, Audition, Jin Orchestra and so on. In these games, according to the changes of sound and pictures, players regulate the operation by keyboard, mouse, game controllers and other tools for games, which coordinates movements of hands and arms with auditory and visual. This helps to improve players' quality of psychomotor skill such as hand-eye coordination and attention. Some aspects have been confirmed by clinical medicine:

- Games can be used in the treatment of schizophrenia [33], and they have significant effect in promoting and strengthening psychomotor skill [34];
- Games can be used to provide the transfer of cognitive attention (such as the treatment of pain and nausea of seasickness, etc.). For example, it is useful for the children who are hit or burned and even ones who receive chemotherapy [35];
- Games can help people who have attention deficits to improve their visual scanning and tracking capabilities [36]. When attention is weakened, if the game is to gradually increase the difficulty, it will be of great help to the focus of attention [37];
- Games can help support the analysis of the development of children's attention: the study of Bangor University concluded that PlayStation 2 games are very useful in the assessment of children's visual processing ability [11].

Games are Conducive to the Practice of Psychomotor Skill. Although computer games have to follow certain rules, they allow players to operate the objects, thus supporting the development of movement proficiency [38] (as shown in Fig. 3). Saunders and Smalley considered that games provide an opportunity of learning technologies within the framework of virtual reality in the study of lifelong learning, which has a meaningful impact on the students who were ready to work [39]. In games, when players have the opportunity to handle real-world problems through

Fig. 3. Learning of First Aid Skills

participating in the content designs, the effectiveness will be strengthened [40]. When the players experience the main areas or situations and form new connections with new ways, his learning and operation in this area will be helpful for the future study and work or even can be migrated to other areas [30].

Internet adventure games and role-playing games provide a range of quite necessary opportunities for experiential learning [41, 42, 30], which arouse great attention of the armed forces. "China National Defense News "reported that in recent years, along with the development of information construction of our army and army-building LAN, some units have driven a variety of simulation "games" such as main battle tanks, fighter aircraft, infantry fighting vehicles and cars to the training practice, and the result is obvious. Through "Online confrontational exercise" and "military games against the training" and other activities, officers and soldiers are allowed to play different "roles" in variety of "virtual battlefields" according to organized, planned and purposeful aim, in order to adapt the "battlefield" environment. These games pave the way for starting real exercise with live ammunition and improve their combat capabilities under the conditions of information technology [43]. The effect of computer games on the training of soldiers was confirmed in the Iraq war. Before the outbreak of the war in Iraq, the U.S. military secretly developed a computer game dedicated to the Marine Corps, in which the terrain, streets, buildings, bridges and other markers are in accordance with the characteristics of the Iraqi capital of Baghdad. Results show that for those pilots who have never participated in actual combat of computer games, the survival probability at the first implementation of mandate is only 60%, while after a computer simulation of combat training, the probability of survival can be increased to 90% [44].

The relationship of games and psychomotor skill is shown in Table 3.

Table 3. The relationship between games and the development of psychomotor skill

First-grade	Second grade	Description
Psychomotor Skill	Quality Skill	Games can be used to help young people develop hand-eye coordination, spatial perception, and visual attention.
	Practice Skill	Games can provide young people with practice environment, related knowledge and a specific training opportunity of psychomotor skill, where practice can be repeated.

5   Games and the Formation of Attitude

Attitude structure includes the cognitive component of an attitude, the emotional component of an attitude and the behavioral component of an attitude. From the perspective of affective component of an attitude, games provide rich visual and spatial aesthetics, musical sound and environment associated with learn and work , which are conducive to causing the interest of young people and triggering their positive learning emotions; from the perspective of behavioral component of an attitude, games provide a virtual environment to support the operation behavior of juvenile behavior, resulting in their behavior similar to the real experience that can be strengthened through the feedback in the game, which are conducive to causing the interest of young people and triggering their positive learning emotions; from the perspective of cognitive component of an attitude, games provide the young people with the process of how they grasp the related objects and operating skills well, which are conducive to causing young people's interest to relevant content and triggering their positive.

5.1   Attitude

The capability which human beings acquire in the "emotional field" is known as "attitude". The attitude is a continuous state which can change the choice of the individual behavior, and it is also a complex internal state which can affect the individual behavior towards people, objects or events and amplify the individual positive or negative reaction [8]. The "internal state" of attitude is deduced from the observations of the individual behavior, instead of the act itself. The objects include people, events, things, systems, the concept of specific events, and every aspect of oneself, all of which can be evaluated, in favor of or against. The objects also include the intuitive state of mind ready to act at the same time. For this definition, it can be understood from the following aspects:

First, the attitude is an internal state of readiness, rather than the actual response itself. The attitude is often behaved as aversion, likes, dislikes and so on. These tendencies can affect the appearance of certain behaviors, but not corresponding.

Second, the attitude is different from the capacity, although both of them are internal tendency. The capacity decides whether the individual can complete the tasks or not, While the attitude decides whether the individual is willing to complete certain the tasks or not, and that is determination of behavior choice.

Third, the attitude is formed through learning, but not innate. Both towards people and towards matter, all kinds of attitudes are shaped and changed by the interaction between the individual and the environment.

Attitude structure involves the cognitive component of an attitude, the emotional component of an attitude and the behavioral component of an attitude:

The Cognitive Component of Attitude. It is a value or a belief with the meaning of the evaluation which the individual has towards the attitude objects. For an object, the attitude of different individual contains different cognitive component. Some people's attitude is mainly based on the understanding of careful consideration; some attitude may be mainly based on emotional impulses; some attitude may be based on the right values and beliefs; and some attitude may be based on wrong ideas and beliefs.

The Emotional Component of Attitude. It reflects the feeling or emotional experience arising from cognitive component of attitudes, and it is the core component of the attitude. Researches have shown that when the attitude changes, the emotion also changes. But different attitude has different emotional component. Some attitudes have more rational elements while some attitudes are non-rational or emotional.

The Behavioral Component of Attitude. It is an intention or purpose which is ready to make some kind of reaction to an object. Generally, the three components of the attitude are coordinated, but sometimes may be inconsistent. For example, the behavioral component and the cognitive component separate. The external behavior is not always the true reflection of the inner attitude, or verbal attitude are often unable to put into action, that is, knowledge out of action.

5.2 Games and the Formation of Attitude

Computer games have the wonderful technology in the display and blending of images and sounds. They can simulate the complex colors, sounds and three-dimensional space of the real world and achieve amazing results (as shown in Fig. 4). Computer games are so attractive and have so much "stickiness". A very important reason is that they have beautiful pictures, sweet sound and perfect 3D effects. Computer games are full of the mystery map scenes, novelty monsters, flamboyance characters and beautiful action skills, and all of them bright players' eyes. In the initial contact, players will be deeply attracted, and full of aspirations to explore the mysteries in games. In games, measures of rewards and punishments and some successful examples provide the effective system of safeguards for regulating play behavior and encouraging players to continue to explore in games. All these elements are useful to players' affective component of an attitude.

The rule, hidden in the images and sound of computer games, is the core component of the attractiveness, and is also the focus of the interaction with players. Players appreciate the pleasure and are willing to continue games. The biggest reason is that games have complex and challenge rules that need use the appropriate response to cope with, which are useful to behavioral component of players' attitude.

Fig. 4. Virtual Life

With the deepening of games, players master the rules step by step through the operation of games, and will change attitudes of relevant knowledge in games with the gradual deepening of understanding, which are useful to behavioral component of players' attitude.

From the above analysis, we can see games' effect on the players' attitude is reflected in affective component, behavioral component, and cognitive component. From the three aspects, we'll discuss t the impacts of games on attitude formation.

Games are Conducive to Attitude Formation from the Perspective of Affection. From the perspective of affection, the effect that computer games act on the players has been recognized by many scholars. Poole considered that the rich visual and spatial sense of beauty will bring you into a very indulgent and virtual world, but it looks just like the real world. Games bring people not only fear but also happiness [45]. Circumstances in games related to the job, can encourage young people, who lack basic skills competency, to participate in highly basic skills courses. Games guide them to learn and get a result through visual stimulation, action sequences and audio-visual feedback [46]. Compared with the traditional classroom approach, games can arouse student's deep interest [11]. Students come to arouse motivation by delight, which is "a part of the natural learning in the process of human development" [47]. When educational games are used in classroom teaching, they can effectively stimulate students' motivation and produce active effect to classroom teaching [48]. Games can enhance the motivation, inspire self-confidence, promote collaborative learning, etc.

Games are Conducive to Attitude Formation from the Perspective of Behavior. Games can provide fully interactive and virtual playing environment, to support the

Table 4. The relationship between games and the formation of attitude

First-grade	Second-grade	Description
Attitude	Affective Component	Games provide rich visual and spatial aesthetics, musical sound and environment associated with learn and work, which are conducive to causing the interest of young people and triggering their positive learning emotions.
	Behavioral Component	Games provide a virtual environment to support the operation behavior of juvenile behavior, resulting in their behavior similar to the real experience that can be strengthened through the feedback in the game, which are conducive to causing the interest of young people and triggering their positive learning emotions.
	Cognitive Component	Games provide the young people with the process of how they grasp the related objects and operating skills well, which are conducive to causing young people's interest to relevant content and triggering their positive.

operation behavior of players. In games, environment information can make person immersed and act similar to real life behavior, and timely feedback can stimulate players to change attitudes in the play behavior and maintain interest in games. In particular, the complex games are very helpful to players in obtaining encouraging attitude change, and they support the development of critical thinking, problem solving and decision making [13, 49, 31, 20]. Players accept the story of the game through the play behavior and experience the story through the characters, which is very contagious [50]. Although game players are to win or to achieve a certain goal, the most critical thing is that they win without losing the game challenging experience of play behavior.

Games are Conducive to Attitude Formation from the Perspective of Cognition. Similar to the real living environment, the attitude of players in games will change gradually with the in-depth understanding. The elements, which encourage players to go on playing the game, exists in the game process itself (some activities and strategies, inherent in the process of games, encourage the player immersed in the game at each stage, and inspire them to finalize the entire game) [51]. For many players, their ultimate goal is the mastery. Not all games are relying on violence to attract people (for example, games of test types). Games' attraction lies in players' master to the game and their striving to improve their skill level [52]. It can be used to encourage the students who are lack of interest, self-confidence, or self-esteem [53], change their attitudes in games to so as to enhance and maintain knowledge.

The relationship between games and the formation of attitude is shown in Table 4.

6 Conclusion and Future Work

Referring to R.M.Gagne's theory of learning outcomes, this paper builds the theoretical system of games and youth development from four aspects: games and the learning of verbal information, games and the development of intellectual skill, games and the development of psychomotor skill, and games and the formation of attitude. But the relevant research work is not perfect, and there are still three aspects of problems as follows:

(1) Games and the development of youth cognitive strategies. This study talks about the games' influence on teenagers from the perspective of the object, so it avoids the problem that is the relationship between games and the development of youth cognitive strategies. However, when we communicated with primary and secondary students, we found games have an indirect effect of cognitive strategy to young people. For example, many middle - primary school pupils think games make them more confident when they deal with the relationship between students. On this issue, there is still very little related research literature at home and abroad. This issue needs further literature and empirical research to improve the theoretical system of games and youth development.

(2) Games and physical activity of youth. Physical games are a good combination of computer games and physical exercise, which are conducive to encouraging young people to participate in physical exercise, thereby enhancing youth fitness. With the rapid development of the physical games' technology, it is highly likely to spread in the next few years, which will have a revolutionized effect on the physical training of young people. Relevant research in this area should be the complement to the theoretical system of games and youth development.

(3) Edu-game and the problem of adolescence game addiction. Although the paper discusses the theory about the relationship between games and youth development, and carries out the design study of edu-game, but it doesn't refers to how to enable young people to enjoy the happiness games bring instead of indulging in the same time. This problem is also an international problem, and it needs great wisdom to deal with. We hope to carry out useful research attempts under the condition of multi-disciplinary collaboration.

Acknowledgments. This project is supported by China Education Science "Eleventh Five-Year Plan" 2009 annual youth issues (Approval No. EEA090388) and Jiangsu Education Science "Eleventh Five-Year Plan" 2008 annual issue "Evaluation index system of people-oriented and developmental educational games" (Approval No. D/2008/01/112). We would like to thank Prof. Yi Li from Nanjing Normal University and Prof. Zhigeng Pan from Zhejiang University for their kind help in this project. They have given us some good suggestions and methods on improving the research work.

References

1. Game Publications Working Committee of Chinese Publishers Association etc.: Report of, Chinese Game Industry, pp. 36–40. Social Sciences Literature Publishing House, Beijing (2008)
2. Natale, M.J.: The Effect of a Male-oriented Computer Gaming Culture on careers in the computer industry. Computers and Society, 24–31 (2002)
3. Klawe, M.M.: The Educational Potential of Electronic Games and the E-GEMS Project. In: Ottman, T., Tomek, I. (eds.) Proceedings of the ED-MEDIA 1994 World Conference on Educational Multimedia and Hypermedia, Vancouver, Canada, June 1994, pp. 25–30 (1994)
4. Ritchie, D., Dodge, B.: Integrating Technology Usage Across the Curriculum. In: Annual Conference on Technology and Teacher Education, Houston, TX, March 1992, pp. 12–15 (1992)
5. Yun, R., Xi, H., Li, Y.: The Experiment of Improving Students' Spatial Ability by Using VGLS. In: Pan, Z., Cheok, D.A.D., Haller, M., Lau, R., Saito, H., Liang, R. (eds.) ICAT 2006. LNCS, vol. 4282, pp. 467–473. Springer, Heidelberg (2006)
6. Clark, D.: Computer Games in Education and Training. In: Clark, D. (ed.) Presentation at LSDA Seminar Learning by Playing: Can Computer Games and Simulations Support Teaching and Learning for Post-16 Learners in Formal, Workplace and Informal Learning Contexts?, London, November 20 (2003),
http://www.bbk.ac.uk/ccs/elearn/events.html (April 2004)
7. Becta: Computer Games in Education Project Report,
http://www.becta.org.uk/research/research.cfm?section=1&id=2835
8. Gagne, R.M.: Principles of Instructional Design. East China Normal University Press (2005)
9. Qi, C., Rude, L.: Contemporary Educational Psychology in Chinese. Beijing Normal University Press (2008)
10. Guixiang, B.: Pedagogic Psychology in Chinese. Beijing Publishing House (2004)
11. Kirriemuir, J.: The Relevance of Video Games and Gaming Consoles to the Higher and Further Education Learning Experience. Techwatch Report TSW 02.01 (2002)
12. Leutner, D.: Guided Discovery Learning with Computer-based Simulation Games: Effects of Adaptive and Non-adaptive Instructional Support. Learning and Instruction, 113–132 (1993)
13. Berson, M.J.: Effectiveness of Computer Technology in Social Studies: a Review of the Literature. Jouunal of Research on Computing in Education, 486–499 (1996)
14. Thomas, R., Cahill, J., Santilli, L.: Using an Interactive Computer Game to Increase Skill and Self-efficacy Regarding Safer Sex Negotiation: Field Test Results. Health Education and Behavior, 71–86 (1997)
15. Sedighian, K.: Playing Styles for Computer and Video Games. In: Ottman, T., Tomek, I. (eds.) Proceedings of the ED-MEDIA 1994 World Conference on Educational Multimedia and Hypermedia, Vancouver, Canada, June 1994, pp. 25–30 (1994)
16. Junjie, S., Shaoyong, Z., Lefang, L., et al.: Discussion on Motivation, Effectiveness and Some Issues of Educational Games. In: ICCE 1998 Proceeding, vol. 6 (2008)
17. Jayakanthan, R.: Application of Computer Games in the Field of Education. The Electronic Library 20(2), 98–102 (2002)
18. VanDeventer, S.S., White, J.A.: Expert Behavior in Children's Video Game Play. Simulation and Gaming 33(1), 28–48 (2002)

19. Randel, J.M., Morris, B.A., Wetzel, C.D., Whitehill, B.V.: The Effectiveness of Games for Educational Purposes: a Review of Recent Research. Simulation and Gaming 23(3), 261–276 (1992)
20. Squire, K., Jenkins, H., Holland, W., Miller, H., et al.: Design Principles of Next-generation Digital Gaming for Education. Educational Technology, 17–23 (September–October 2003)
21. Pillay, H., Brownlee, J., Wilss, L.: Cognition and Recreational Computer Games: Implications for Educational Technology. Journal of Research on Computing in Education 32(1), 203–216 (1999)
22. Ko, S.: An Empirical Analysis of Children's Thinking and Learning Using a Computer Game Context. Educational Psychology 22(2), 219–233 (2002)
23. Green, C., Bavelier, D.: Action Video Game Modifies Visual Selective Attention. Nature 423, 534–537 (2003)
24. Greenfield, P.M., Camaioni, L., Ercolani, P., et al.: Cognitive Socialization by Computer Games in Two Cultures: Inductive Discovery or Mastery of an Iconic Code. Journal of Applied Developmental Psychology, 59–85 (1994)
25. Doolittle, J.H.: Using Riddles and Interactive Computer Games to Teach Problem-Solving Skills. Teaching of Psychology 22(1), 33–36 (1995)
26. Pillay, H.: An Investigation of Cognitive Processes Engaged in by Recreational Computer Games Players: Implications for Skills of the Future. Journal of Research on Technology in Education, 336–350 (2003)
27. Griffiths, M.D.: The Educational Benefits of Videogames. Education and Health, 47–51 (2002)
28. Halff, H.M.: Adventure Games for Science Education: Generative Methods in Exploratory Environments
29. Shangyong, W.: From Game Addiction to See Young New Media Literacy Education in Chinese. Chongqing University Journals (Social Science edn.) (February 2008)
30. Gee, J.P.: What Video Games Have to Teach Us about Learning and Literacy. Palgrave Macmillan, New York (2003)
31. Hollins, P.: Playing is the New Learning E.Learning Age, 16–19 (December-January 2003)
32. Rose, R.: Game Design—Principles and Practice. Electronic Industry Press (2003)
33. Samoilovich, S., Ricccitelli, C., Scheil, A., et al.: Attitude of Schizophrenics to Computer Videogames. Psychopathology, 117–119 (1992)
34. Sietsema, J.M., Nelson, D.L., Mulder, R.M., et al.: The Use of a Game to Promote Arm Reach in Persons with Traumatic Brain Injury. American Journal of Occupational Therapy, 19–24 (1993)
35. Vasterling, J., Jenkins, R.A., Tope, D.M., et al.: Cognitive Distraction and Relaxation Training for the Control of Side Effects Due to Cancer Chemotherapy. Journal of Behavioural Medicine, 65—80 (1993)
36. Larose, S., Gagnon, S., Ferland, C., et al.: Psychology of Computers, XIV. Cognitive Rehabilitation Through Computer Games. Perceptual and Motor Skills, 851–858 (1989)
37. Pope, A.T., Bogart, E.H.: Extended Attention Span Training System: Video Game Neurotherapy for Attention Deficit Disorder. Child Study Journal, 39–50 (1996)
38. Fabricatore, C.: Learning and Videogames: An Unexploited Synergy, http://www.learndev.org/dl/FabricatoreAECT2000.pdf
39. Saunders, D., Smalley, N.: Simulations and Games for Transition and Change in Lifelong Learning. In: Saunders, D., Smalley, N. (eds.) The International Simulation and Gaming Research Yearbook, London, pp. 1–9 (2000)

40. Kusunoki, F., Sugimoto, M., Hashizume, H.: Discovering How Other Pupils Think by Collaborative Learning in a Classroom. Paper Presented to the Fourth International Conference on Knowledge-based Intelligent Engineering Systems and Allied Technologies. 30 August–1 September (2000)
41. Filipczak, B.: Training Gets Doomed. Training, 24–31 (August 1997)
42. Griffiths, M.D., Davies, M.N.O.: Research Note–excessive Online Computer Gaming: Implications for Education. Journal of Computer Assisted Learning, 379–380 (2002)
43. Chinaview,
    http://news.xinhuanet.com/mil/2008-01/28/content_7511071.htm
44. Chinaview,
    http://news.xinhuanet.com/mil/2007-05/14/content_6092748.htm
45. Poole, S.: Rigger happy, Video Games and the Entertainment Revolution, New York (2000)
46. Brownfield, S., Vik, G.: Teaching Basic Skills with Computer Games. Training and Developmental Journal, 52–56 (1983)
47. Bisson, C., Luckner, J.: Fun in Learning: the Pedagogical Role of Fun in Adventure Education. Journal of Experimental Education, 108–112 (1996)
48. Rosas, R., Nussbaum, M., Cumsile, P., Marianov, V., et al.: Beyond Nintendo: Design and Assessment of Educational Video Games for First and Second Grade Students. Computers and Education, 71–94 (2003)
49. Helliar, C.V., Michaelson, R., Power, D.M., et al.: Using a Portfolio Management Game (Finesse) to Teach Finance. Accounting Education, 37–51 (2000)
50. McLellan, H.: Magical Stories: Blending Virtual Reality and Artificial Intelligence. In: Beauchamp, D.G., Braden, R.A., Griffin, R.E. (eds.) Imagery and Visual Literacy: Annual Conference of the International Visual and Literacy Association, pp. 76–80 (1994)
51. Prensky, M.: The Motivation of Game Play-The Real Twenty-First Century Learning Revolution. On the Horizon, 5–11 (2002)
52. Mitchell, A.: Exploring the Potential of a Games-Oriented Implementation for M-portal. Paper Presented to the MLEARN 2003 Conference –Learning with Mobile Devices, London, pp. 19–20 (May 2003)
53. Dempsey, J.V., Rasmussen, K., Lucassen, B.: Instructional Gaming: Implications for Instructional Technology. Paper Presented at the Annual Meeting of the Association for Educational Communications and Technology, pp. 16–20 (1994); Pillay H, Brownlee J, Wilss L: Cognition and recreational computer games: implications for educational technology. Journal of Research on Computing in Education, 32(1), 203–216 (February 1999)

Author Index